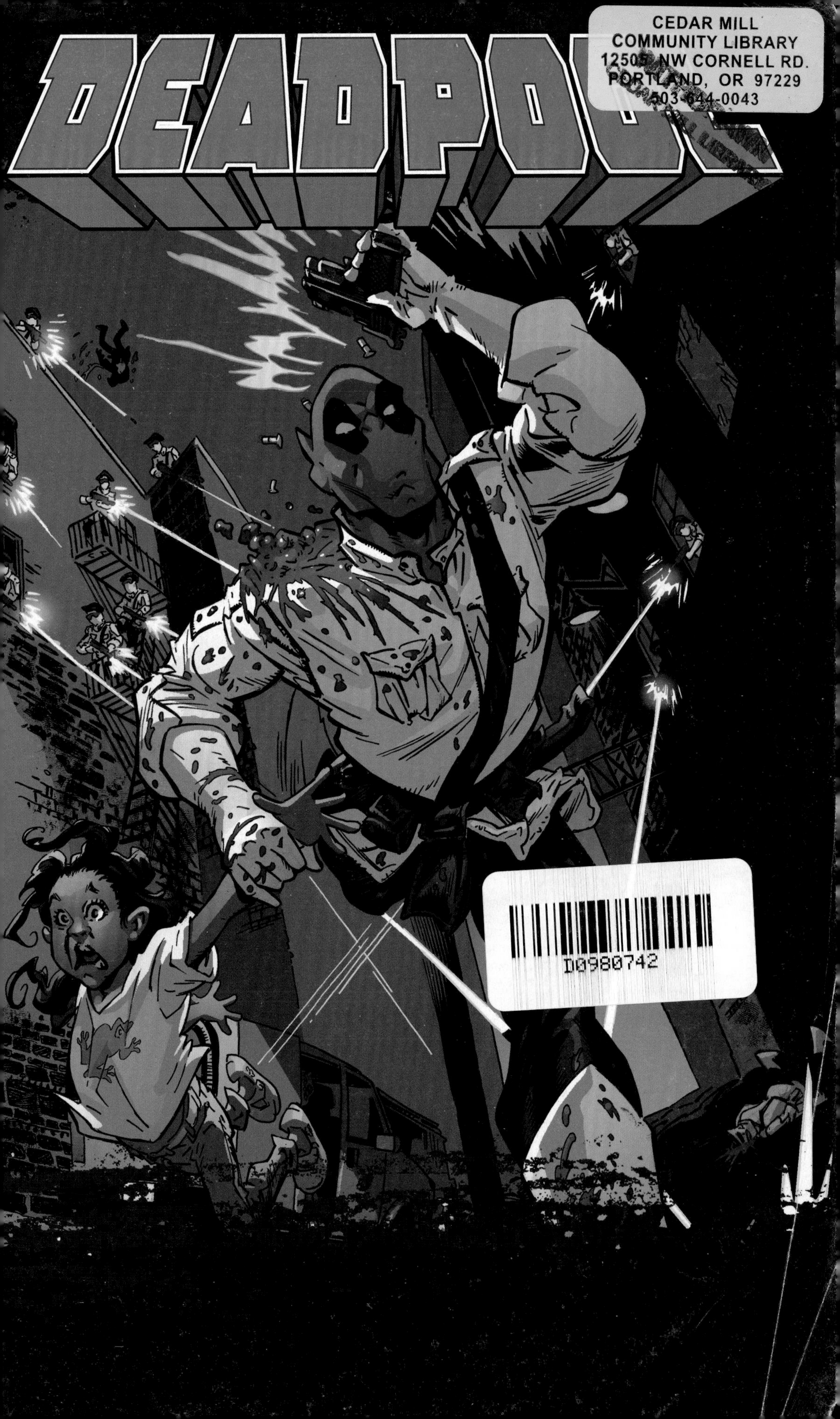

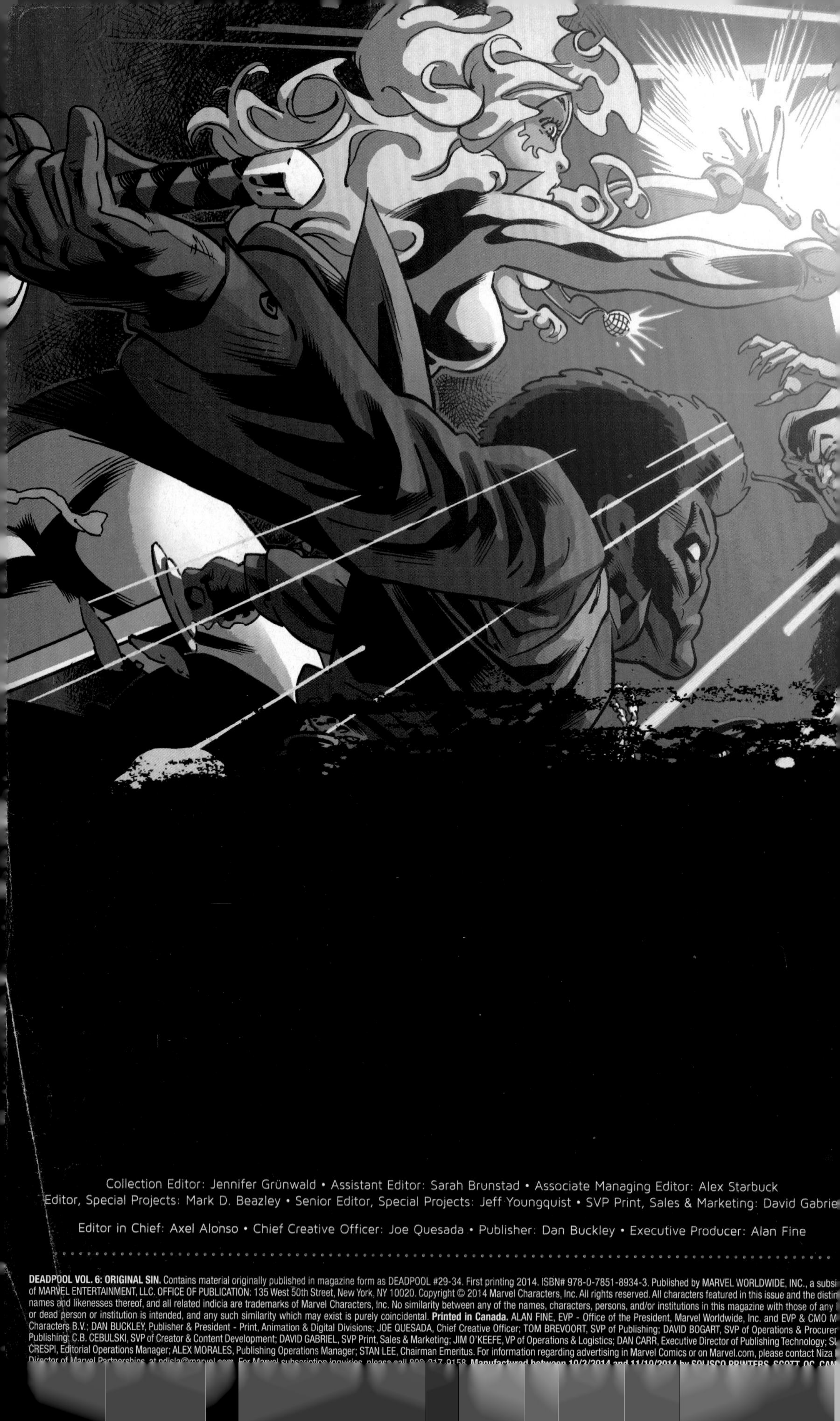

Collection Editor: Jennifer Grünwald • Assistant Editor: Sarah Brunstad • Associate Managing Editor: Alex Starbuck
Editor, Special Projects: Mark D. Beazley • Senior Editor, Special Projects: Jeff Youngquist • SVP Print, Sales & Marketing: David Gabrie

Editor in Chief: Axel Alonso • Chief Creative Officer: Joe Quesada • Publisher: Dan Buckley • Executive Producer: Alan Fine

DEADPOOL VOL. 6: ORIGINAL SIN. Contains material originally published in magazine form as DEADPOOL #29-34. First printing 2014. ISBN# 978-0-7851-8934-3. Published by MARVEL WORLDWIDE, INC., a subsi of MARVEL ENTERTAINMENT, LLC. OFFICE OF PUBLICATION: 135 West 50th Street, New York, NY 10020. **Printed in Canada.** ALAN FINE, EVP - Office of the President, Marvel Worldwide, Inc. and EVP & CMO M Characters B.V.; DAN BUCKLEY, Publisher & President - Print, Animation & Digital Divisions; JOE QUESADA, Chief Creative Officer; TOM BREVOORT, SVP of Publishing; DAVID BOGART, SVP of Operations & Procurer Publishing; C.B. CEBULSKI, SVP of Creator & Content Development; DAVID GABRIEL, SVP Print, Sales & Marketing; JIM O'KEEFE, VP of Operations & Logistics; DAN CARR, Executive Director of Publishing Technology; S CRESPI, Editorial Operations Manager; ALEX MORALES, Publishing Operations Manager; STAN LEE, Chairman Emeritus. For information regarding advertising in Marvel Comics or on Marvel.com, please contact Niza Director of Marvel Partnerships, at ndisla@marvel.com. For Marvel subscription inquiries, please call 800-217-9158. **Manufactured between 10/3/2014 and 11/10/2014 by SOLISCO PRINTERS, SCOTT, QC, CAN**

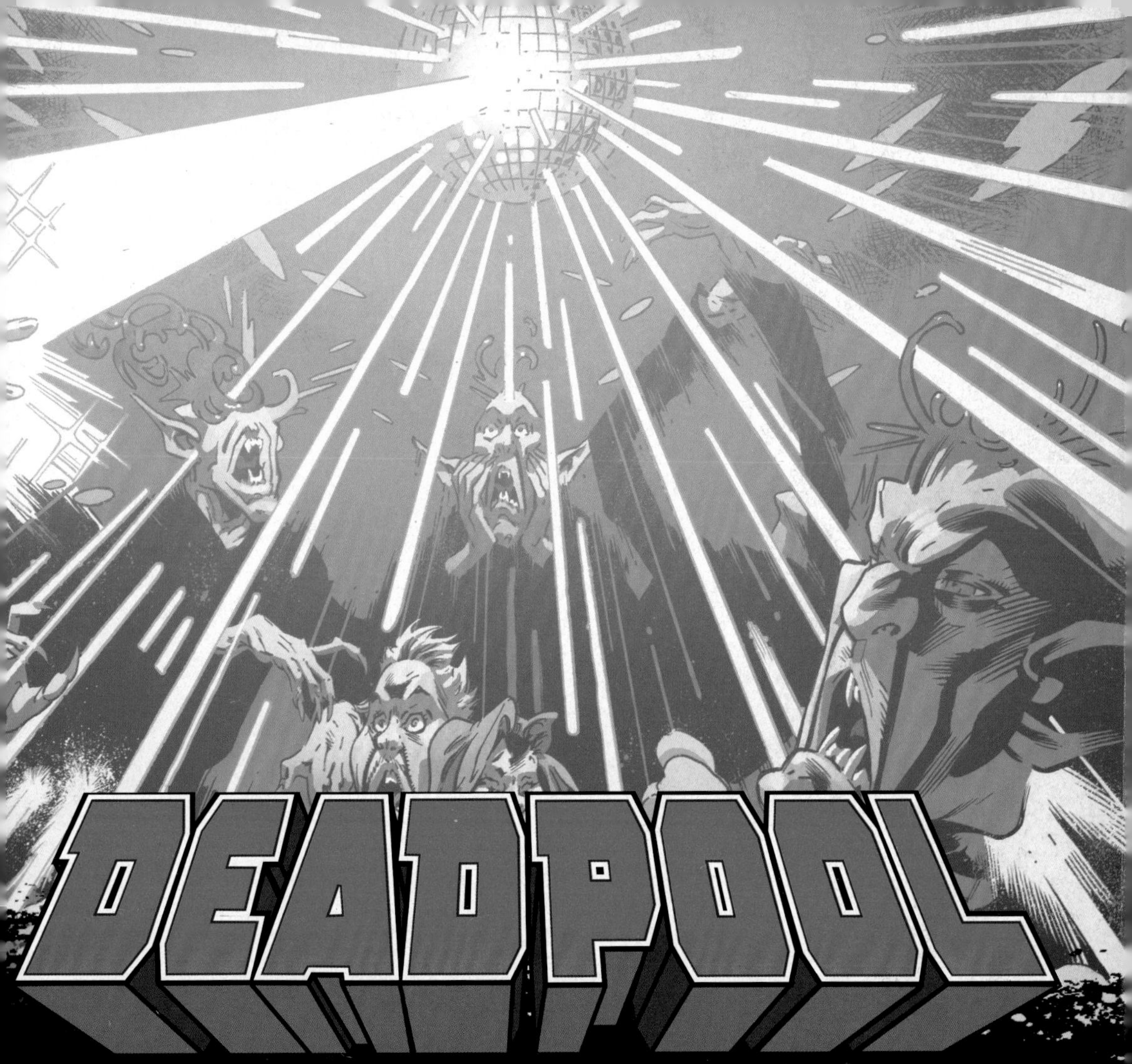

DEADPOOL

WRITERS
GERRY DUGGAN & BRIAN POSEHN

ARTISTS
JOHN LUCAS (#29-33) & SCOTT KOBLISH (#34)

COLORIST
VAL STAPLES

LETTERER
VC'S JOE SABINO

COVER ART
DECLAN SHALVEY & JORDAN BELLAIRE (#29), MARK BROOKS (#30-31 & #34), CARLO BARBERI & ANDRES MOSSA (#32) AND MIKE DEL MUNDO (#33)

ASSISTANT EDITOR
FRANKIE JOHNSON

EDITOR
JORDAN D. WHITE

X-MEN GROUP EDITOR
MIKE MARTS

DEADPOOL CREATED BY ROB LIEFELD AND FABIAN NICIEZA

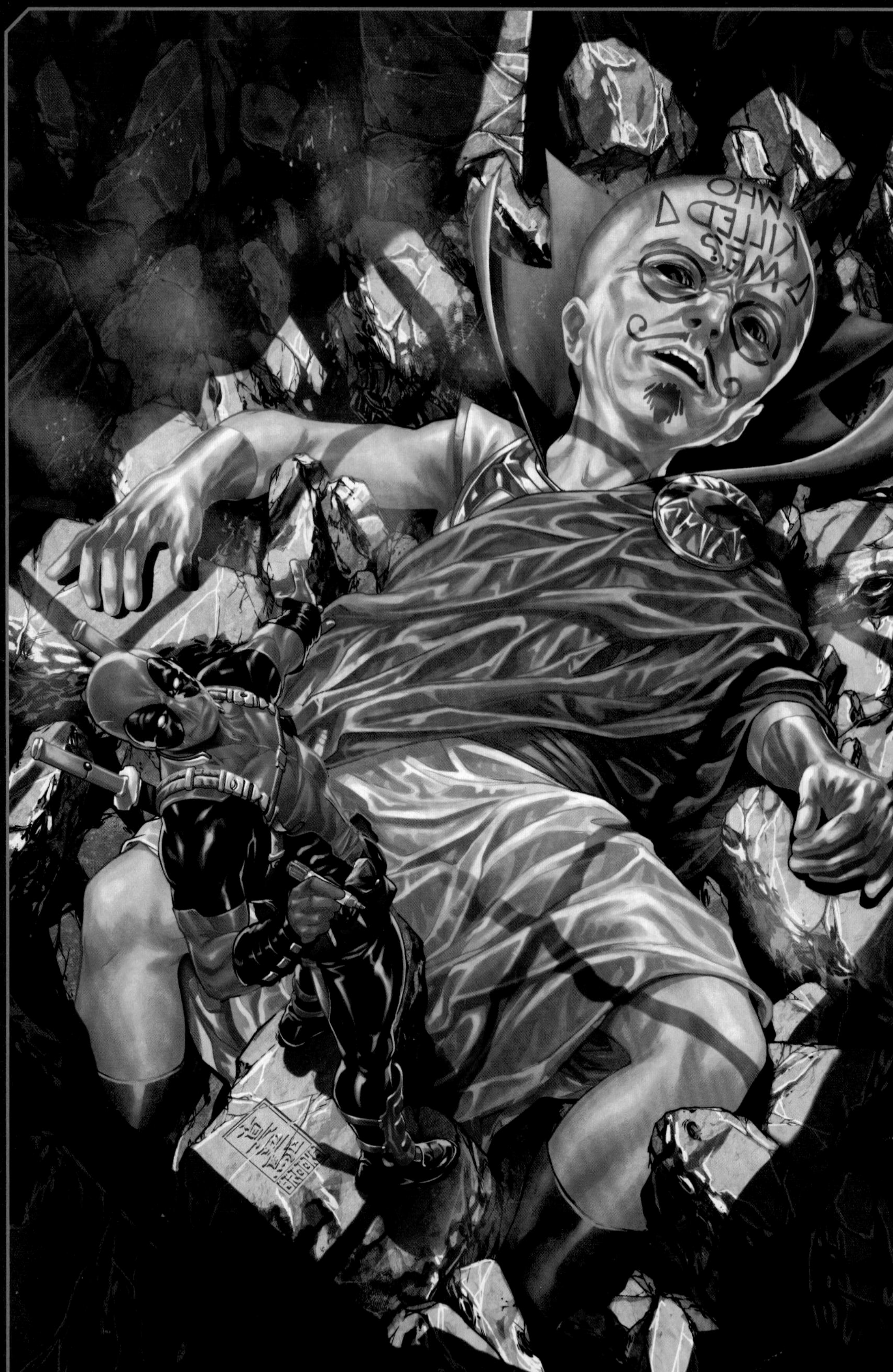

#29 VARIANT
BY MARK BROOKS

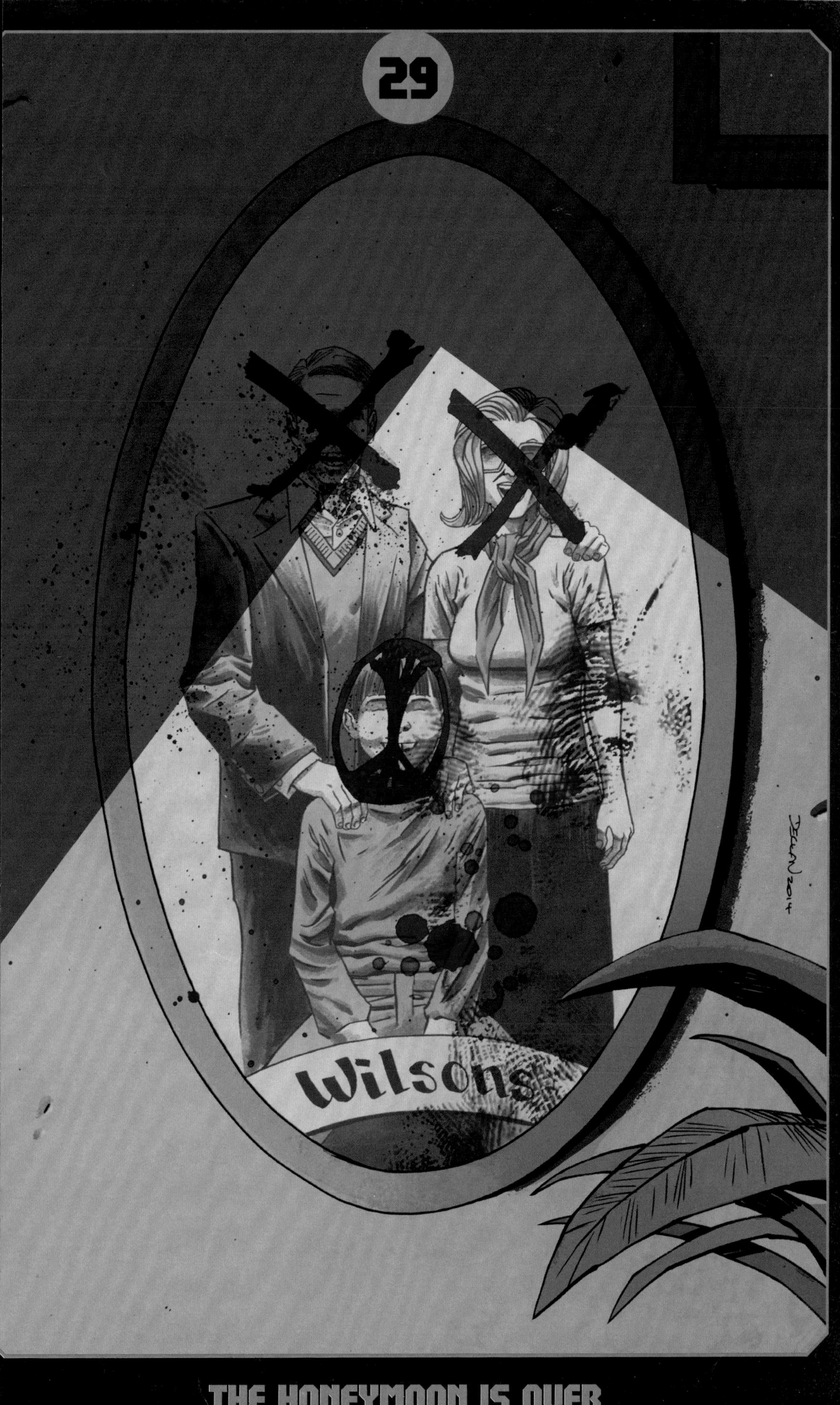
29
Wilsons

THE HONEYMOON IS OVER

Possibly the world's most skilled mercenary, definitely the world's most annoyin[g]
Wade Wilson was chosen for a top-secret government program that gave him [a]
healing factor allowing him to heal from any wound. Now, Wade makes his way [as]
a gun for hire, shooting his prey's faces off while talking his friends' ears off. C[all]
him the Merc with the Mouth...call him the Regeneratin' Degenerate...call him...

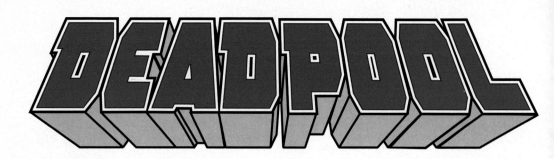

HEY THERE, PEEPS! *DEADPOOL* HERE--THE *MARRIED MAN* WITH THE *MOUTH.*

AND *WHAT A MOUTH* IT IS.

THANK YOU, SWEETIE. THIS IS *SHIKLAH,* MY WIFE-- THE *QUEEN OF THE MONSTER METROPOLIS!* WHICH MAKES ME THEIR *KING!*

I'M AFRAID NOT. *CONSORT TO THE QUEEN,* MY LOVE. I CAN MAKE YOU A PRINCE, PERHAPS?

WE'LL DISCUSS THIS IN PRIVATE.

ANYWAY--BEFORE WE WERE MARRIED, SHIKLAH WAS ENGAGED TO THAT OL' BLOODSUCKER HIMSELF, *DRACULA!* IT WAS PART OF SOME WORLD- RULING SCHEME OF HIS. WE FOILED IT WITH OUR HOLY MATRIMONY.

LAST WE HEARD, DRAC WAS PISSED, SWEARING *REVENGE.*

OH, AND A WHILE BACK I FOUND OUT I HAD A *DAUGHTER* WHO MIGHT BE DEAD. OR...SHE MIGHT NOT. MY S.H.I.E.L.D. BUDDY *AGENT PRESTON* (IN HER UN-SHINY NEW ROBOT BODY) IS LOOKING INTO IT FOR ME.

LI'L DEADPOOL ART BY
IRENE Y. LEE

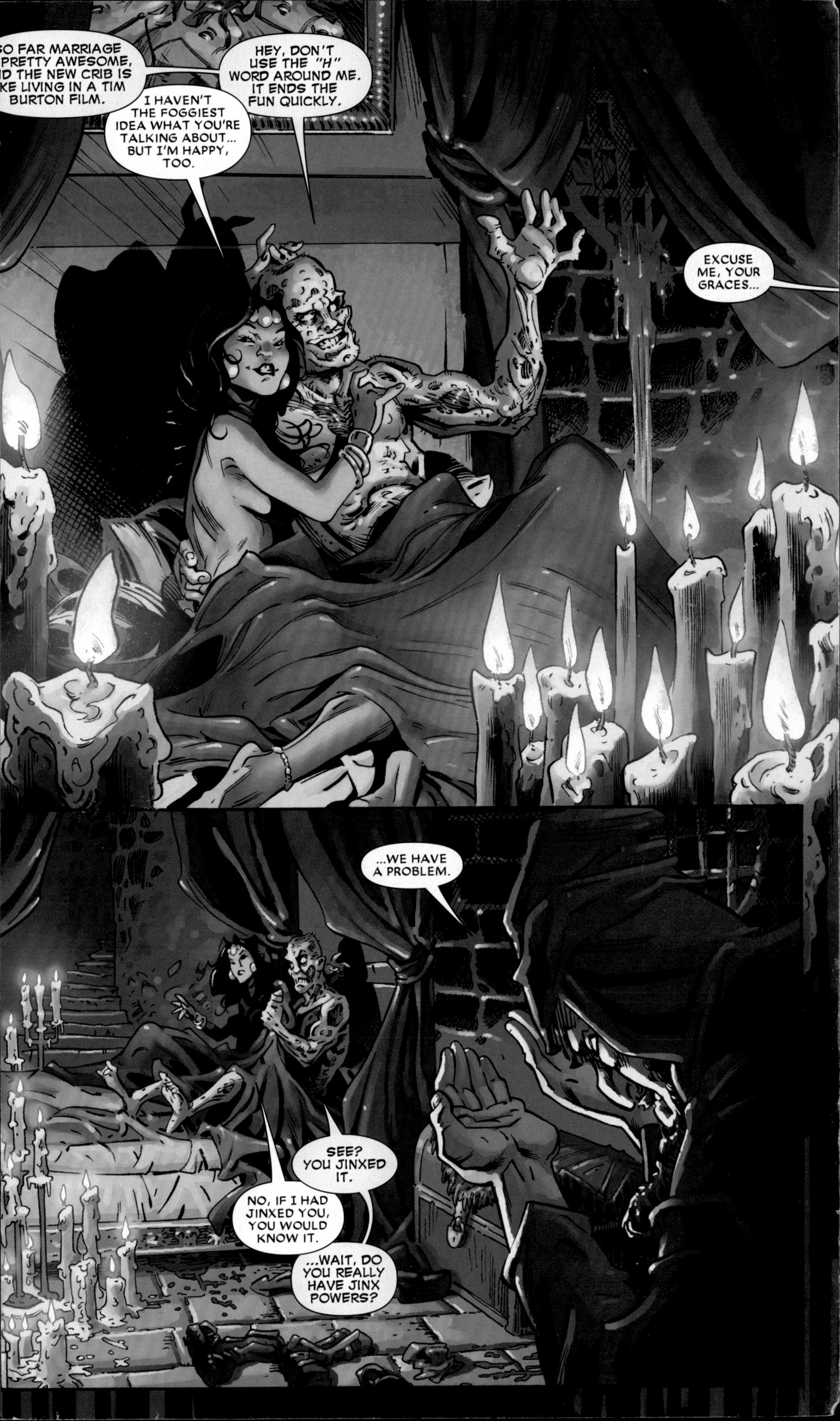
SO FAR MARRIAGE PRETTY AWESOME, ND THE NEW CRIB IS KE LIVING IN A TIM BURTON FILM.
I HAVEN'T THE FOGGIEST IDEA WHAT YOU'RE TALKING ABOUT... BUT I'M HAPPY, TOO.
HEY, DON'T USE THE "H" WORD AROUND ME. IT ENDS THE FUN QUICKLY.
EXCUSE ME, YOUR GRACES...
...WE HAVE A PROBLEM.
SEE? YOU JINXED IT.
NO, IF I HAD JINXED YOU, YOU WOULD KNOW IT.
...WAIT, DO YOU REALLY HAVE JINX POWERS?

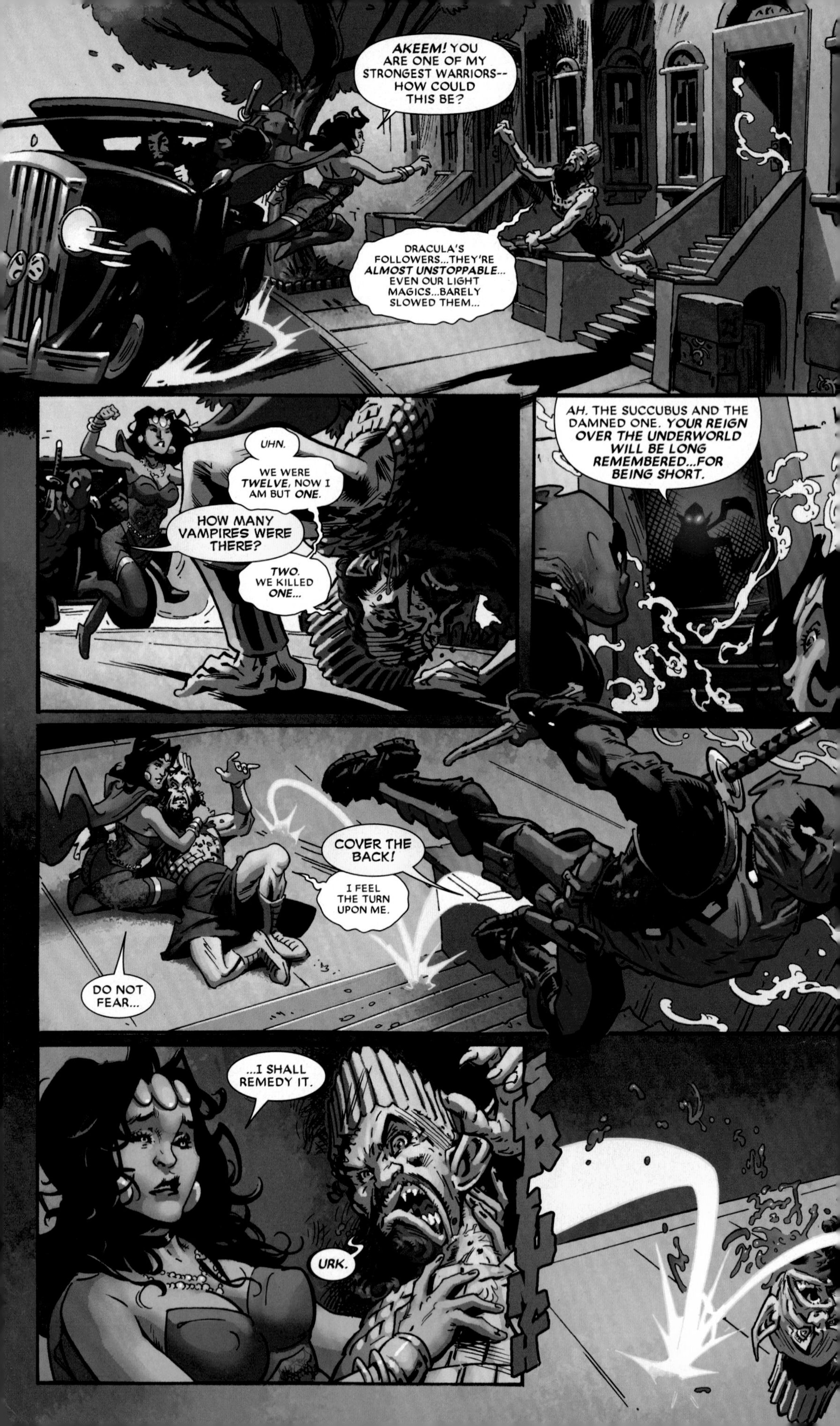
AKEEM! YOU ARE ONE OF MY STRONGEST WARRIORS-- HOW COULD THIS BE?
DRACULA'S FOLLOWERS...THEY'RE ALMOST UNSTOPPABLE... EVEN OUR LIGHT MAGICS...BARELY SLOWED THEM...
UHN.
WE WERE TWELVE, NOW I AM BUT ONE.
HOW MANY VAMPIRES WERE THERE?
TWO. WE KILLED ONE...
AH. THE SUCCUBUS AND THE DAMNED ONE. YOUR REIGN OVER THE UNDERWORLD WILL BE LONG REMEMBERED...FOR BEING SHORT.
COVER THE BACK!
I FEEL THE TURN UPON ME.
DO NOT FEAR...
...I SHALL REMEDY IT.
URK.

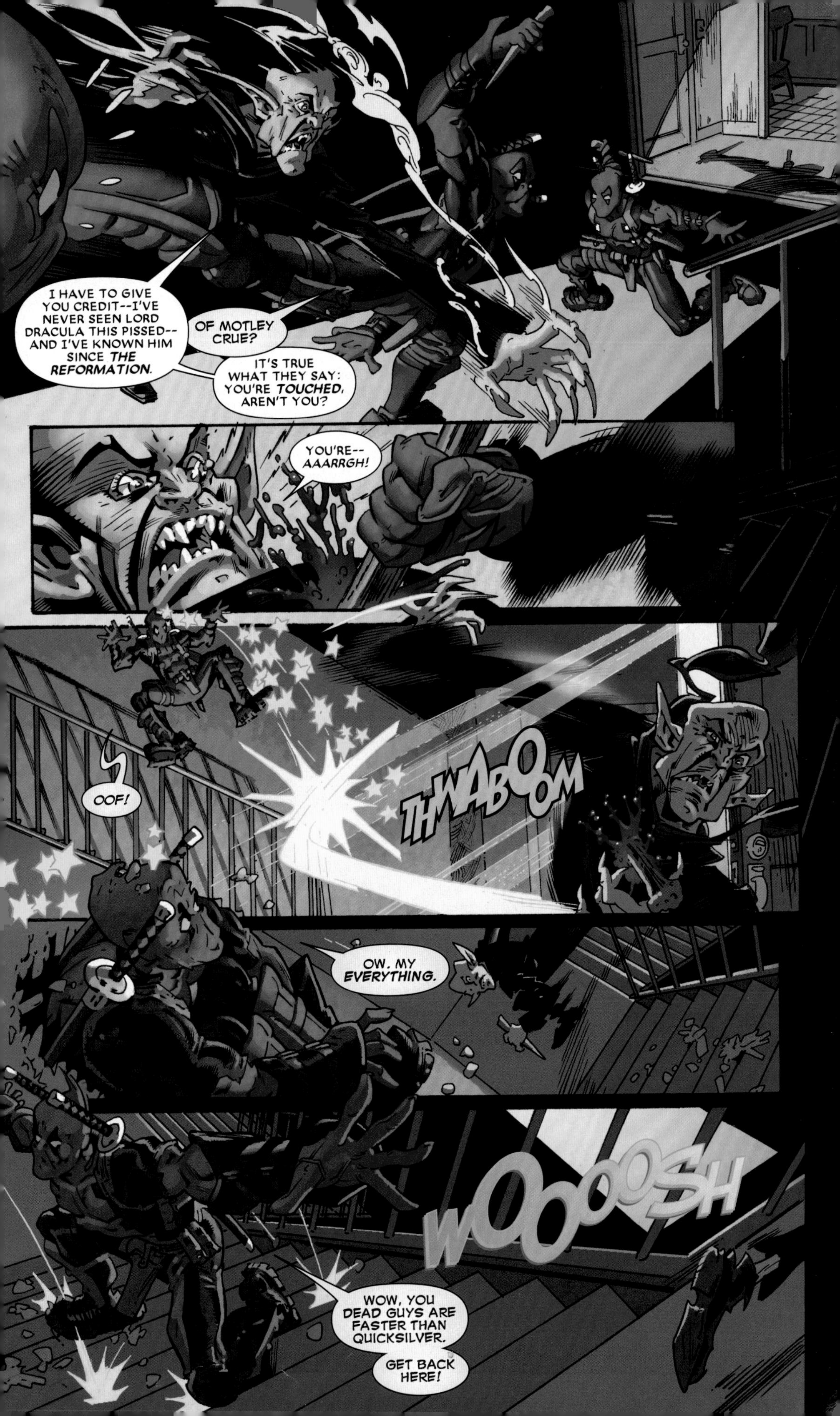
I HAVE TO GIVE YOU CREDIT--I'VE NEVER SEEN LORD DRACULA THIS PISSED--AND I'VE KNOWN HIM SINCE *THE REFORMATION*.
OF MOTLEY CRUE?
IT'S TRUE WHAT THEY SAY: YOU'RE *TOUCHED*, AREN'T YOU?
YOU'RE--AAAARRGH!
OOF!
THWABOOM
OW. MY *EVERYTHING*.
WOOOOSH
WOW, YOU DEAD GUYS ARE FASTER THAN QUICKSILVER.
GET BACK HERE!

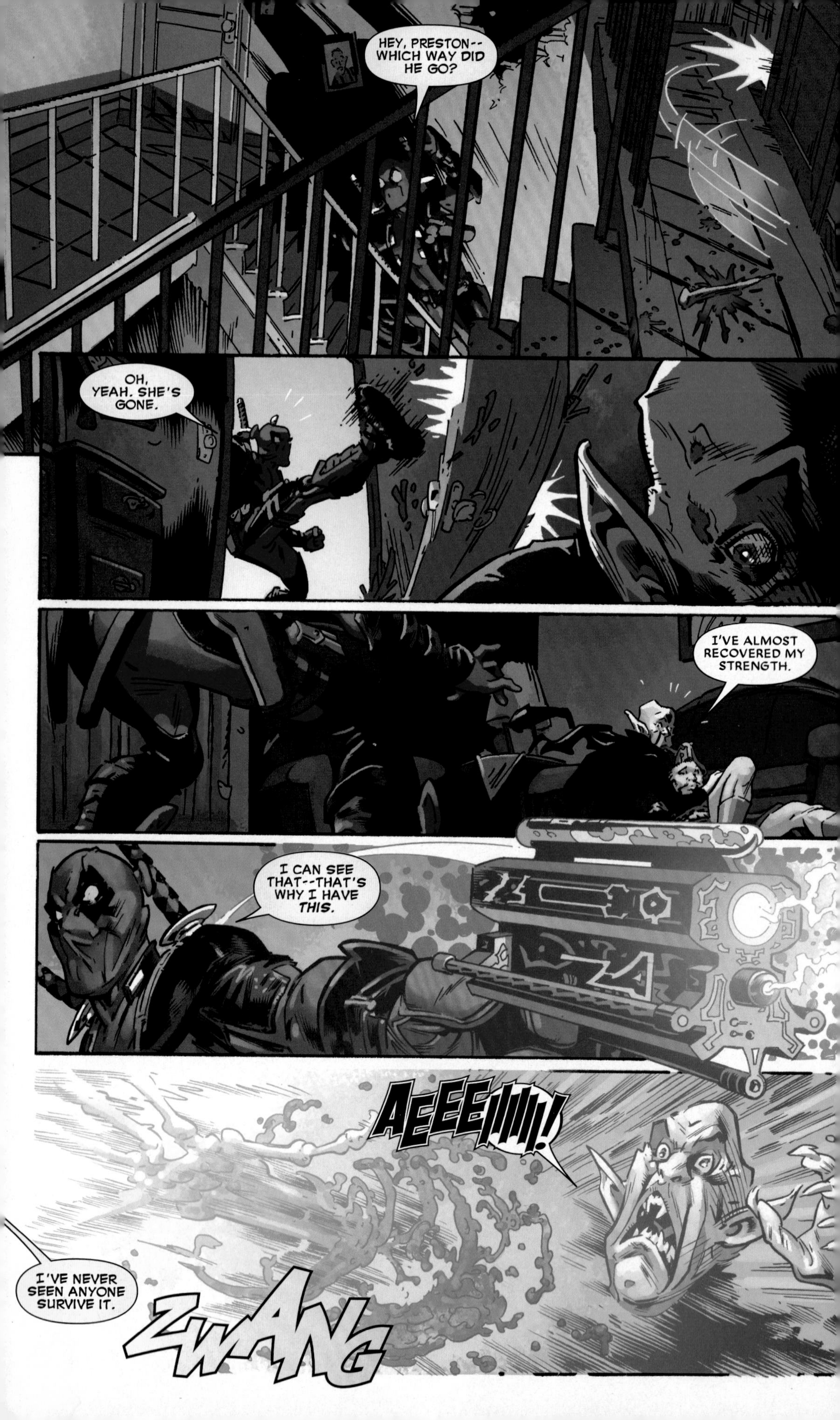
HEY, PRESTON--
WHICH WAY DID
HE GO?
OH,
YEAH. SHE'S
GONE.
I'VE ALMOST
RECOVERED MY
STRENGTH.
I CAN SEE
THAT--THAT'S
WHY I HAVE
THIS.
AEEEIIIII!
I'VE NEVER
SEEN ANYONE
SURVIVE IT.
ZWANG

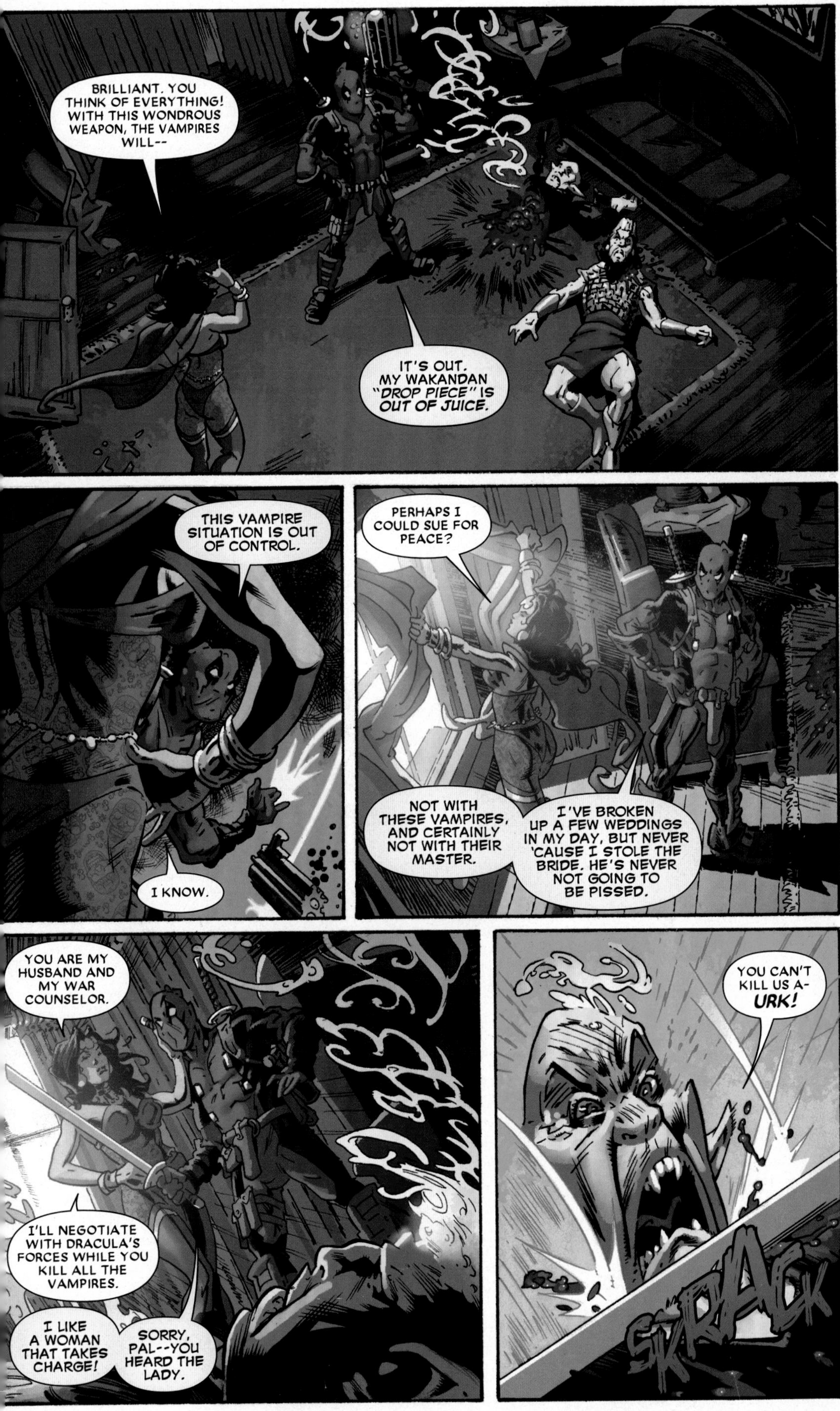
BRILLIANT. YOU THINK OF EVERYTHING! WITH THIS WONDROUS WEAPON, THE VAMPIRES WILL--
IT'S OUT. MY WAKANDAN "DROP PIECE" IS OUT OF JUICE.
THIS VAMPIRE SITUATION IS OUT OF CONTROL.
I KNOW.
PERHAPS I COULD SUE FOR PEACE?
NOT WITH THESE VAMPIRES, AND CERTAINLY NOT WITH THEIR MASTER.
I'VE BROKEN UP A FEW WEDDINGS IN MY DAY, BUT NEVER 'CAUSE I STOLE THE BRIDE. HE'S NEVER NOT GOING TO BE PISSED.
YOU ARE MY HUSBAND AND MY WAR COUNSELOR.
I'LL NEGOTIATE WITH DRACULA'S FORCES WHILE YOU KILL ALL THE VAMPIRES.
I LIKE A WOMAN THAT TAKES CHARGE!
SORRY, PAL--YOU HEARD THE LADY.
YOU CAN'T KILL US A- URK!
SKRACK

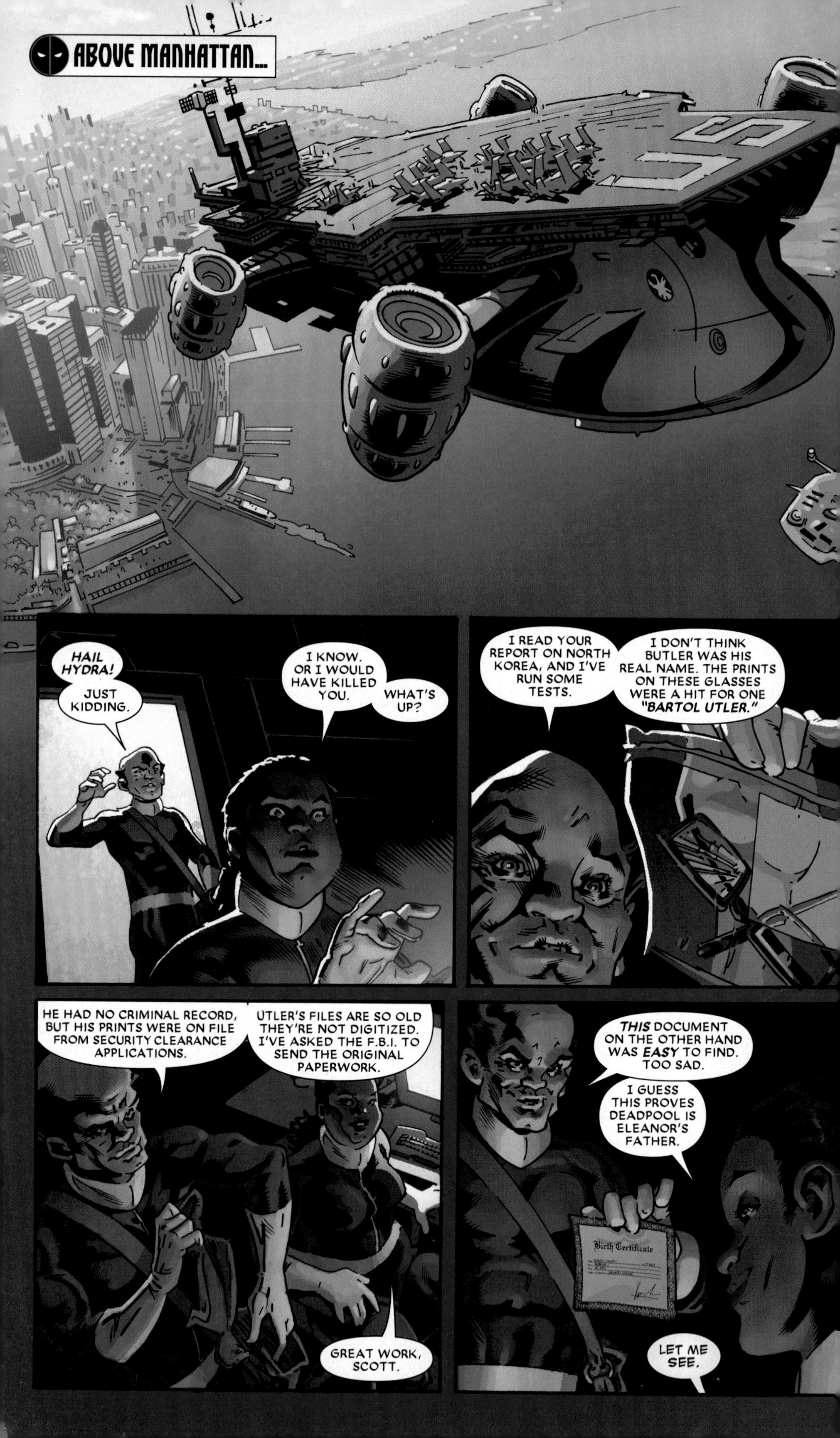
ABOVE MANHATTAN...
HAIL HYDRA!
JUST KIDDING.
I KNOW. OR I WOULD HAVE KILLED YOU.
WHAT'S UP?
I READ YOUR REPORT ON NORTH KOREA, AND I'VE RUN SOME TESTS.
I DON'T THINK BUTLER WAS HIS REAL NAME. THE PRINTS ON THESE GLASSES WERE A HIT FOR ONE "BARTOL UTLER."
HE HAD NO CRIMINAL RECORD, BUT HIS PRINTS WERE ON FILE FROM SECURITY CLEARANCE APPLICATIONS.
UTLER'S FILES ARE SO OLD THEY'RE NOT DIGITIZED. I'VE ASKED THE F.B.I. TO SEND THE ORIGINAL PAPERWORK.
GREAT WORK, SCOTT.
THIS DOCUMENT ON THE OTHER HAND WAS EASY TO FIND. TOO SAD.
I GUESS THIS PROVES DEADPOOL IS ELEANOR'S FATHER.
Birth Certificate
LET ME SEE.

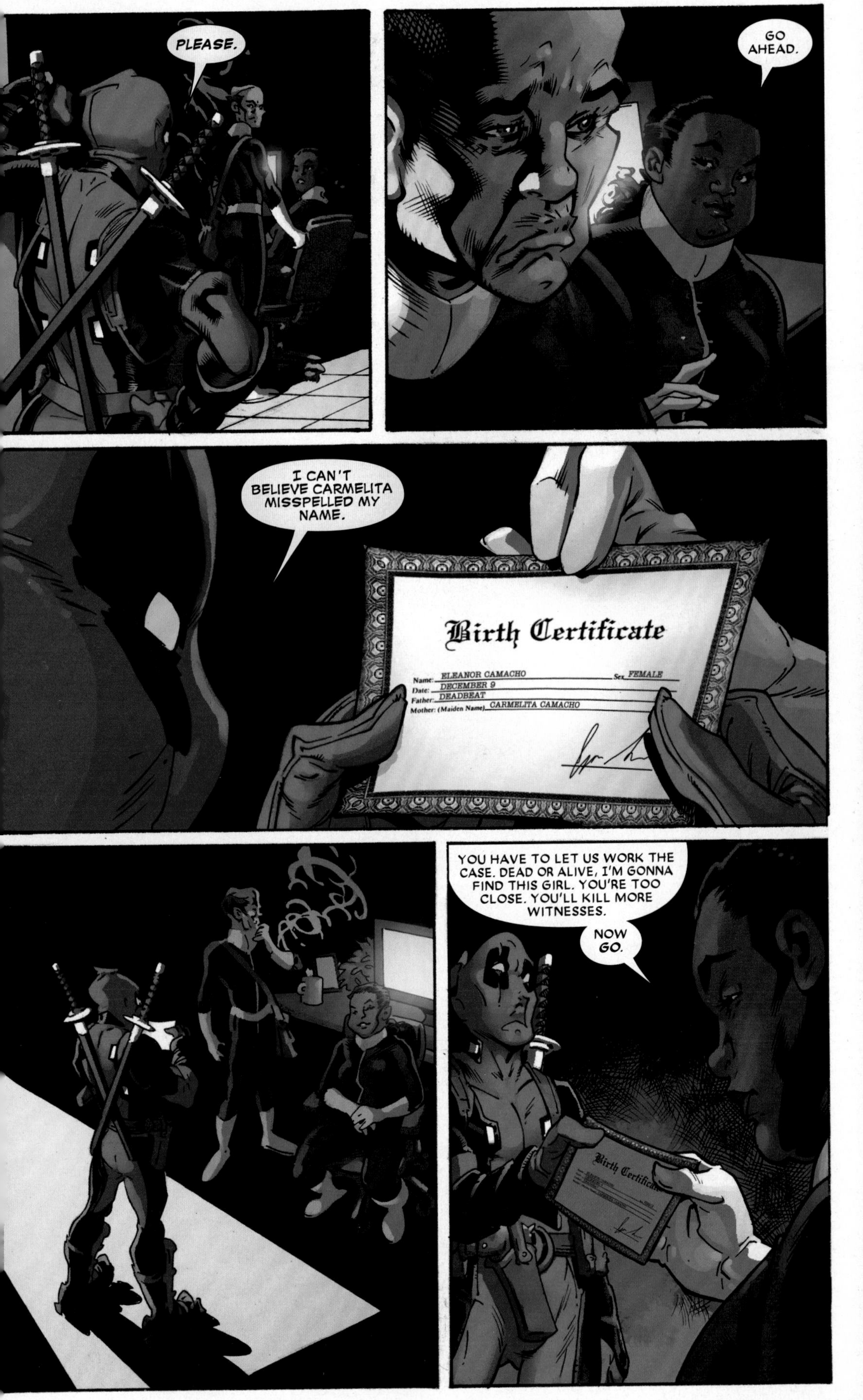
PLEASE.
GO AHEAD.
I CAN'T BELIEVE CARMELITA MISSPELLED MY NAME.
Birth Certificate
Name: ELEANOR CAMACHO
Sex FEMALE
Date: DECEMBER 9
Father: DEADBEAT
Mother: (Maiden Name) CARMELITA CAMACHO
YOU HAVE TO LET US WORK THE CASE. DEAD OR ALIVE, I'M GONNA FIND THIS GIRL. YOU'RE TOO CLOSE. YOU'LL KILL MORE WITNESSES.
NOW GO.
Birth Certificate

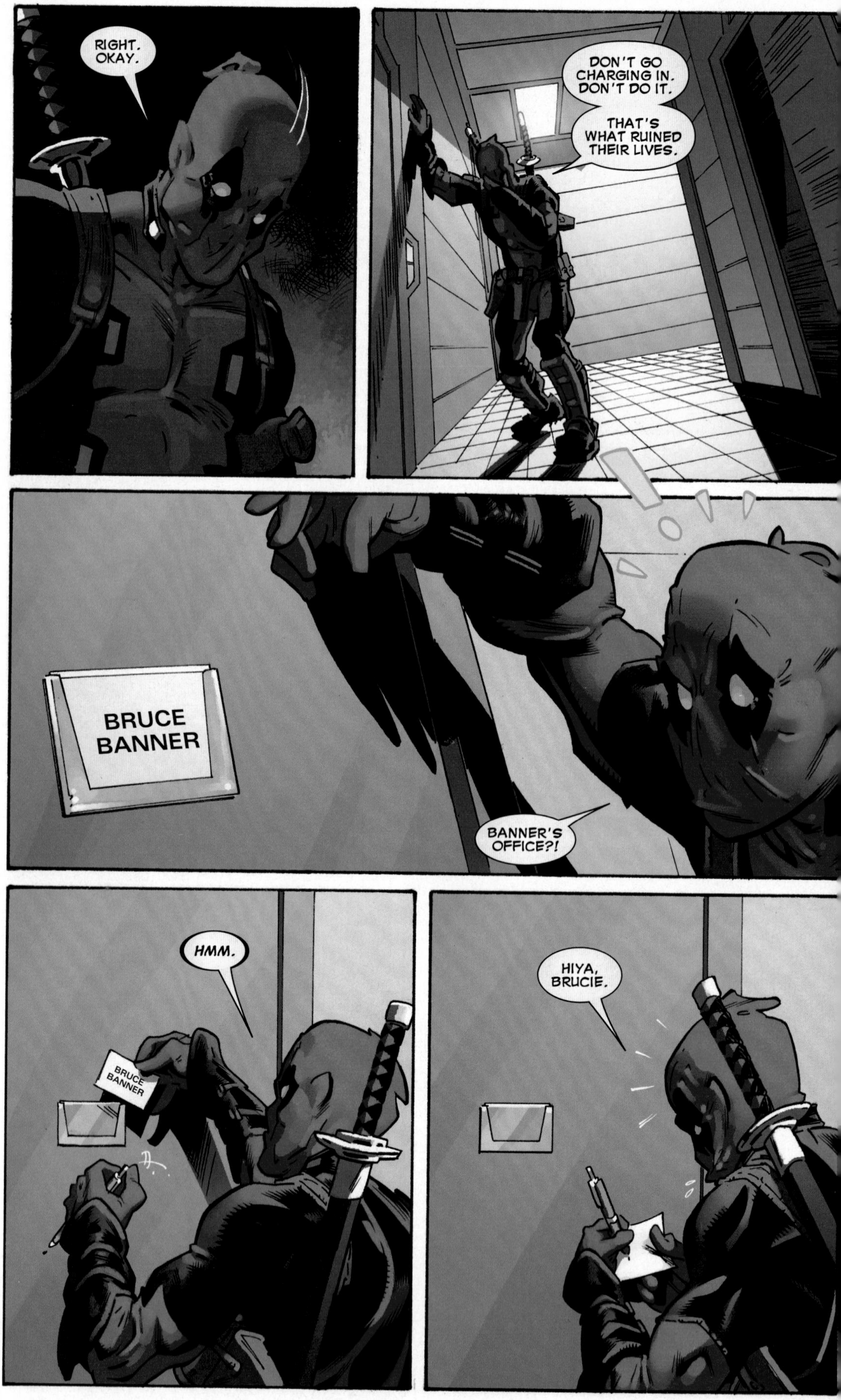
RIGHT. OKAY.
DON'T GO CHARGING IN. DON'T DO IT.
THAT'S WHAT RUINED THEIR LIVES.
BRUCE BANNER
BANNER'S OFFICE?!
HMM.
BRUCE BANNER
HIYA, BRUCIE.

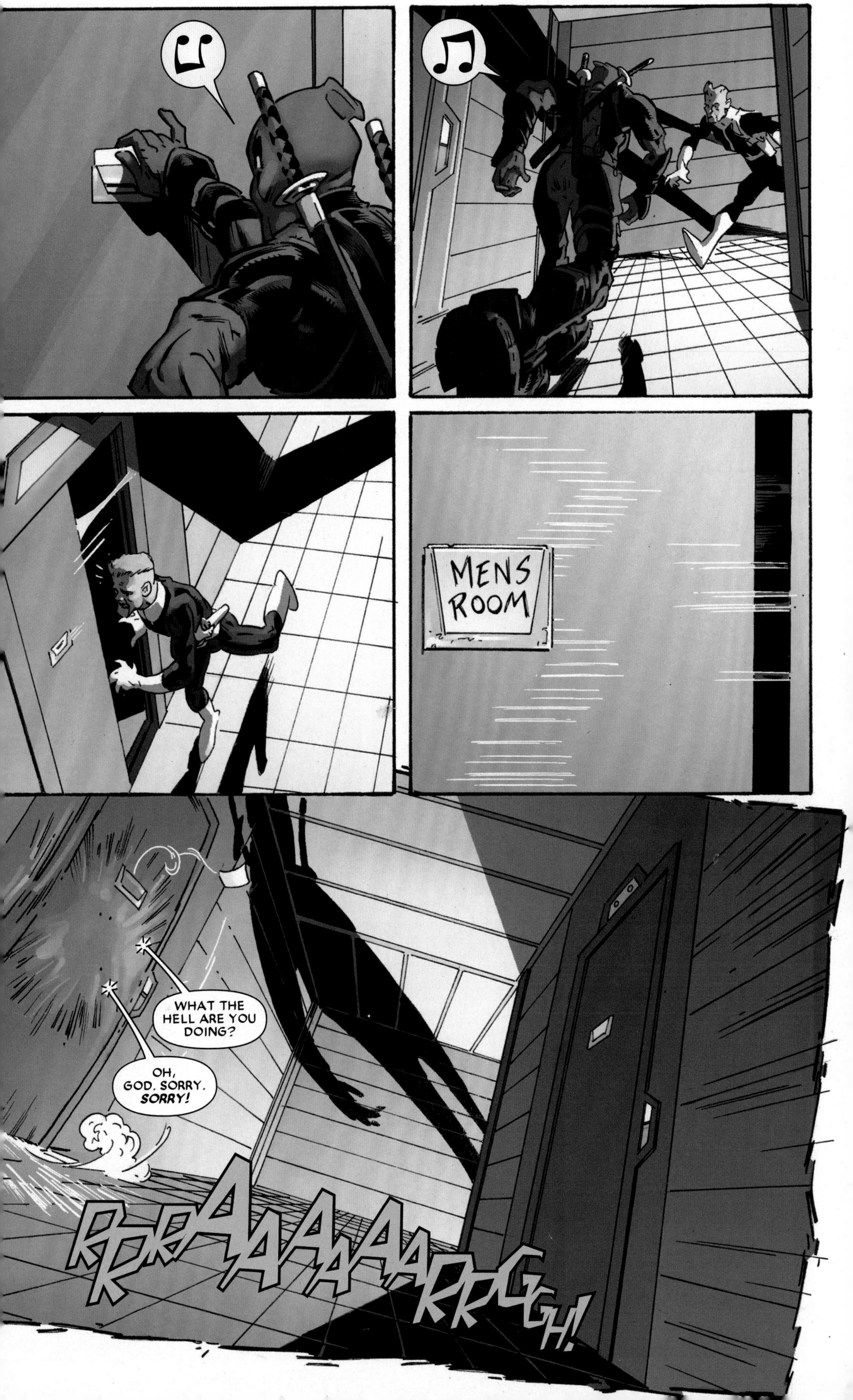
MENS
ROOM
WHAT THE HELL ARE YOU DOING?
OH, GOD. SORRY. SORRY!
RRRRAAAAAAAARRRGGH!

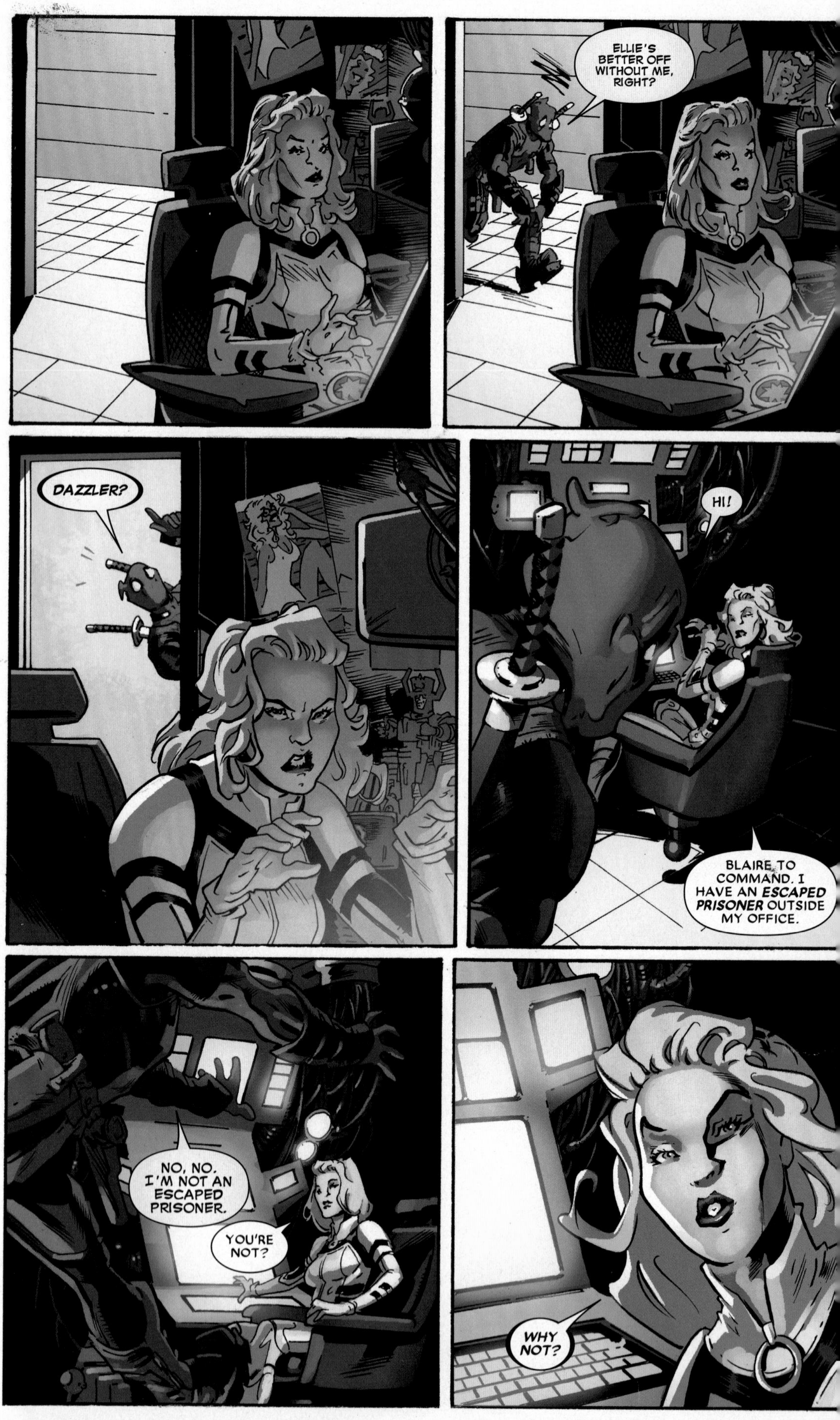
ELLIE'S BETTER OFF WITHOUT ME, RIGHT?
DAZZLER?
HI!
BLAIRE TO COMMAND. I HAVE AN *ESCAPED PRISONER* OUTSIDE MY OFFICE.
NO, NO. I'M NOT AN ESCAPED PRISONER.
YOU'RE NOT?
WHY NOT?

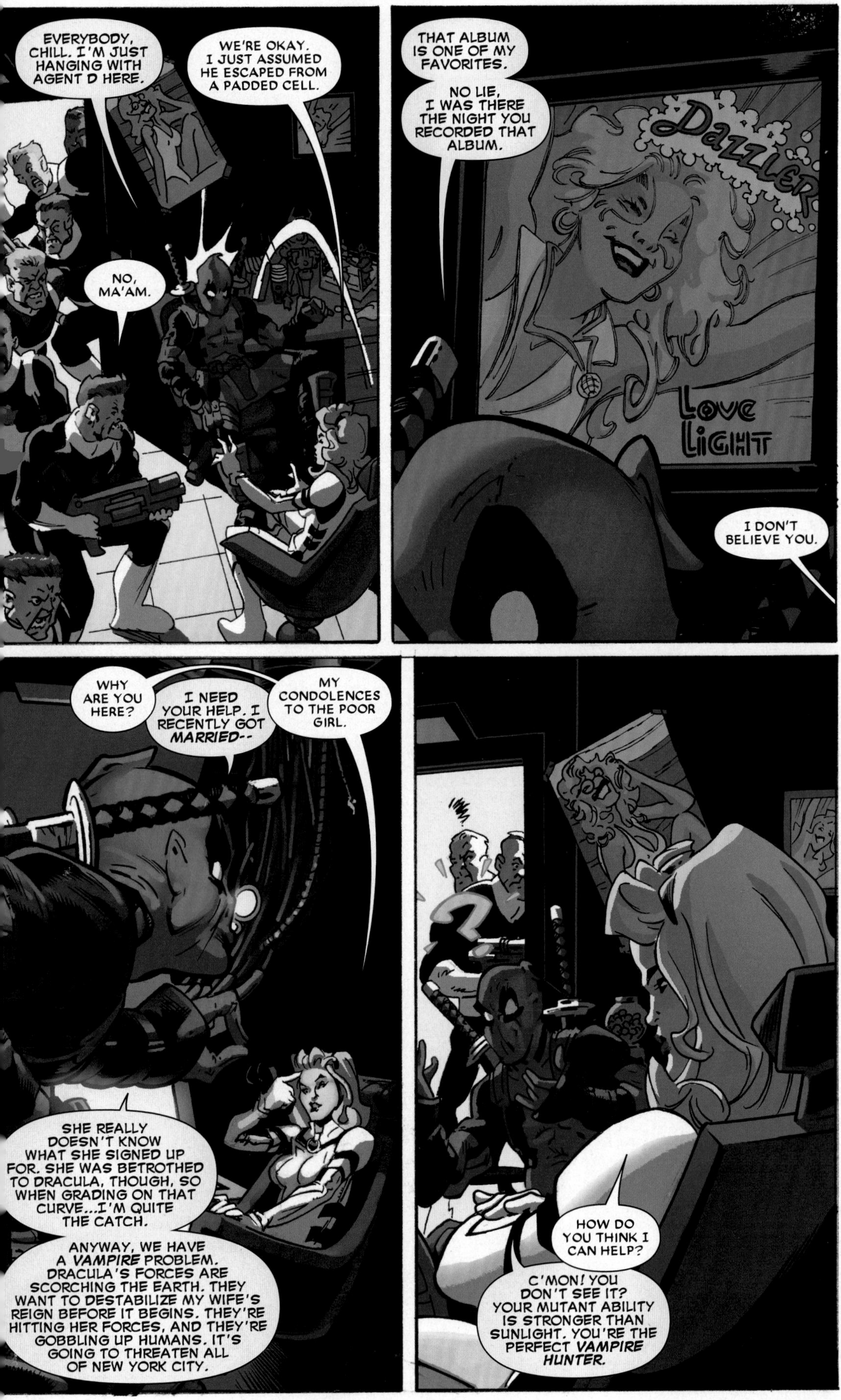
EVERYBODY, CHILL. I'M JUST HANGING WITH AGENT D HERE.
WE'RE OKAY. I JUST ASSUMED HE ESCAPED FROM A PADDED CELL.
NO, MA'AM.
THAT ALBUM IS ONE OF MY FAVORITES.
NO LIE, I WAS THERE THE NIGHT YOU RECORDED THAT ALBUM.
DAZZLER
LOVE LIGHT
I DON'T BELIEVE YOU.
WHY ARE YOU HERE?
I NEED YOUR HELP. I RECENTLY GOT MARRIED--
MY CONDOLENCES TO THE POOR GIRL.
SHE REALLY DOESN'T KNOW WHAT SHE SIGNED UP FOR. SHE WAS BETROTHED TO DRACULA, THOUGH, SO WHEN GRADING ON THAT CURVE...I'M QUITE THE CATCH.
ANYWAY, WE HAVE A VAMPIRE PROBLEM. DRACULA'S FORCES ARE SCORCHING THE EARTH. THEY WANT TO DESTABILIZE MY WIFE'S REIGN BEFORE IT BEGINS. THEY'RE HITTING HER FORCES, AND THEY'RE GOBBLING UP HUMANS. IT'S GOING TO THREATEN ALL OF NEW YORK CITY.
HOW DO YOU THINK I CAN HELP?
C'MON! YOU DON'T SEE IT? YOUR MUTANT ABILITY IS STRONGER THAN SUNLIGHT. YOU'RE THE PERFECT VAMPIRE HUNTER.

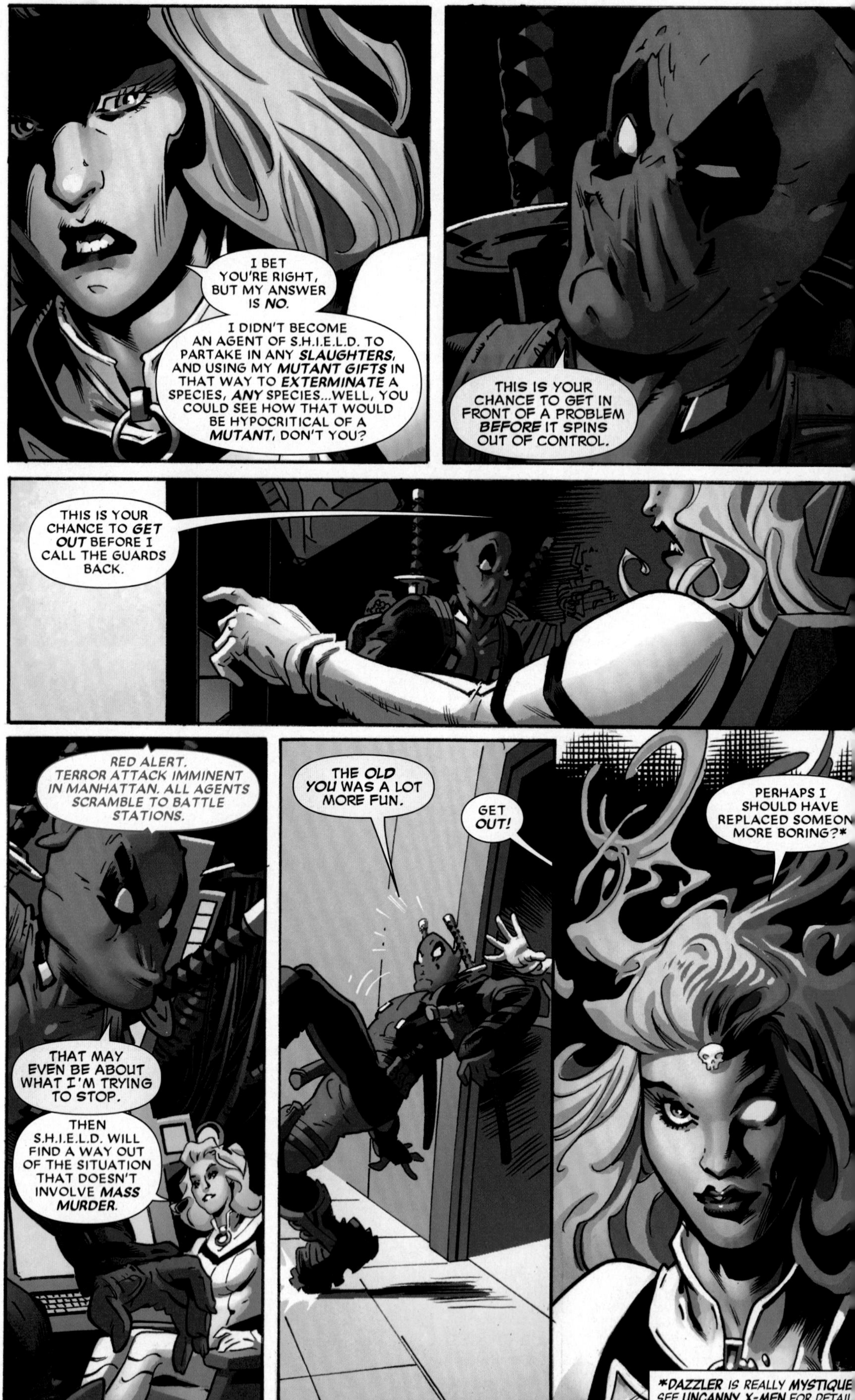
I BET YOU'RE RIGHT, BUT MY ANSWER IS NO.
I DIDN'T BECOME AN AGENT OF S.H.I.E.L.D. TO PARTAKE IN ANY SLAUGHTERS, AND USING MY MUTANT GIFTS IN THAT WAY TO EXTERMINATE A SPECIES, ANY SPECIES...WELL, YOU COULD SEE HOW THAT WOULD BE HYPOCRITICAL OF A MUTANT, DON'T YOU?
THIS IS YOUR CHANCE TO GET IN FRONT OF A PROBLEM BEFORE IT SPINS OUT OF CONTROL.
THIS IS YOUR CHANCE TO GET OUT BEFORE I CALL THE GUARDS BACK.
RED ALERT. TERROR ATTACK IMMINENT IN MANHATTAN. ALL AGENTS SCRAMBLE TO BATTLE STATIONS.
THAT MAY EVEN BE ABOUT WHAT I'M TRYING TO STOP.
THEN S.H.I.E.L.D. WILL FIND A WAY OUT OF THE SITUATION THAT DOESN'T INVOLVE MASS MURDER.
THE OLD YOU WAS A LOT MORE FUN.
GET OUT!
PERHAPS I SHOULD HAVE REPLACED SOMEON MORE BORING?*
*DAZZLER IS REALLY MYSTIQUE SEE UNCANNY X-MEN FOR DETAIL --JORDAN

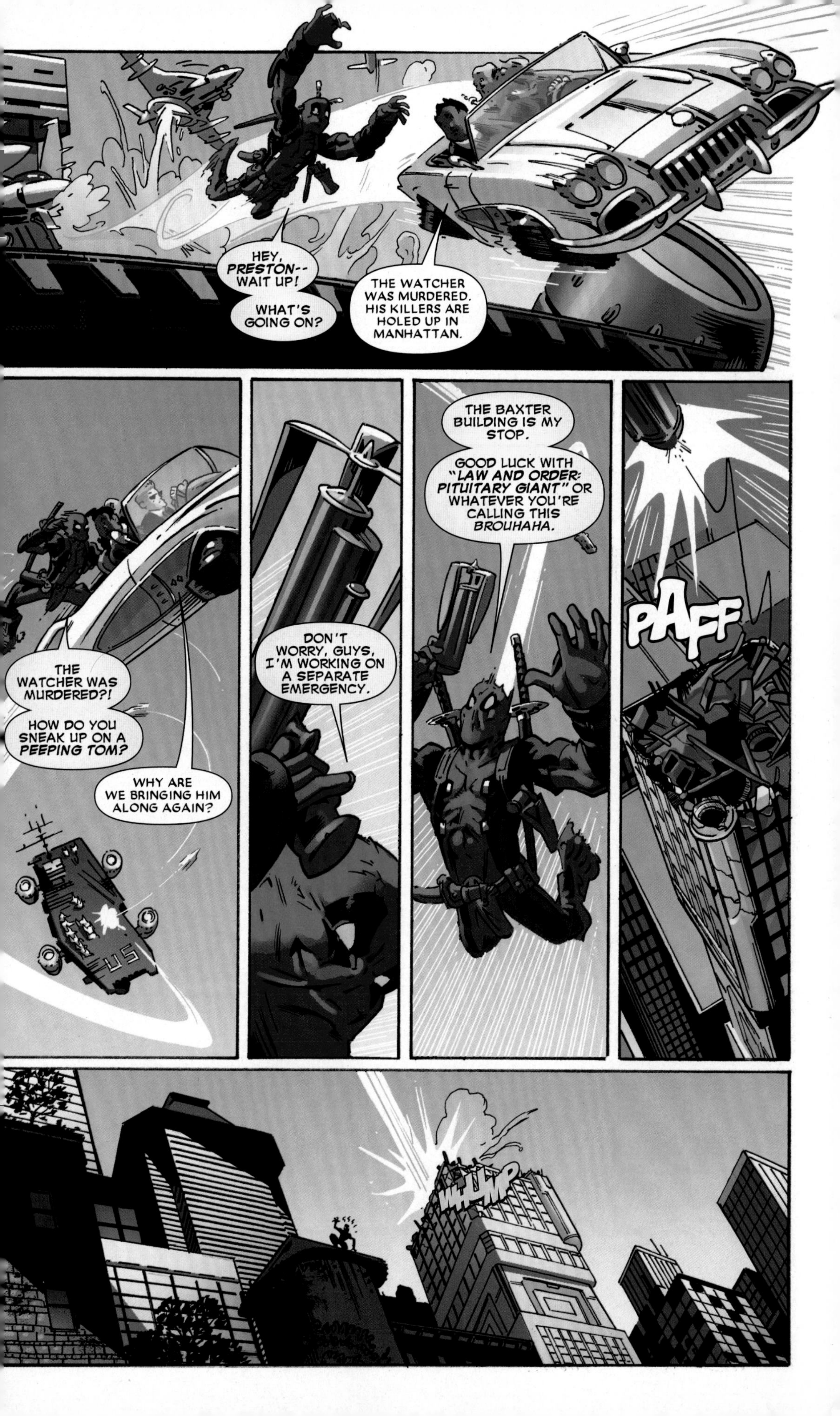

HEY, PRESTON-- WAIT UP!
WHAT'S GOING ON?
THE WATCHER WAS MURDERED. HIS KILLERS ARE HOLED UP IN MANHATTAN.
THE WATCHER WAS MURDERED?!
HOW DO YOU SNEAK UP ON A PEEPING TOM?
WHY ARE WE BRINGING HIM ALONG AGAIN?
DON'T WORRY, GUYS, I'M WORKING ON A SEPARATE EMERGENCY.
THE BAXTER BUILDING IS MY STOP.
GOOD LUCK WITH "LAW AND ORDER: PITUITARY GIANT" OR WHATEVER YOU'RE CALLING THIS BROUHAHA.
PAFF
WHUMP

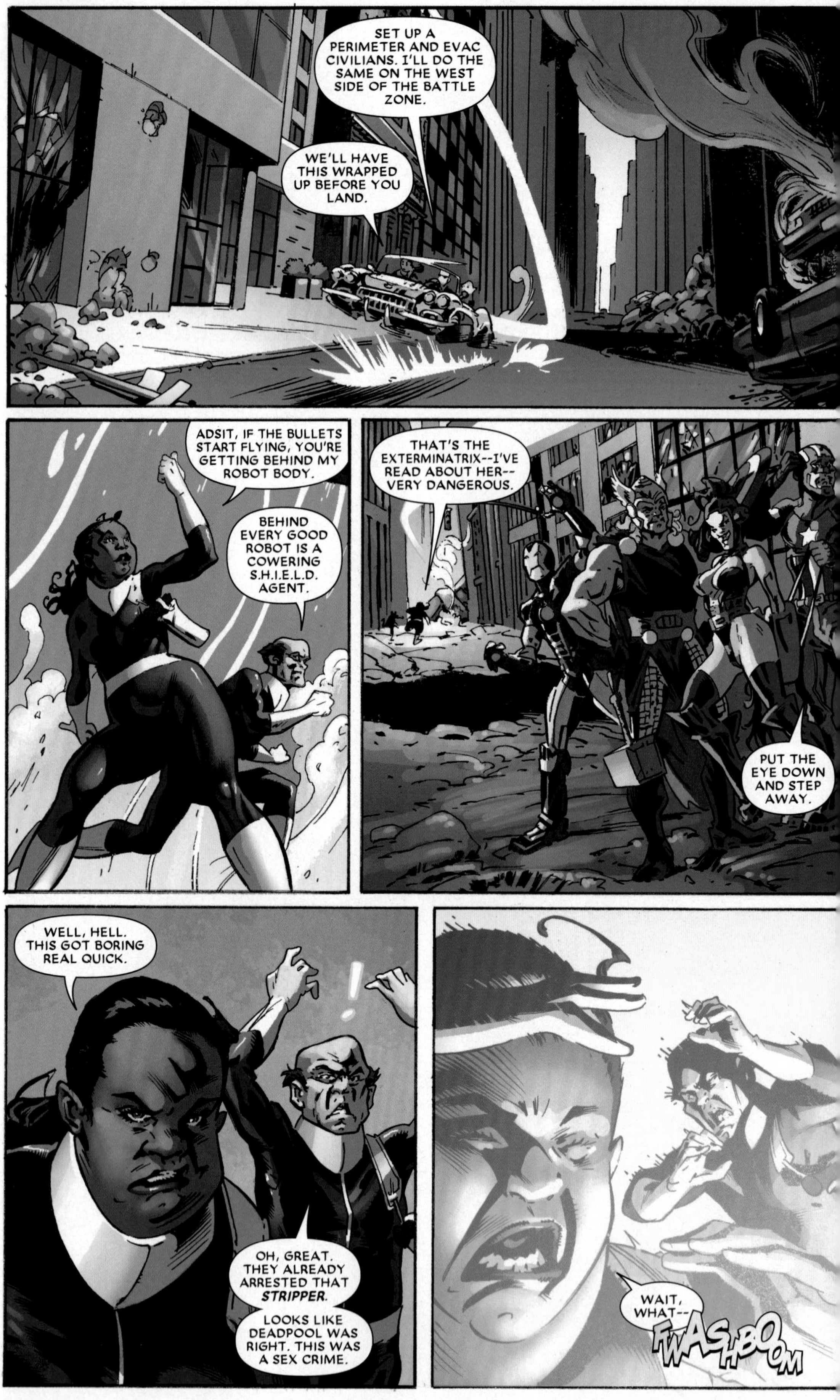
SET UP A PERIMETER AND EVAC CIVILIANS. I'LL DO THE SAME ON THE WEST SIDE OF THE BATTLE ZONE.
WE'LL HAVE THIS WRAPPED UP BEFORE YOU LAND.
ADSIT, IF THE BULLETS START FLYING, YOU'RE GETTING BEHIND MY ROBOT BODY.
BEHIND EVERY GOOD ROBOT IS A COWERING S.H.I.E.L.D. AGENT.
THAT'S THE EXTERMINATRIX--I'VE READ ABOUT HER--VERY DANGEROUS.
PUT THE EYE DOWN AND STEP AWAY.
WELL, HELL. THIS GOT BORING REAL QUICK.
!
OH, GREAT. THEY ALREADY ARRESTED THAT *STRIPPER*.
LOOKS LIKE DEADPOOL WAS RIGHT. THIS WAS A SEX CRIME.
WAIT, WHAT--
FWASHBOOM

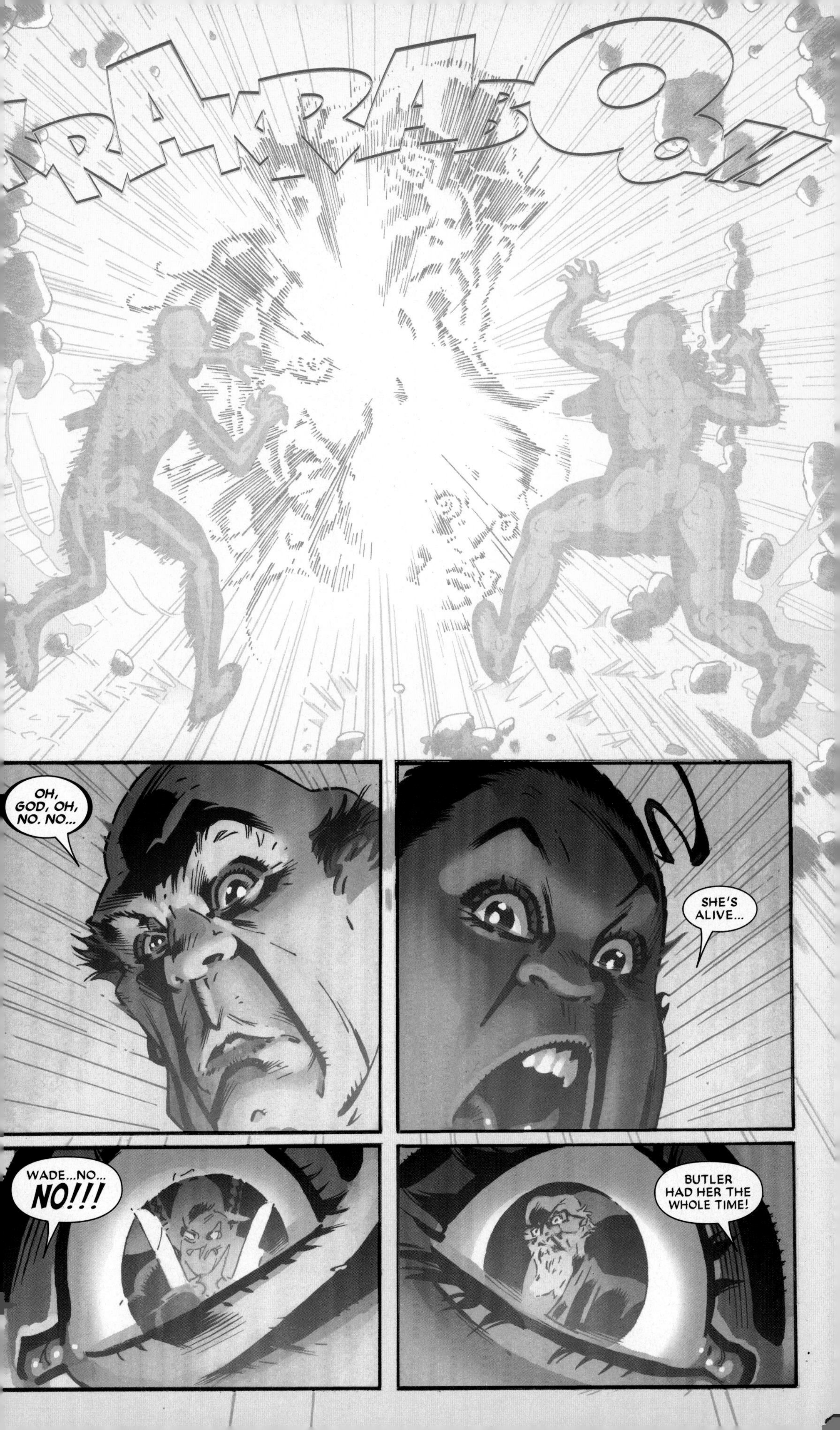
KRAKABOOM!!
OH, GOD, OH, NO. NO...
SHE'S ALIVE...
WADE...NO... NO!!!
BUTLER HAD HER THE WHOLE TIME!

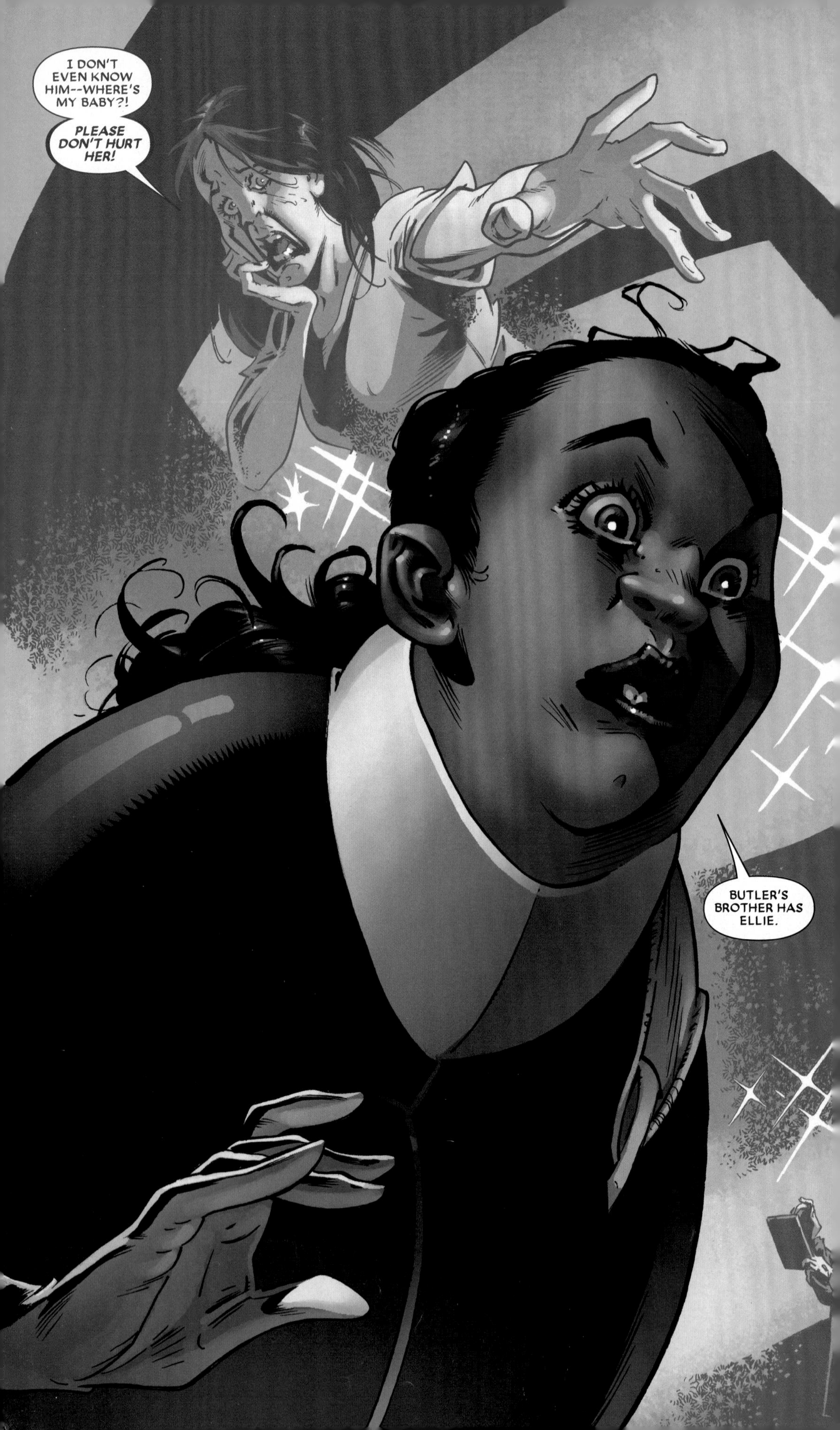
I DON'T EVEN KNOW HIM--WHERE'S MY BABY?!
PLEASE DON'T HURT HER!
BUTLER'S BROTHER HAS ELLIE.

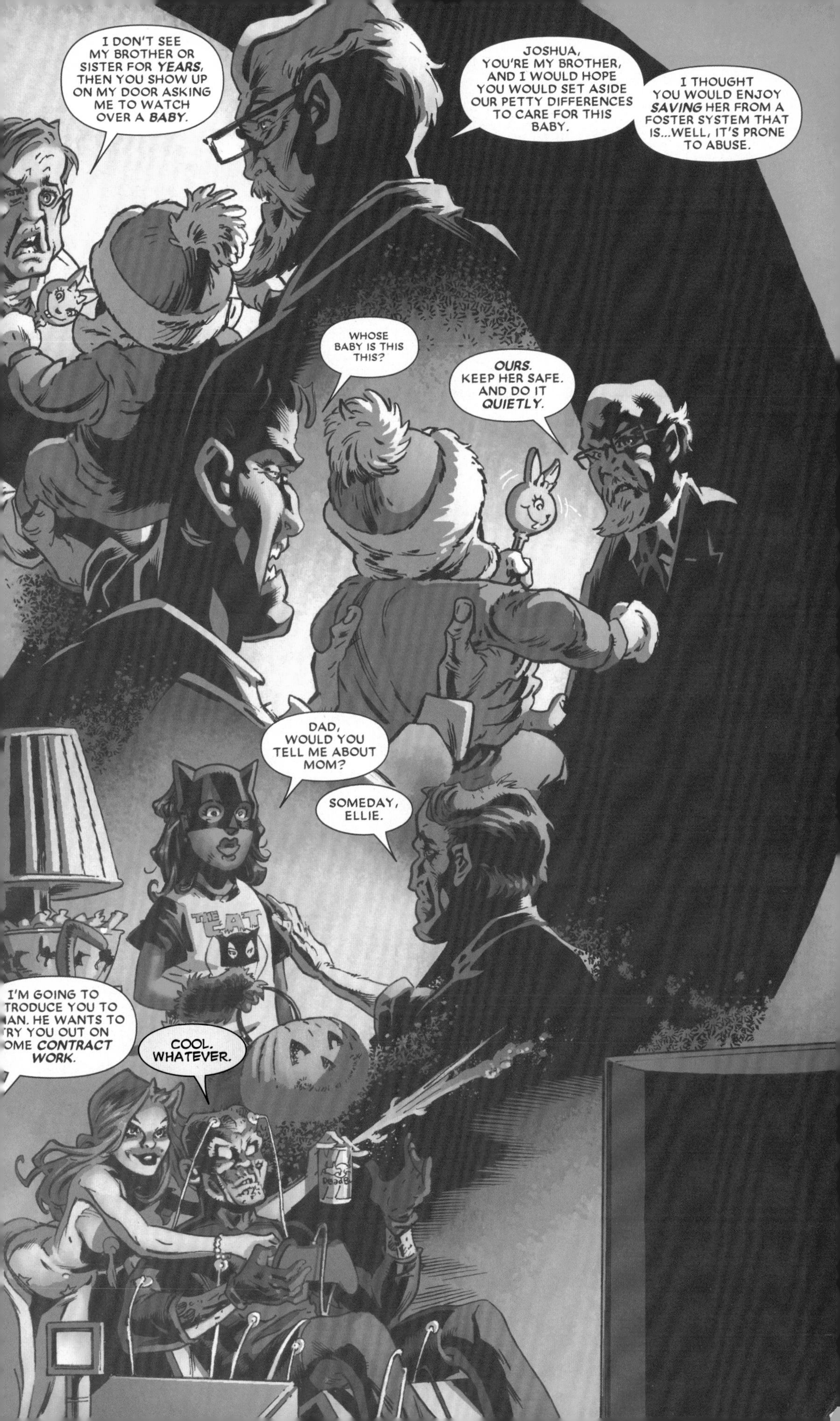
I DON'T SEE MY BROTHER OR SISTER FOR *YEARS*, THEN YOU SHOW UP ON MY DOOR ASKING ME TO WATCH OVER A *BABY*.
JOSHUA, YOU'RE MY BROTHER, AND I WOULD HOPE YOU WOULD SET ASIDE OUR PETTY DIFFERENCES TO CARE FOR THIS BABY.
I THOUGHT YOU WOULD ENJOY *SAVING* HER FROM A FOSTER SYSTEM THAT IS...WELL, IT'S PRONE TO ABUSE.
WHOSE BABY IS THIS THIS?
OURS. KEEP HER SAFE. AND DO IT *QUIETLY*.
DAD, WOULD YOU TELL ME ABOUT MOM?
SOMEDAY, ELLIE.
I'M GOING TO TRODUCE YOU TO IAN. HE WANTS TO TRY YOU OUT ON OME *CONTRACT WORK*.
COOL. WHATEVER.

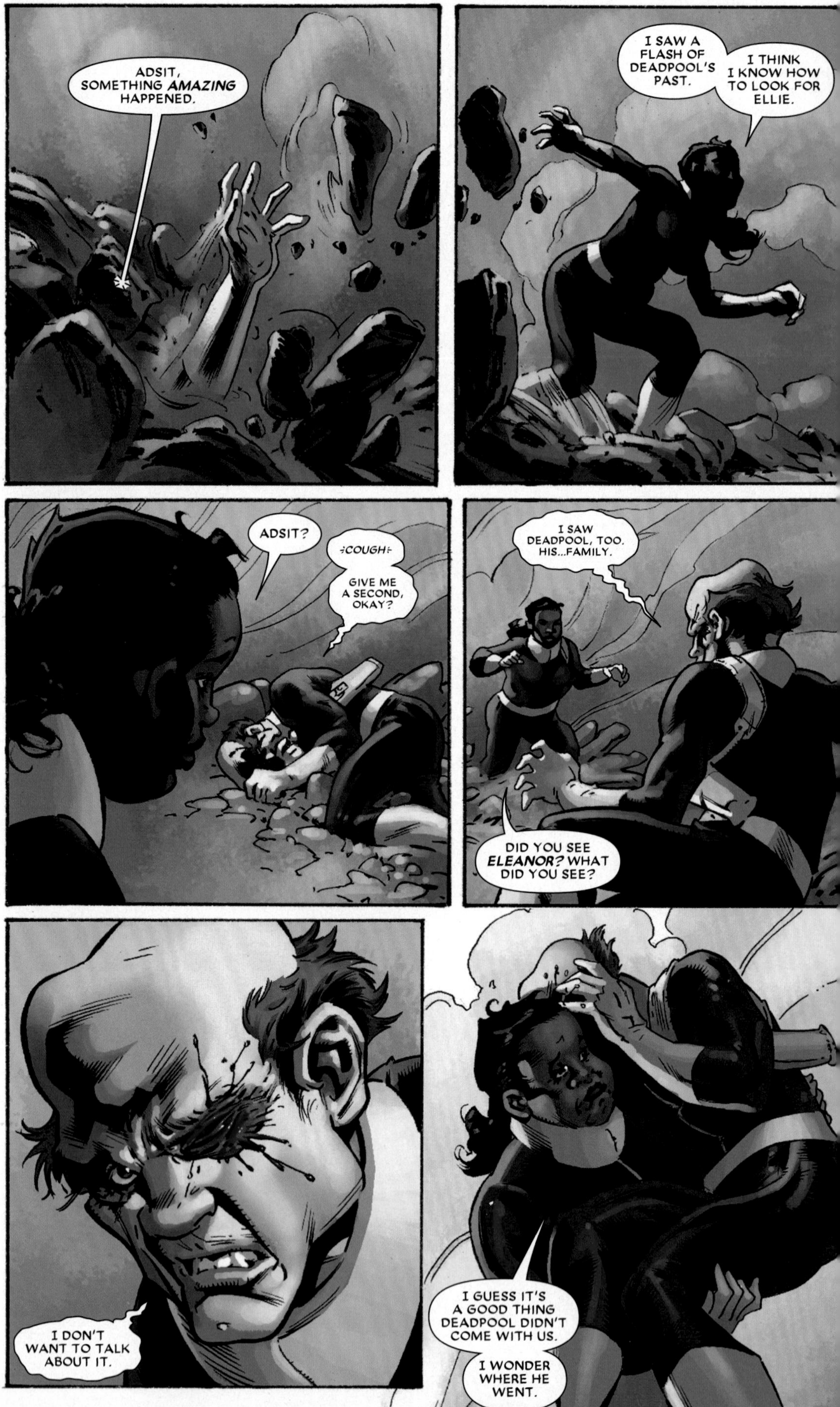
ADSIT, SOMETHING *AMAZING* HAPPENED.
I SAW A FLASH OF DEADPOOL'S PAST.
I THINK I KNOW HOW TO LOOK FOR ELLIE.
ADSIT?
÷COUGH÷
GIVE ME A SECOND, OKAY?
I SAW DEADPOOL, TOO. HIS...FAMILY.
DID YOU SEE *ELEANOR?* WHAT DID YOU SEE?
I DON'T WANT TO TALK ABOUT IT.
I GUESS IT'S A GOOD THING DEADPOOL DIDN'T COME WITH US.
I WONDER WHERE HE WENT.

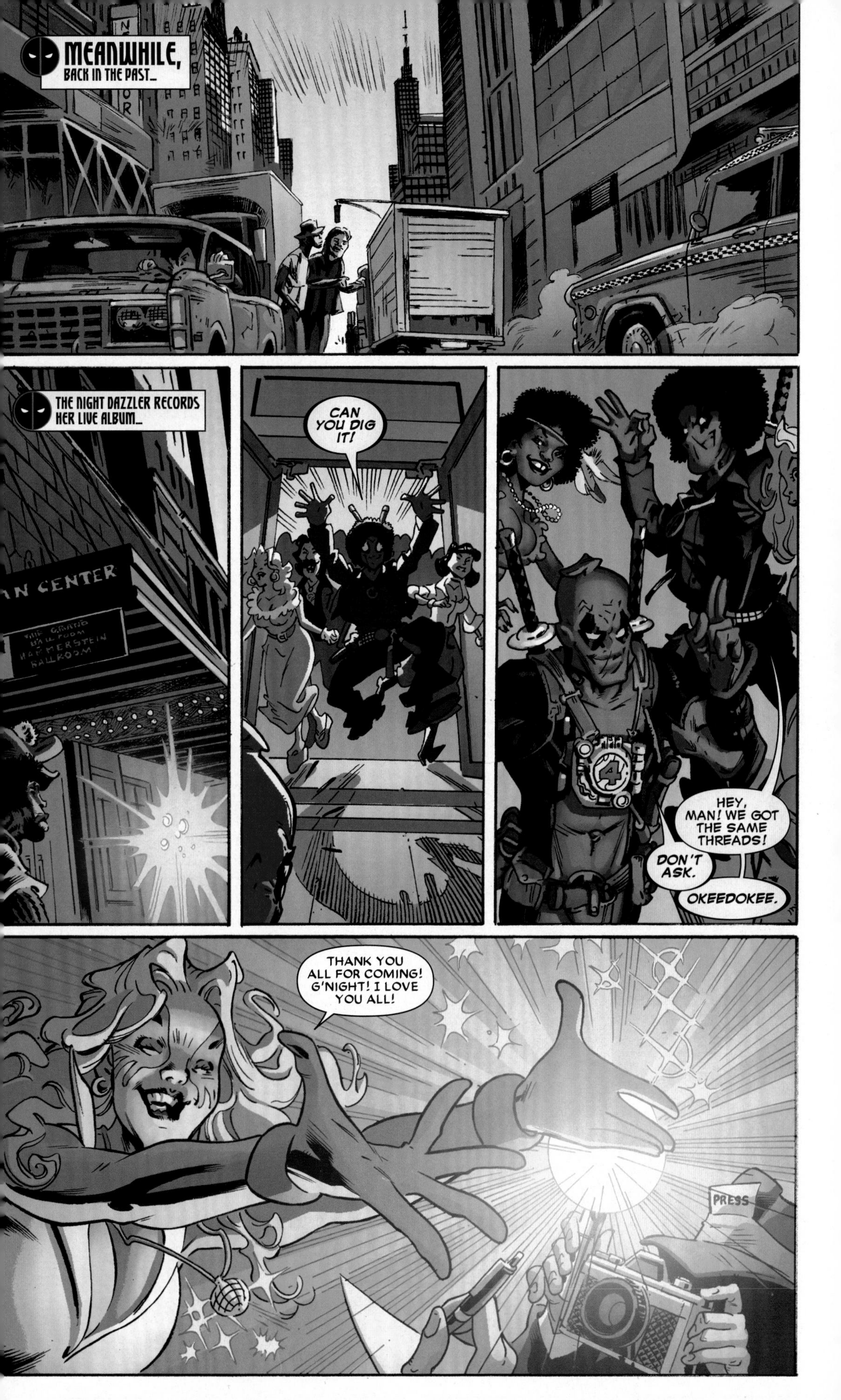
MEANWHILE, BACK IN THE PAST...
THE NIGHT DAZZLER RECORDS HER LIVE ALBUM...
AN CENTER
THE GRAND BALLROOM HAMMERSTEIN BALLROOM
CAN YOU DIG IT!
HEY, MAN! WE GOT THE SAME THREADS!
DON'T ASK.
OKEEDOKEE.
THANK YOU ALL FOR COMING! G'NIGHT! I LOVE YOU ALL!
PRESS

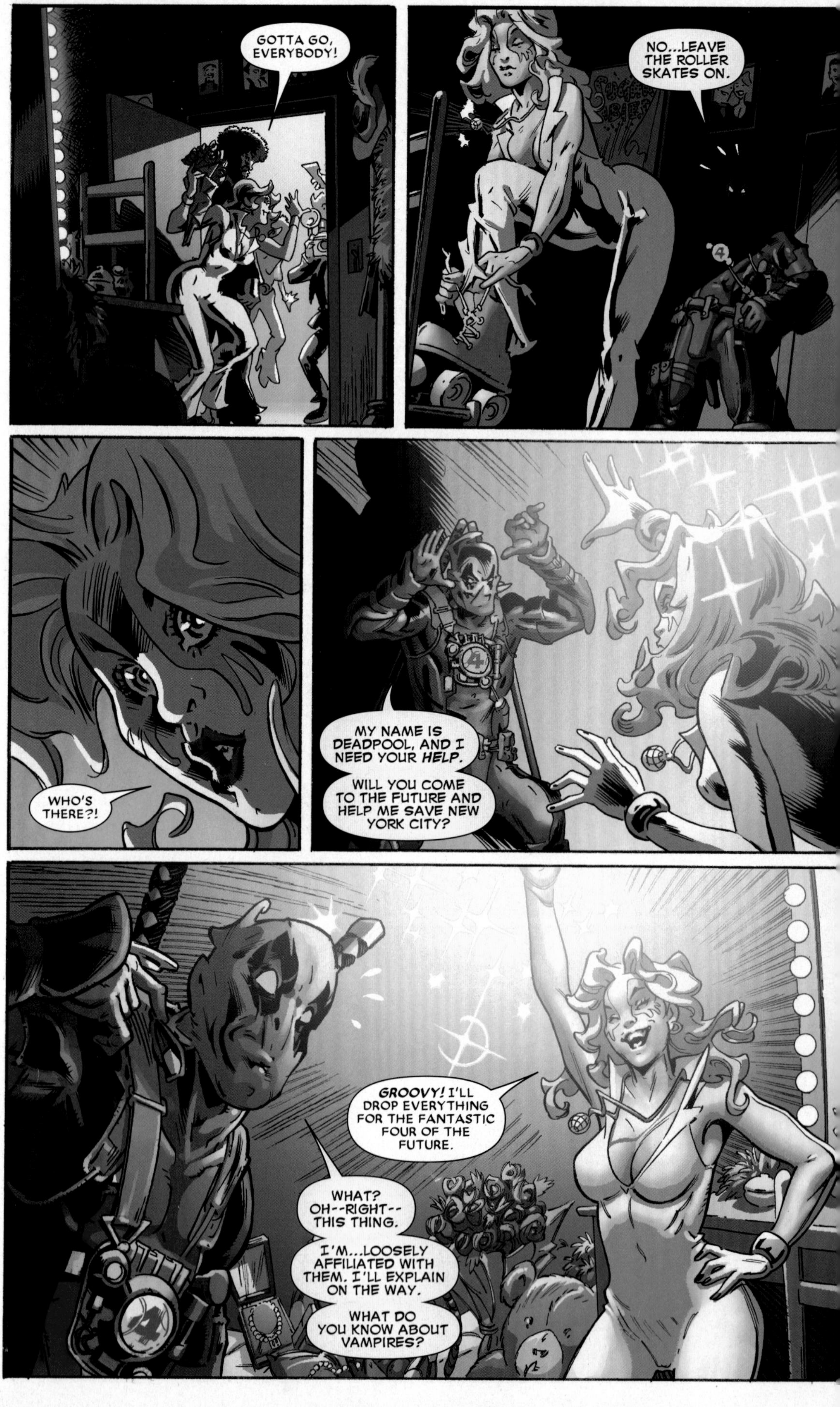

GOTTA GO, EVERYBODY!
NO...LEAVE THE ROLLER SKATES ON.
WHO'S THERE?!
MY NAME IS DEADPOOL, AND I NEED YOUR HELP.
WILL YOU COME TO THE FUTURE AND HELP ME SAVE NEW YORK CITY?
GROOVY! I'LL DROP EVERYTHING FOR THE FANTASTIC FOUR OF THE FUTURE.
WHAT? OH--RIGHT-- THIS THING.
I'M...LOOSELY AFFILIATED WITH THEM. I'LL EXPLAIN ON THE WAY.
WHAT DO YOU KNOW ABOUT VAMPIRES?

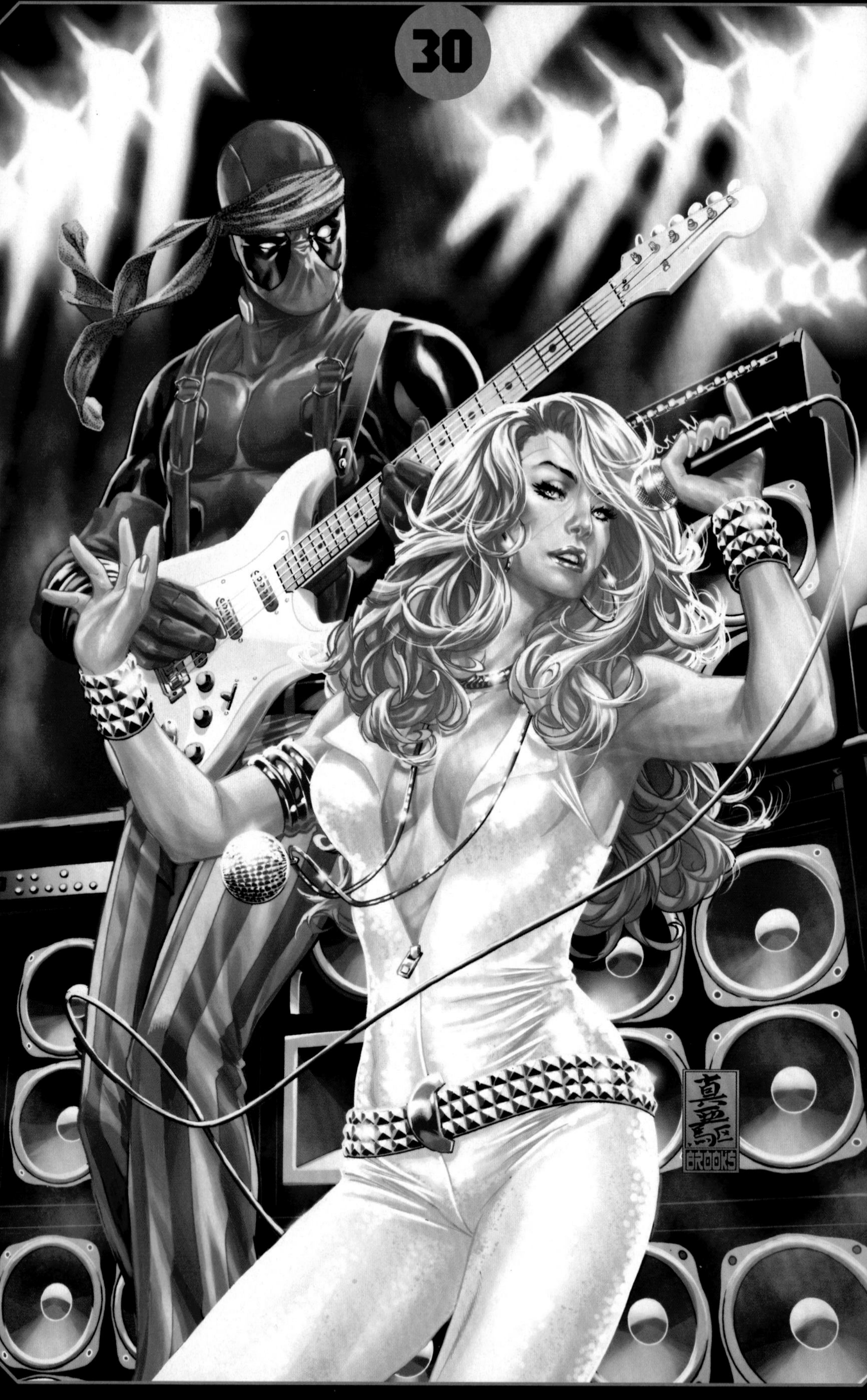
BROOKS

THE BRAVE AND THE BLONDE

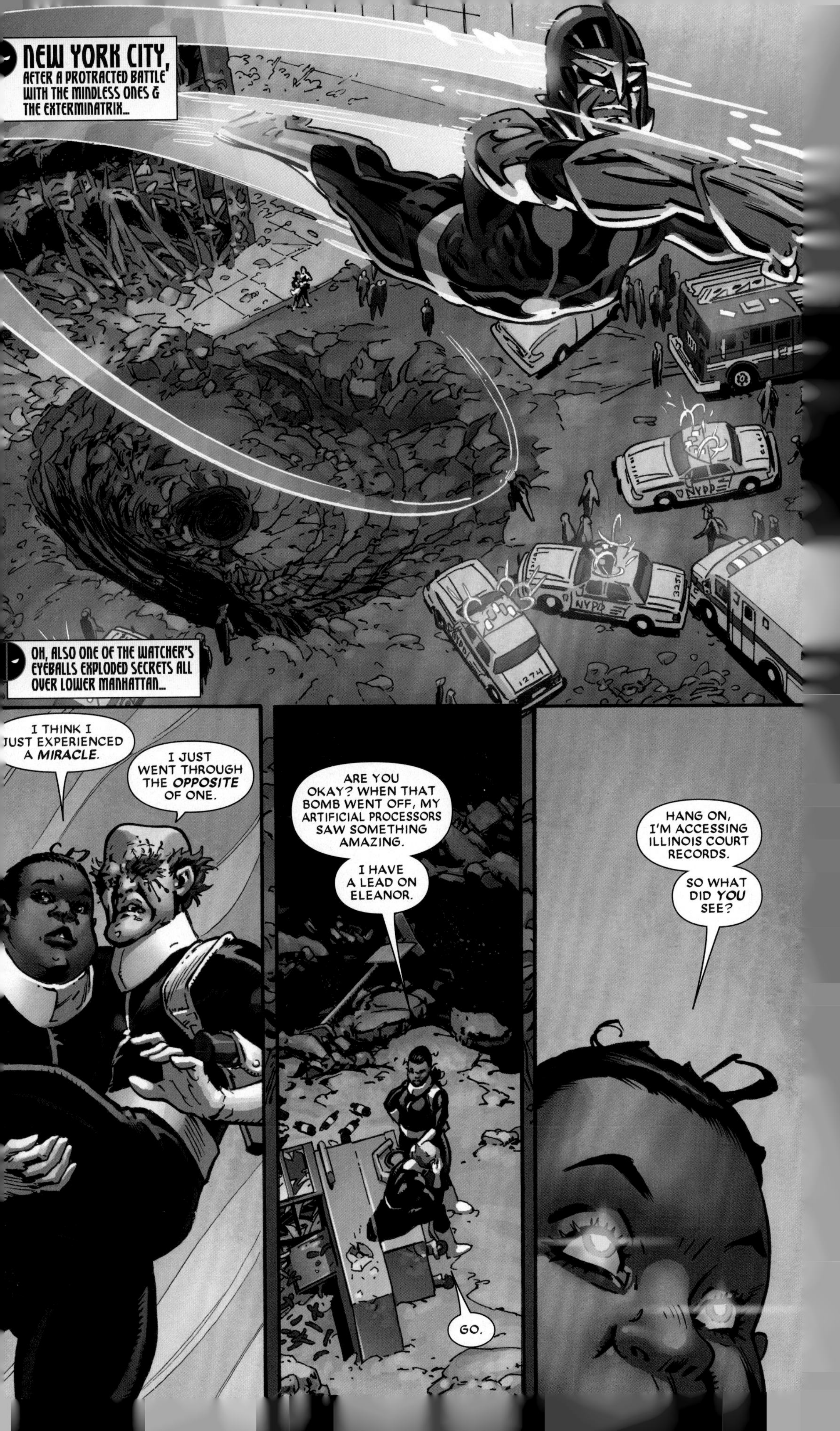
NEW YORK CITY, AFTER A PROTRACTED BATTLE WITH THE MINDLESS ONES & THE EXTERMINATRIX...
OH, ALSO ONE OF THE WATCHER'S EYEBALLS EXPLODED SECRETS ALL OVER LOWER MANHATTAN...
I THINK I JUST EXPERIENCED A *MIRACLE*.
I JUST WENT THROUGH THE *OPPOSITE* OF ONE.
ARE YOU OKAY? WHEN THAT BOMB WENT OFF, MY ARTIFICIAL PROCESSORS SAW SOMETHING AMAZING.
I HAVE A LEAD ON ELEANOR.
GO.
HANG ON, I'M ACCESSING ILLINOIS COURT RECORDS.
SO WHAT DID *YOU* SEE?

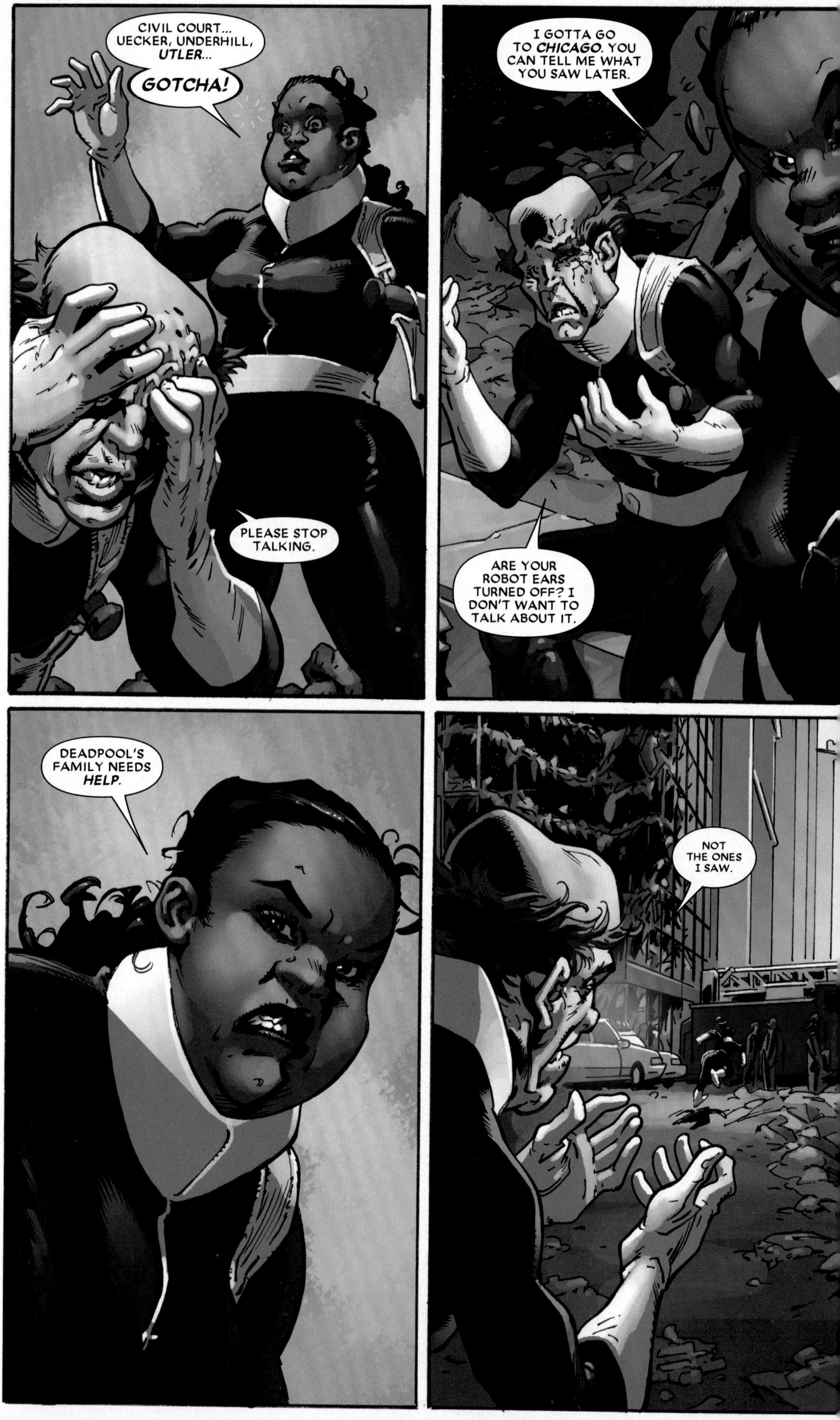
CIVIL COURT... UECKER, UNDERHILL, UTLER...
GOTCHA!
PLEASE STOP TALKING.
I GOTTA GO TO CHICAGO. YOU CAN TELL ME WHAT YOU SAW LATER.
ARE YOUR ROBOT EARS TURNED OFF? I DON'T WANT TO TALK ABOUT IT.
DEADPOOL'S FAMILY NEEDS HELP.
NOT THE ONES I SAW.

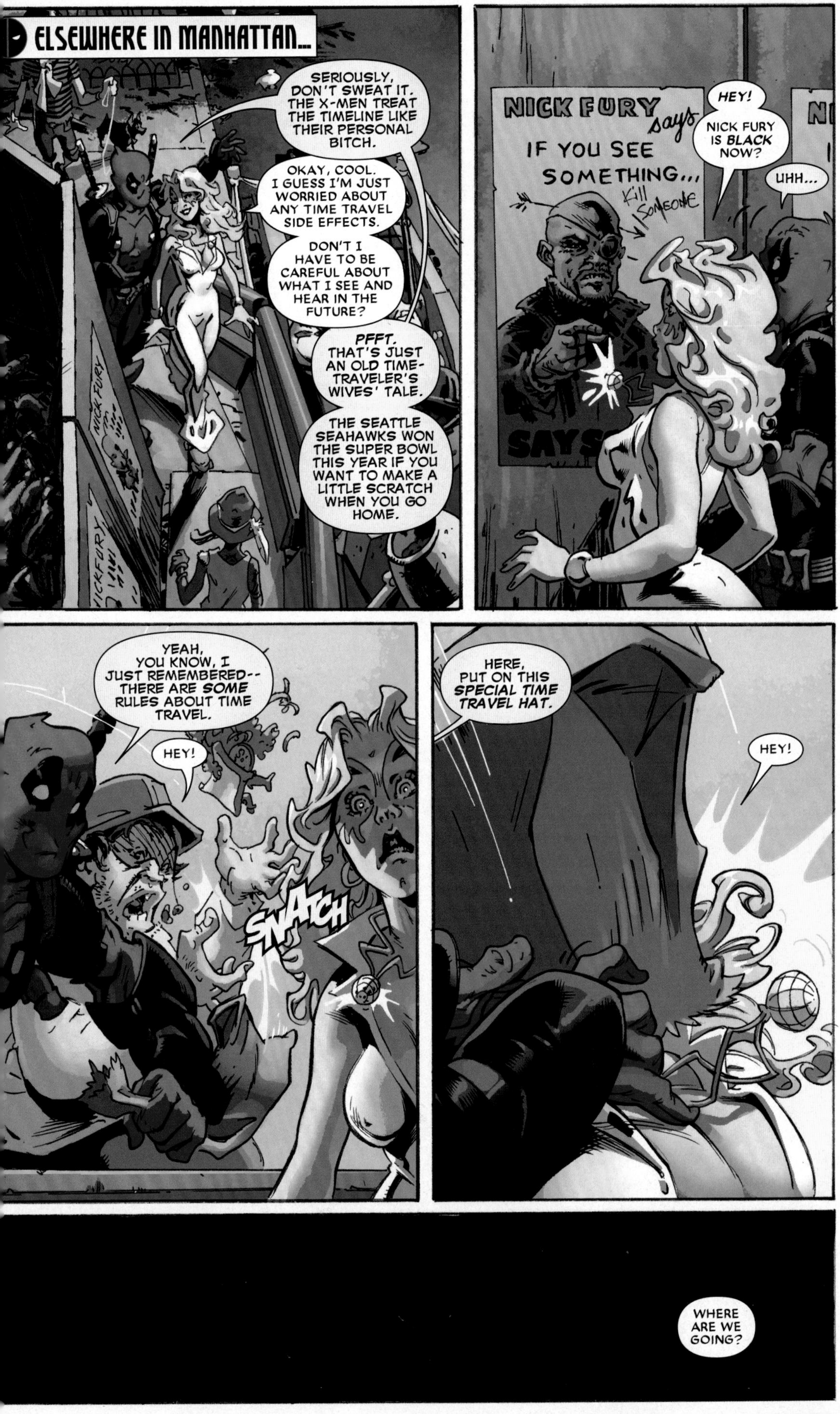
ELSEWHERE IN MANHATTAN...
SERIOUSLY, DON'T SWEAT IT. THE X-MEN TREAT THE TIMELINE LIKE THEIR PERSONAL BITCH.
OKAY, COOL. I GUESS I'M JUST WORRIED ABOUT ANY TIME TRAVEL SIDE EFFECTS.
DON'T I HAVE TO BE CAREFUL ABOUT WHAT I SEE AND HEAR IN THE FUTURE?
PFFT. THAT'S JUST AN OLD TIME-TRAVELER'S WIVES' TALE.
THE SEATTLE SEAHAWKS WON THE SUPER BOWL THIS YEAR IF YOU WANT TO MAKE A LITTLE SCRATCH WHEN YOU GO HOME.
NICK FURY says IF YOU SEE SOMETHING... Kill SOMEONE
HEY!
NICK FURY IS BLACK NOW?
UHH...
YEAH, YOU KNOW, I JUST REMEMBERED-- THERE ARE SOME RULES ABOUT TIME TRAVEL.
HEY!
SNATCH
HERE, PUT ON THIS SPECIAL TIME TRAVEL HAT.
HEY!
WHERE ARE WE GOING?

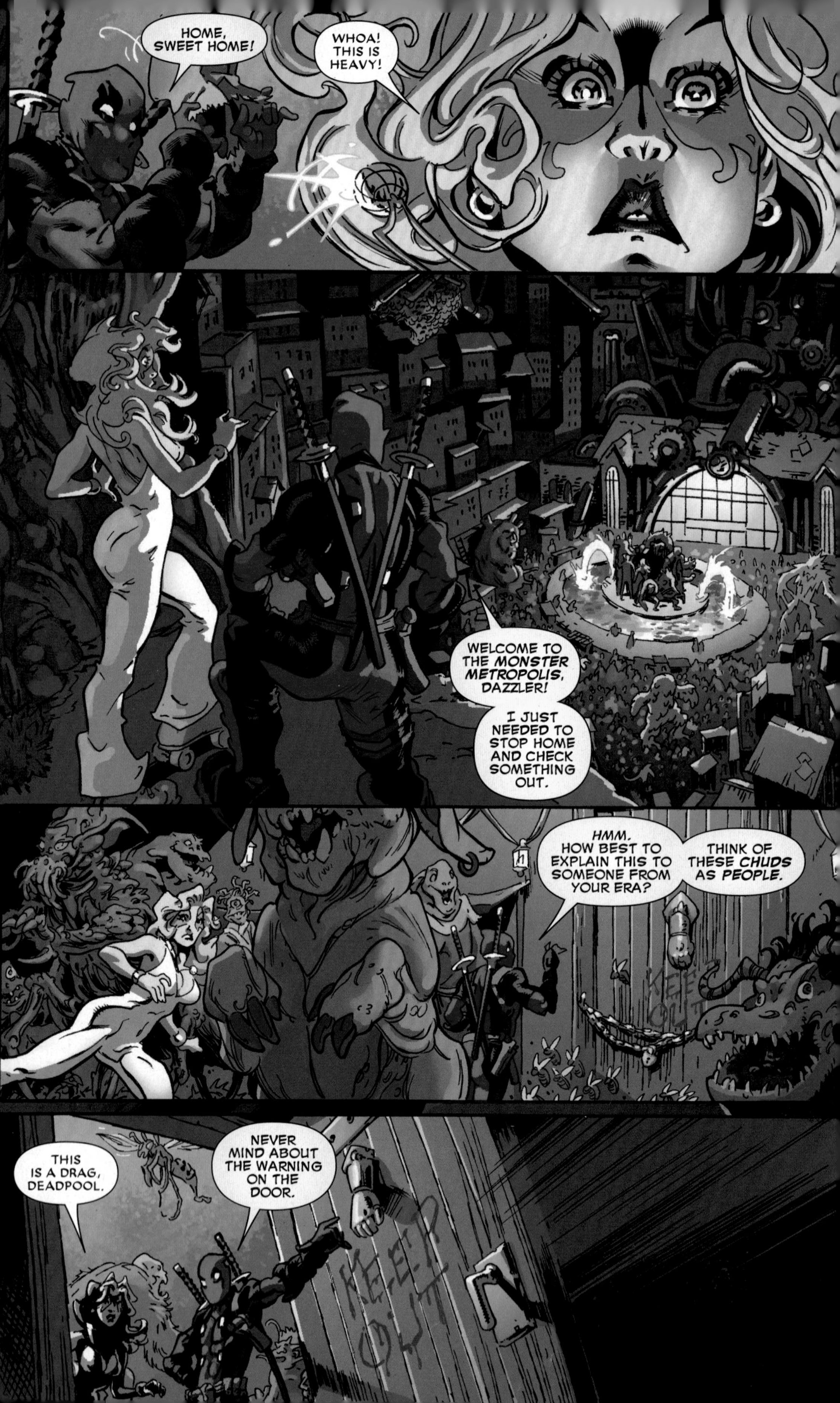
HOME, SWEET HOME!
WHOA! THIS IS HEAVY!
WELCOME TO THE *MONSTER METROPOLIS*, DAZZLER!
I JUST NEEDED TO STOP HOME AND CHECK SOMETHING OUT.
HMM. HOW BEST TO EXPLAIN THIS TO SOMEONE FROM YOUR ERA?
THINK OF THESE *CHUDS* AS *PEOPLE.*
THIS IS A DRAG, DEADPOOL.
NEVER MIND ABOUT THE WARNING ON THE DOOR.
KEEP OUT

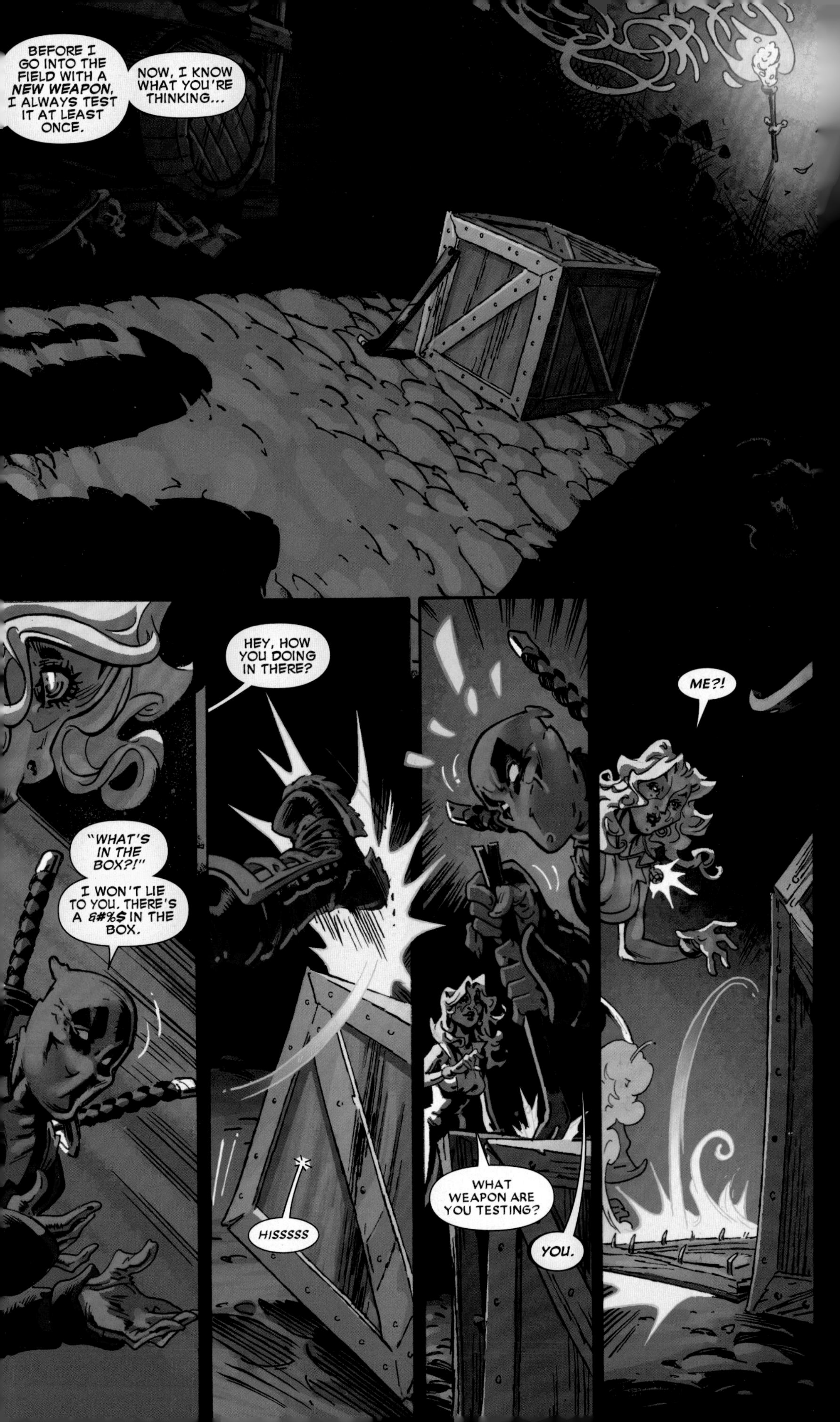
BEFORE I GO INTO THE FIELD WITH A *NEW WEAPON*, I ALWAYS TEST IT AT LEAST ONCE.
NOW, I KNOW WHAT YOU'RE THINKING...
"WHAT'S IN THE BOX?!"
I WON'T LIE TO YOU. THERE'S A &#%$ IN THE BOX.
HEY, HOW YOU DOING IN THERE?
HISSSSS
WHAT WEAPON ARE YOU TESTING?
YOU.
ME?!

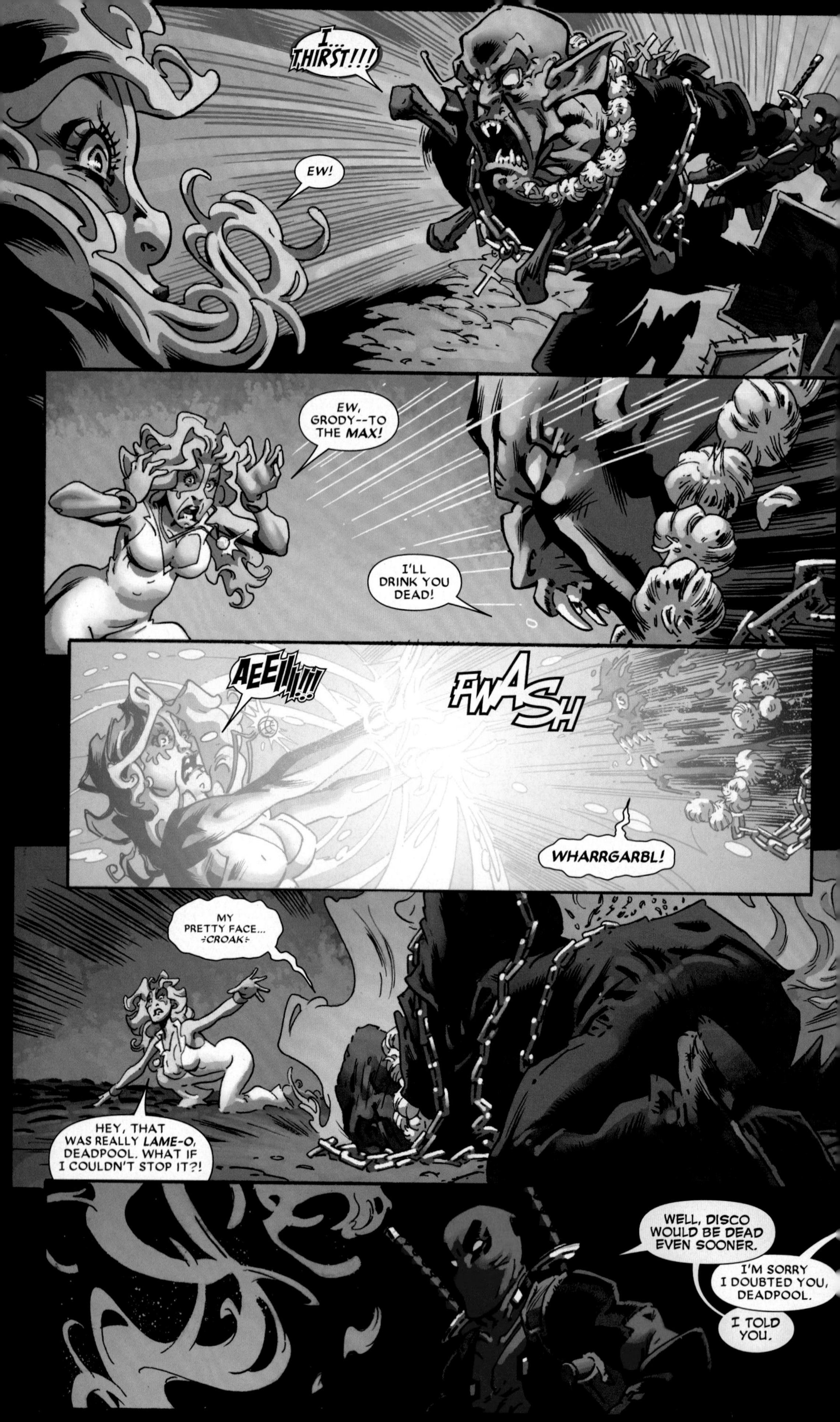

I... THIRST!!!
EW!
EW, GRODY--TO THE MAX!
I'LL DRINK YOU DEAD!
AEEIIII!!!
FWASH
WHARRGARBL!
MY PRETTY FACE... ÷CROAK÷
HEY, THAT WAS REALLY LAME-O, DEADPOOL. WHAT IF I COULDN'T STOP IT?!
WELL, DISCO WOULD BE DEAD EVEN SOONER.
I'M SORRY I DOUBTED YOU, DEADPOOL.
I TOLD YOU.

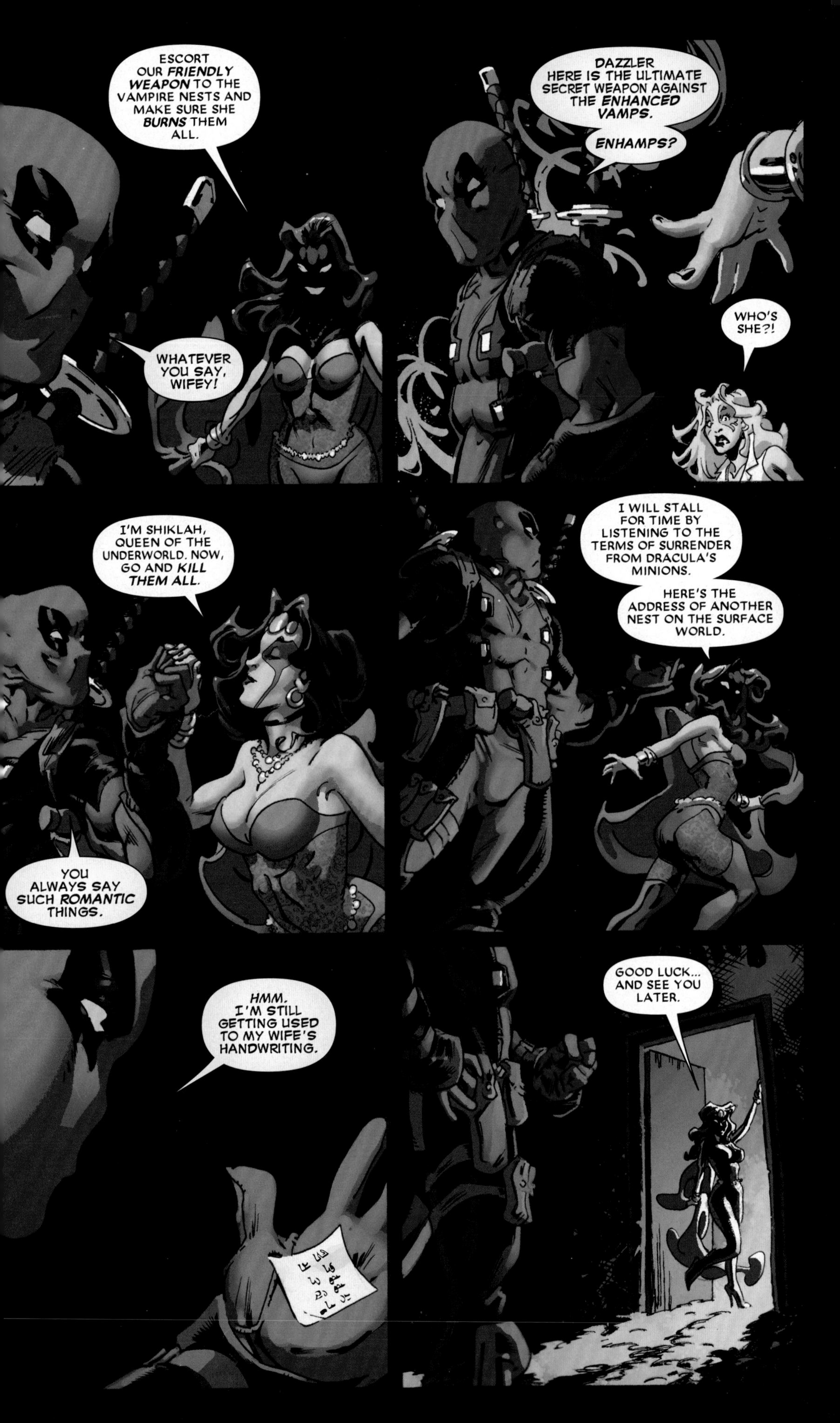
ESCORT OUR FRIENDLY WEAPON TO THE VAMPIRE NESTS AND MAKE SURE SHE BURNS THEM ALL.
WHATEVER YOU SAY, WIFEY!
DAZZLER HERE IS THE ULTIMATE SECRET WEAPON AGAINST THE ENHANCED VAMPS.
ENHAMPS?
WHO'S SHE?!
I'M SHIKLAH, QUEEN OF THE UNDERWORLD. NOW, GO AND KILL THEM ALL.
YOU ALWAYS SAY SUCH ROMANTIC THINGS.
I WILL STALL FOR TIME BY LISTENING TO THE TERMS OF SURRENDER FROM DRACULA'S MINIONS.
HERE'S THE ADDRESS OF ANOTHER NEST ON THE SURFACE WORLD.
HMM. I'M STILL GETTING USED TO MY WIFE'S HANDWRITING.
GOOD LUCK... AND SEE YOU LATER.

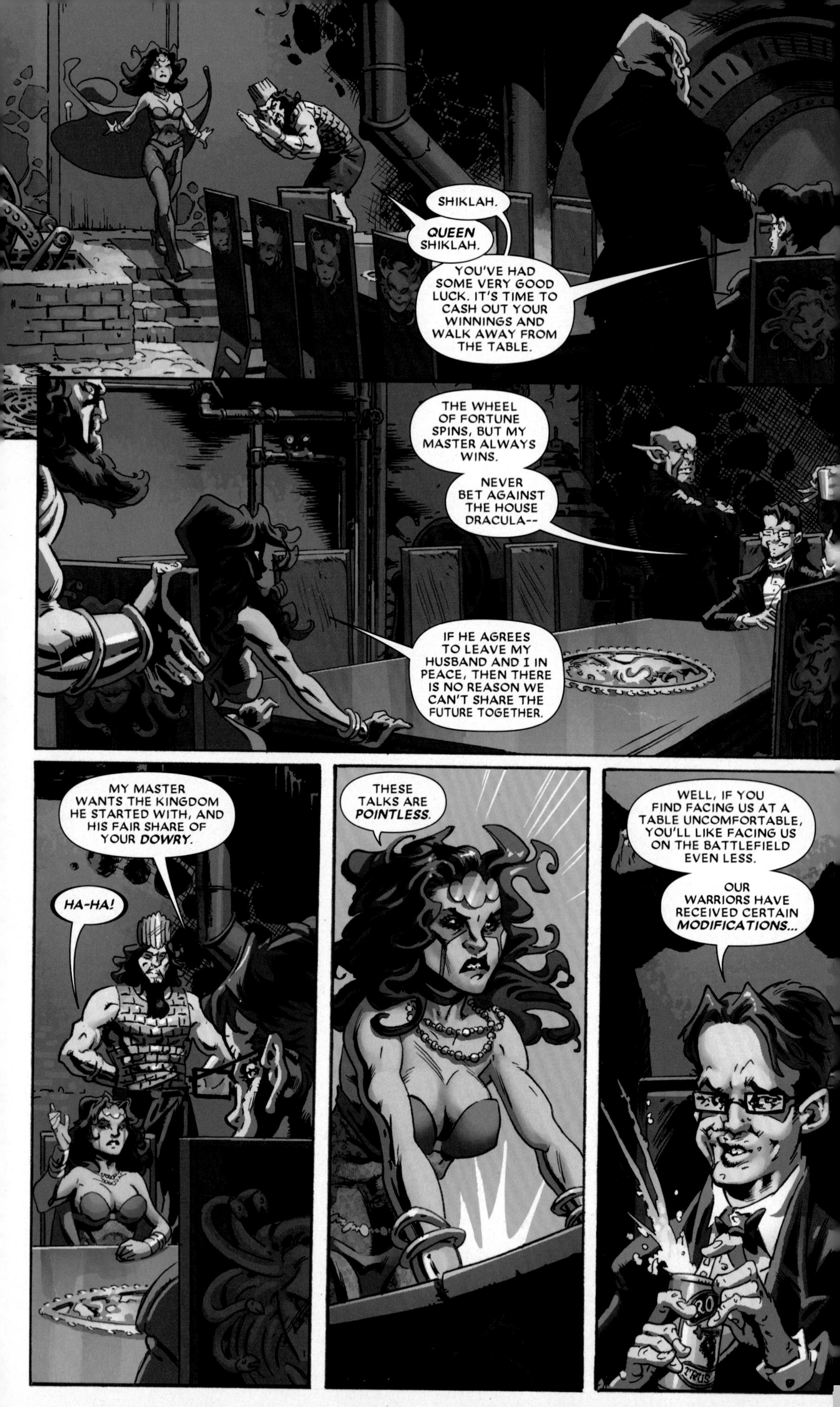
SHIKLAH.
QUEEN SHIKLAH.
YOU'VE HAD SOME VERY GOOD LUCK. IT'S TIME TO CASH OUT YOUR WINNINGS AND WALK AWAY FROM THE TABLE.
THE WHEEL OF FORTUNE SPINS, BUT MY MASTER ALWAYS WINS.
NEVER BET AGAINST THE HOUSE DRACULA--
IF HE AGREES TO LEAVE MY HUSBAND AND I IN PEACE, THEN THERE IS NO REASON WE CAN'T SHARE THE FUTURE TOGETHER.
MY MASTER WANTS THE KINGDOM HE STARTED WITH, AND HIS FAIR SHARE OF YOUR DOWRY.
HA-HA!
THESE TALKS ARE POINTLESS.
WELL, IF YOU FIND FACING US AT A TABLE UNCOMFORTABLE, YOU'LL LIKE FACING US ON THE BATTLEFIELD EVEN LESS.
OUR WARRIORS HAVE RECEIVED CERTAIN MODIFICATIONS...

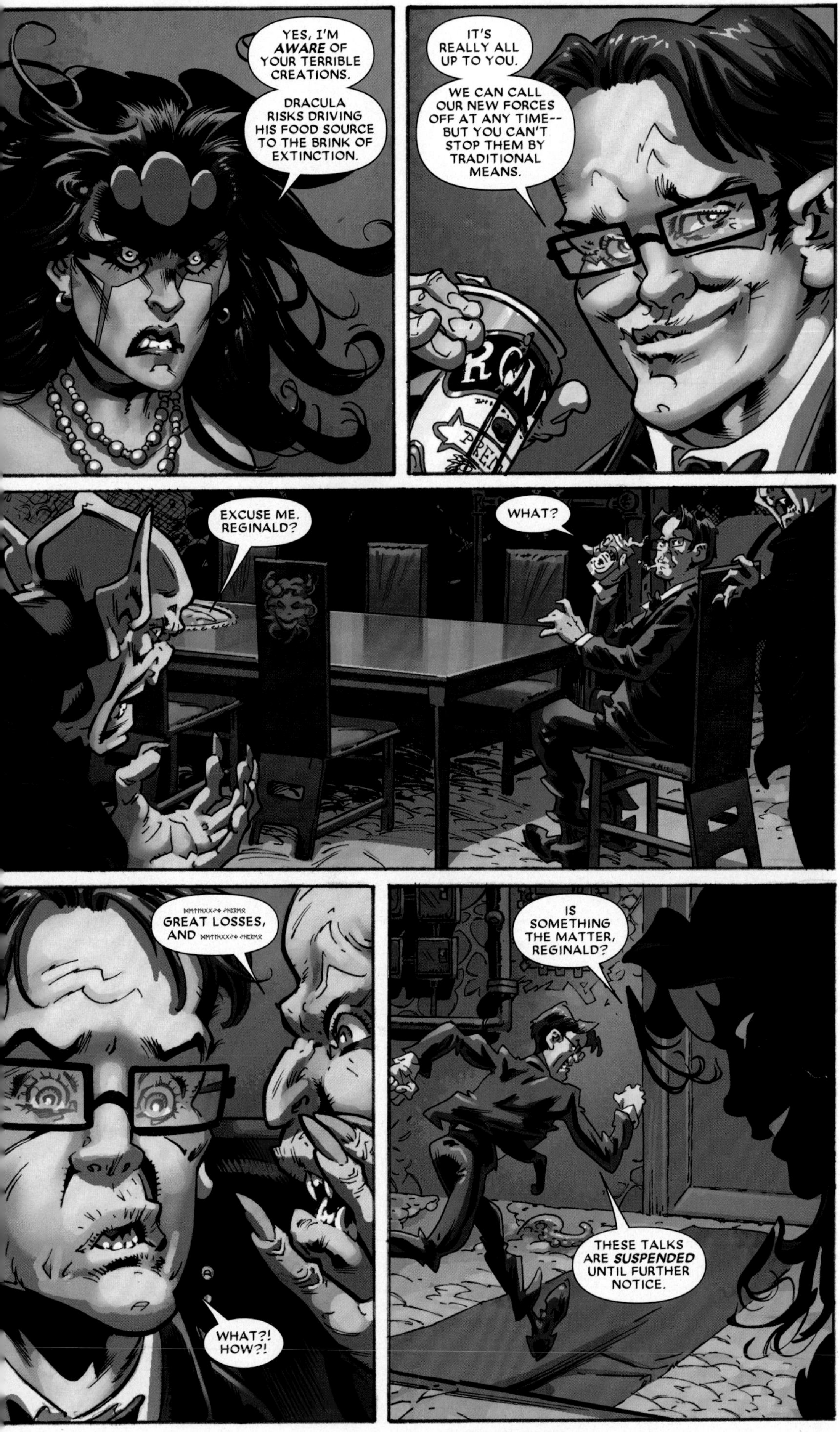
YES, I'M *AWARE* OF YOUR TERRIBLE CREATIONS.
DRACULA RISKS DRIVING HIS FOOD SOURCE TO THE BRINK OF EXTINCTION.
IT'S REALLY ALL UP TO YOU.
WE CAN CALL OUR NEW FORCES OFF AT ANY TIME-- BUT YOU CAN'T STOP THEM BY TRADITIONAL MEANS.
EXCUSE ME. REGINALD?
WHAT?
GREAT LOSSES, AND
WHAT?! HOW?!
IS SOMETHING THE MATTER, REGINALD?
THESE TALKS ARE *SUSPENDED* UNTIL FURTHER NOTICE.

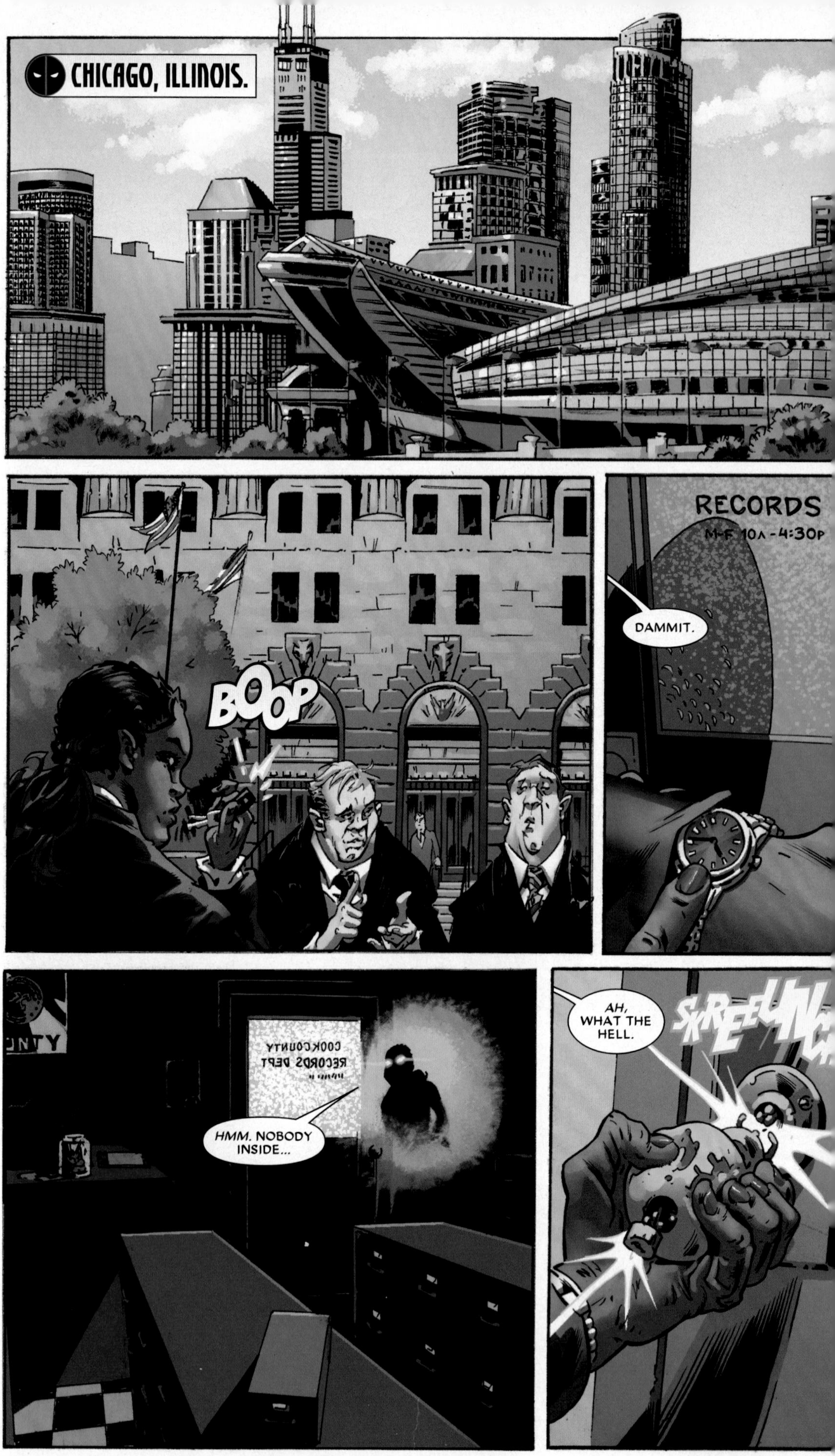
CHICAGO, ILLINOIS.
BOOP
RECORDS
M-F 10A-4:30P
DAMMIT.
COOK COUNTY
RECORDS DEPT
HMM. NOBODY INSIDE...
AH, WHAT THE HELL.

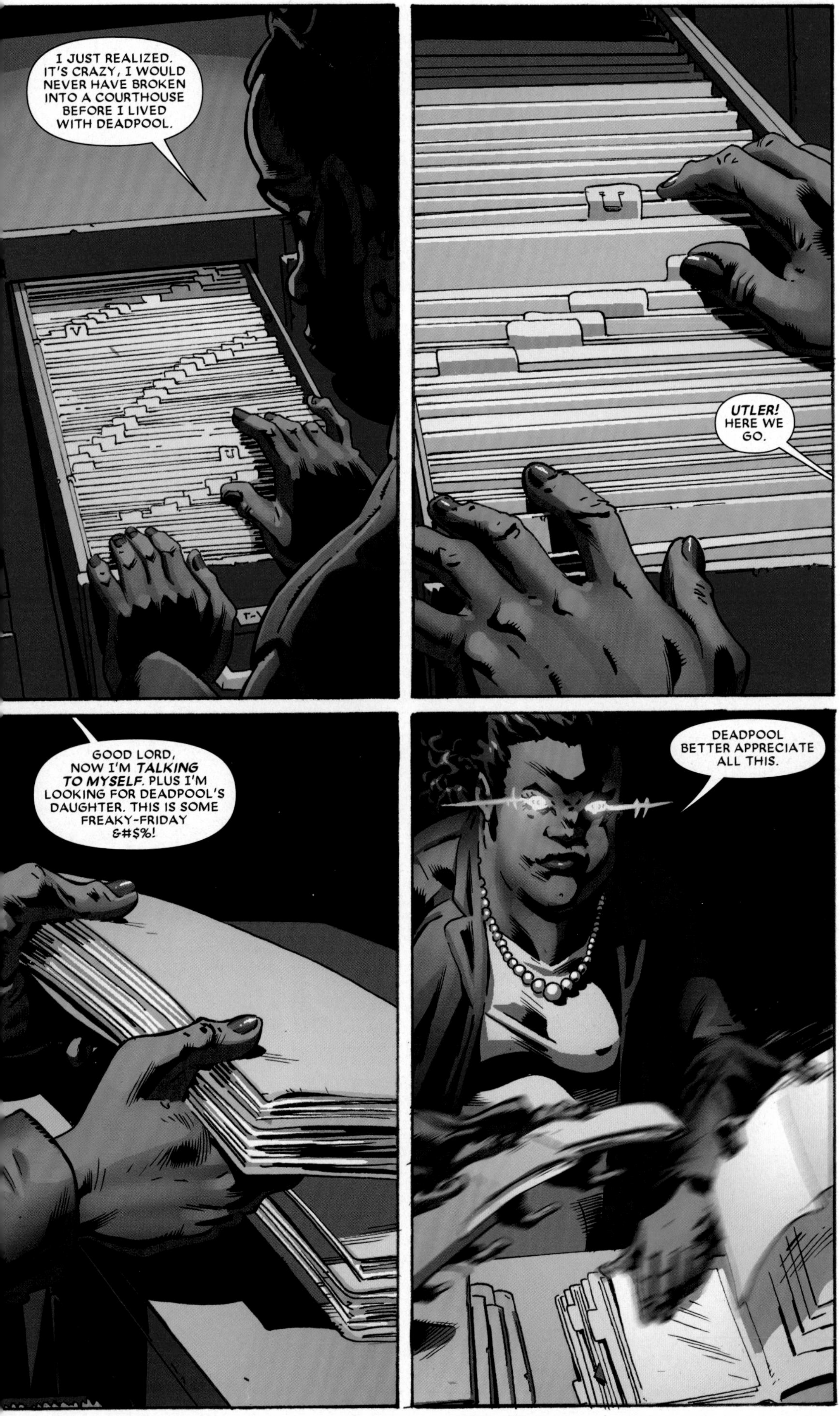
I JUST REALIZED. IT'S CRAZY, I WOULD NEVER HAVE BROKEN INTO A COURTHOUSE BEFORE I LIVED WITH DEADPOOL.
UTLER! HERE WE GO.
GOOD LORD, NOW I'M TALKING TO MYSELF. PLUS I'M LOOKING FOR DEADPOOL'S DAUGHTER. THIS IS SOME FREAKY-FRIDAY &#$%!
DEADPOOL BETTER APPRECIATE ALL THIS.

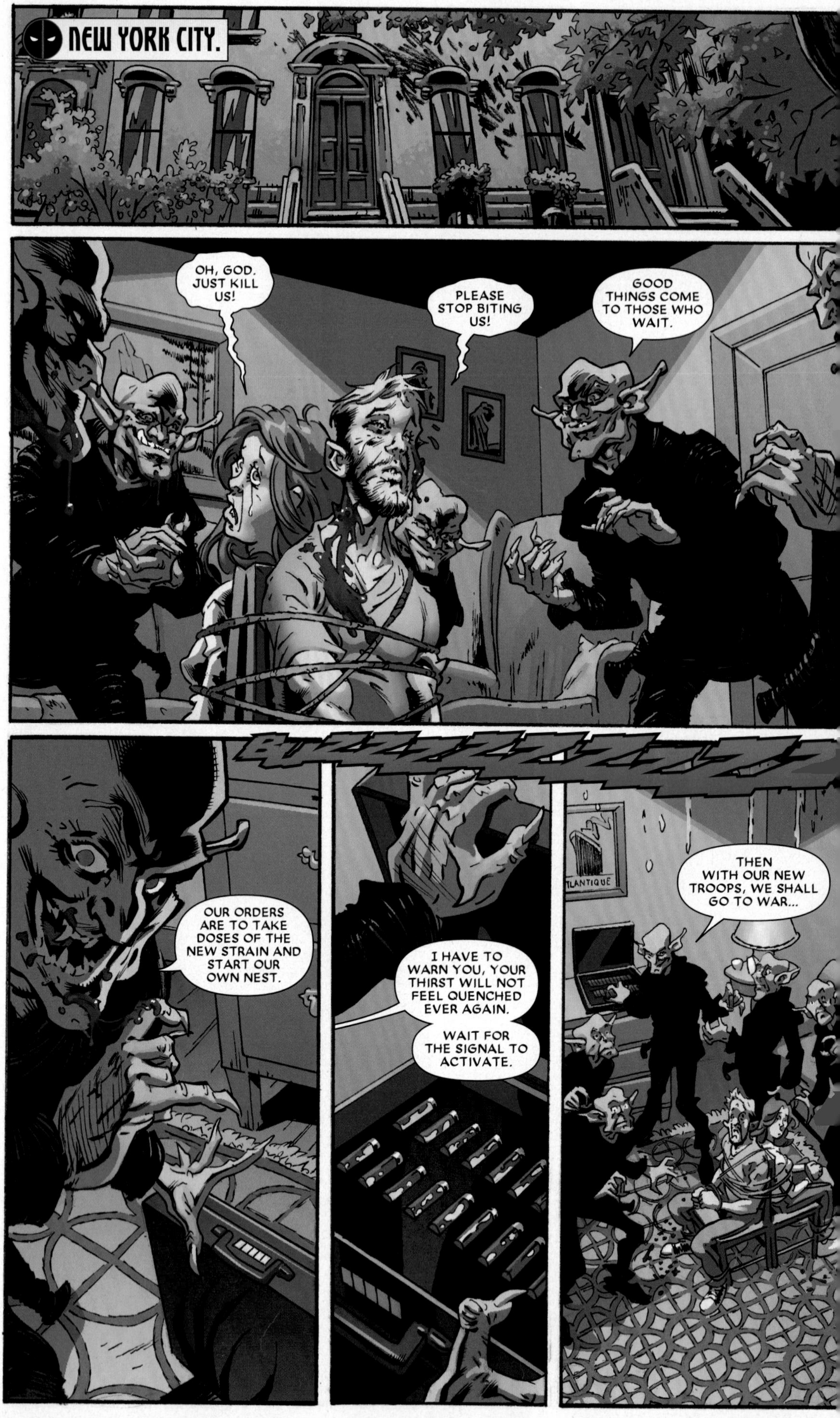
NEW YORK CITY.
OH, GOD. JUST KILL US!
PLEASE STOP BITING US!
GOOD THINGS COME TO THOSE WHO WAIT.
OUR ORDERS ARE TO TAKE DOSES OF THE NEW STRAIN AND START OUR OWN NEST.
I HAVE TO WARN YOU, YOUR THIRST WILL NOT FEEL QUENCHED EVER AGAIN.
WAIT FOR THE SIGNAL TO ACTIVATE.
THEN WITH OUR NEW TROOPS, WE SHALL GO TO WAR...

WHAT IN THE HELL?

I THOUGHT DISCO WAS DEAD.

HA HA HA HAHAH HA HA HA HA

NOT AS DEAD AS YOU GUYS.

KLIK KLIK KLIK

AARGH!

BRAKOM

READY, DAZZLER?

READY, DEADY.

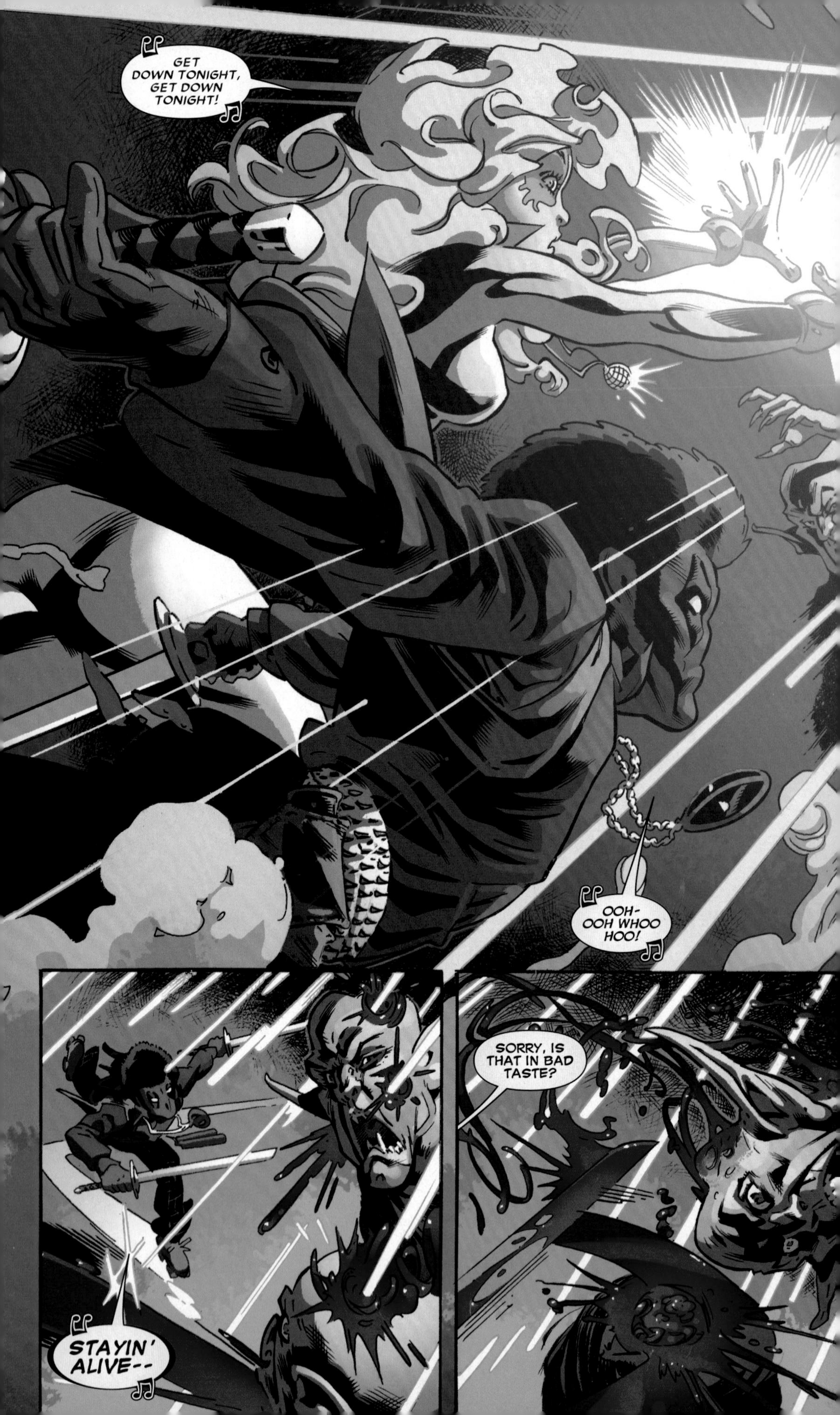
GET DOWN TONIGHT, GET DOWN TONIGHT!
OOH- OOH WHOO HOO!
STAYIN' ALIVE--
SORRY, IS THAT IN BAD TASTE?

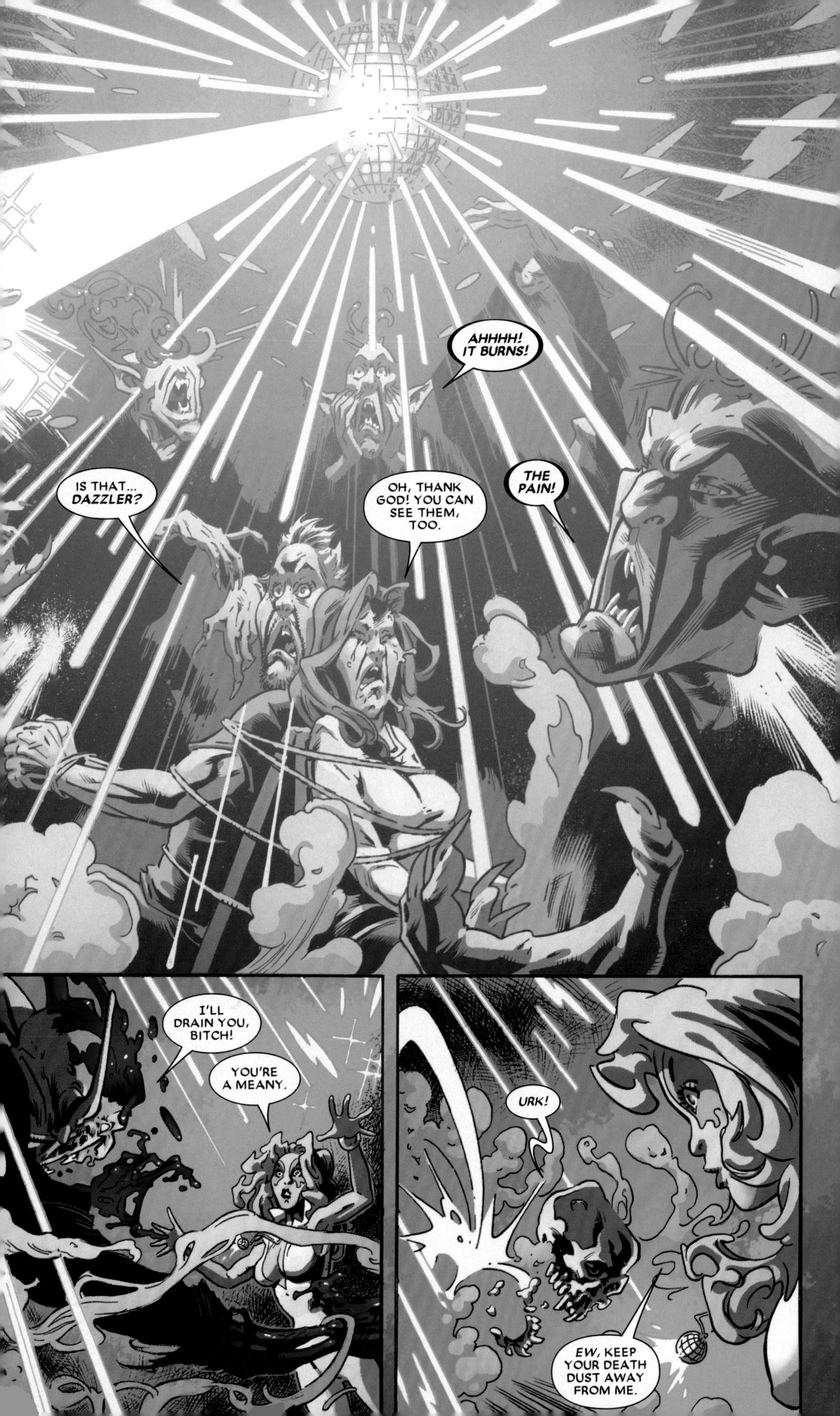
AHHHH! IT BURNS!
IS THAT... DAZZLER?
OH, THANK GOD! YOU CAN SEE THEM, TOO.
THE PAIN!
I'LL DRAIN YOU, BITCH!
YOU'RE A MEANY.
URK!
EW, KEEP YOUR DEATH DUST AWAY FROM ME.

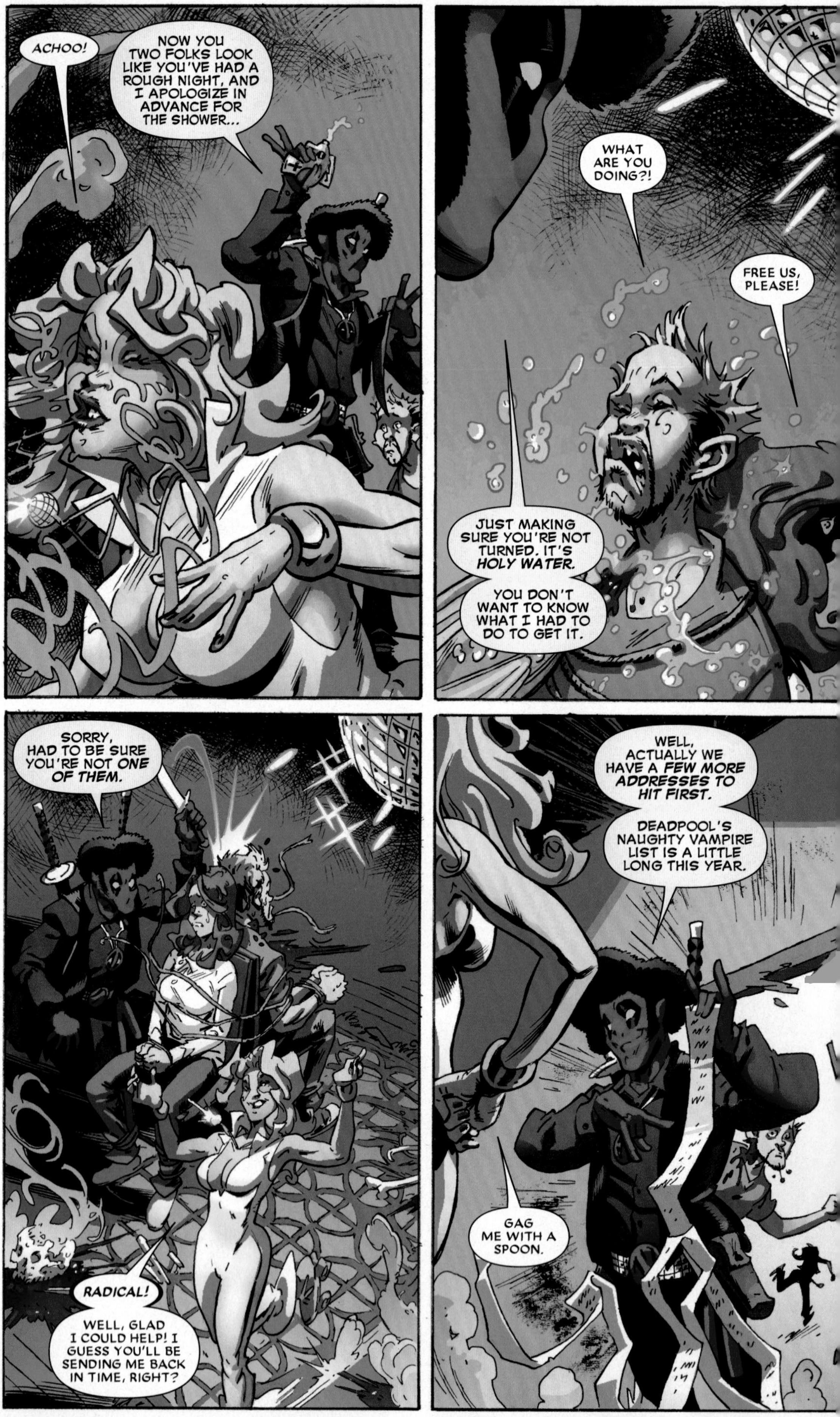
ACHOO!
NOW YOU TWO FOLKS LOOK LIKE YOU'VE HAD A ROUGH NIGHT, AND I APOLOGIZE IN ADVANCE FOR THE SHOWER...
WHAT ARE YOU DOING?!
FREE US, PLEASE!
JUST MAKING SURE YOU'RE NOT TURNED. IT'S HOLY WATER.
YOU DON'T WANT TO KNOW WHAT I HAD TO DO TO GET IT.
SORRY, HAD TO BE SURE YOU'RE NOT ONE OF THEM.
RADICAL!
WELL, GLAD I COULD HELP! I GUESS YOU'LL BE SENDING ME BACK IN TIME, RIGHT?
WELL, ACTUALLY WE HAVE A FEW MORE ADDRESSES TO HIT FIRST.
DEADPOOL'S NAUGHTY VAMPIRE LIST IS A LITTLE LONG THIS YEAR.
GAG ME WITH A SPOON.

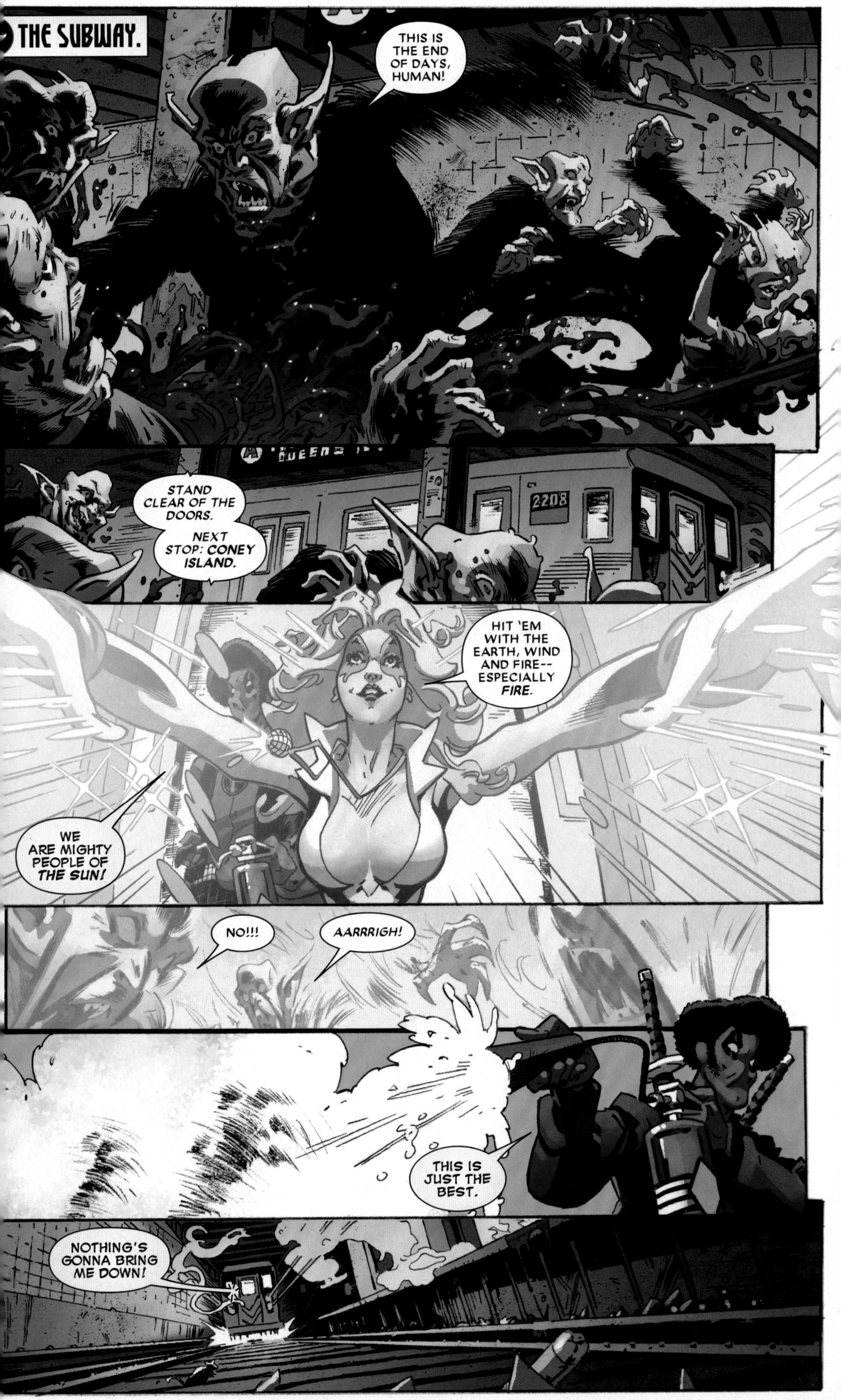
THE SUBWAY.
THIS IS THE END OF DAYS, HUMAN!
STAND CLEAR OF THE DOORS.
NEXT STOP: CONEY ISLAND.
HIT 'EM WITH THE EARTH, WIND AND FIRE-- ESPECIALLY FIRE.
WE ARE MIGHTY PEOPLE OF THE SUN!
NO!!!
AARRRIGH!
THIS IS JUST THE BEST.
NOTHING'S GONNA BRING ME DOWN!

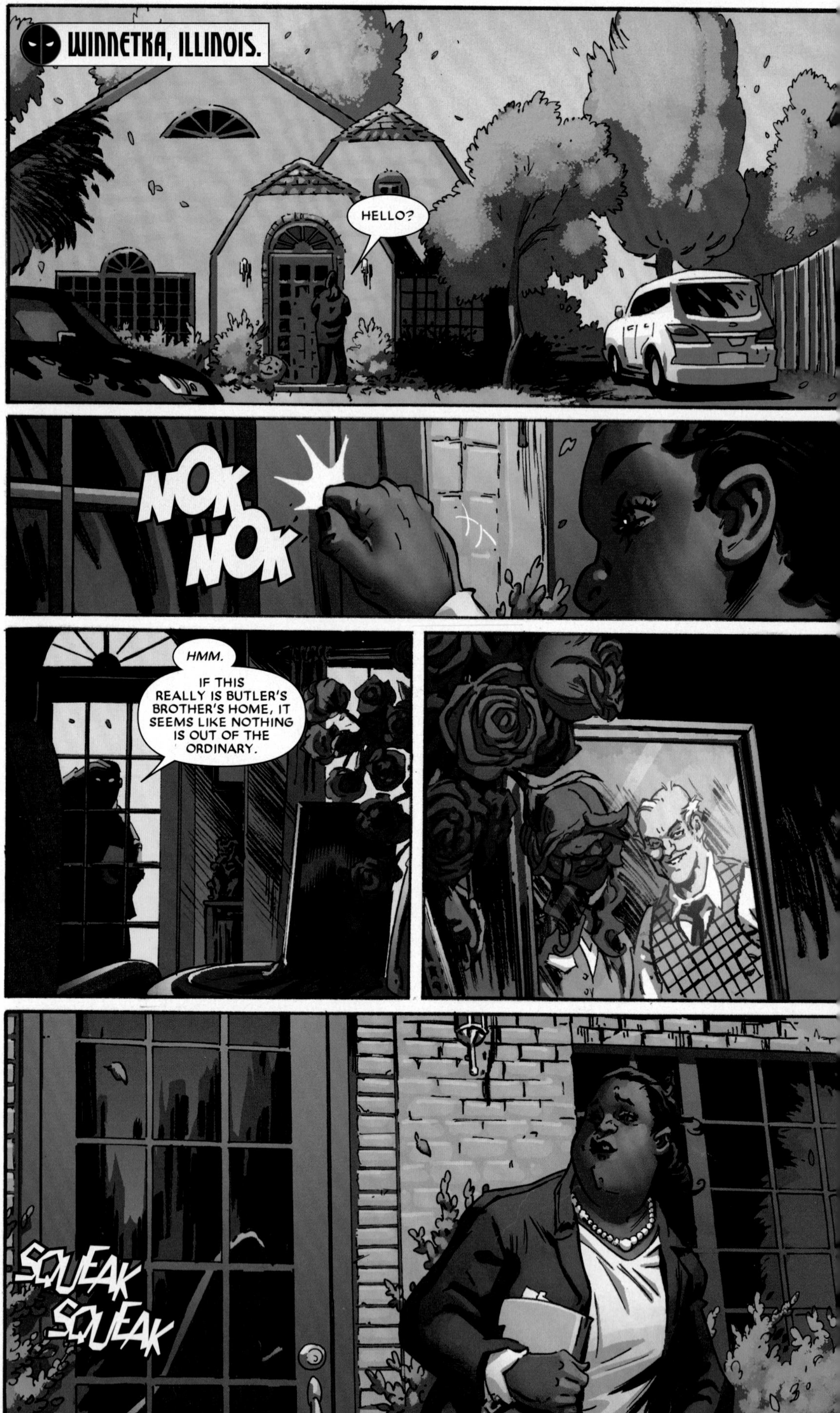
WINNETKA, ILLINOIS.
HELLO?
NOK NOK
HMM.
IF THIS REALLY IS BUTLER'S BROTHER'S HOME, IT SEEMS LIKE NOTHING IS OUT OF THE ORDINARY.
SQUEAK SQUEAK

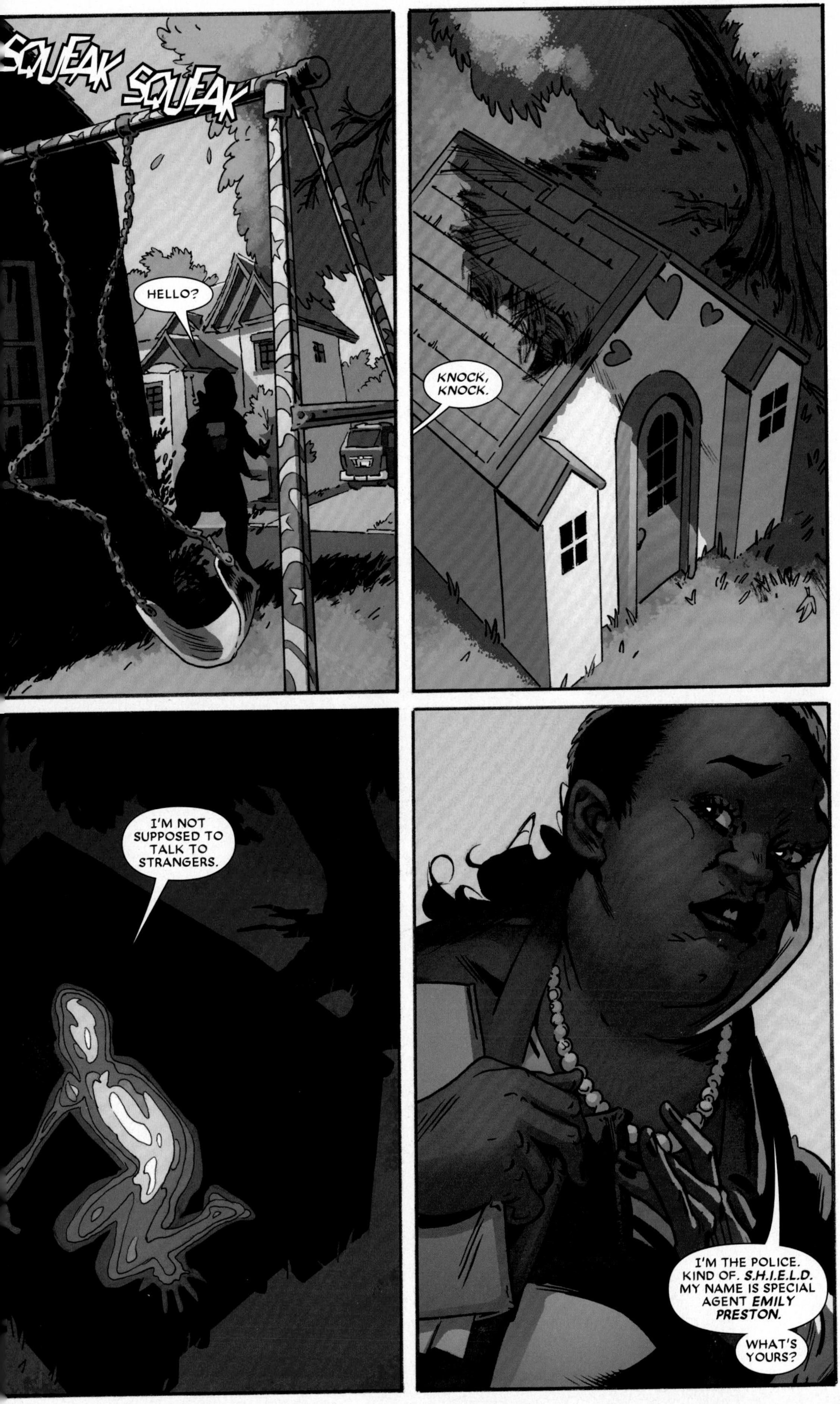
SQUEAK SQUEAK
HELLO?
KNOCK, KNOCK.
I'M NOT SUPPOSED TO TALK TO STRANGERS.
I'M THE POLICE. KIND OF. S.H.I.E.L.D. MY NAME IS SPECIAL AGENT EMILY PRESTON.
WHAT'S YOURS?

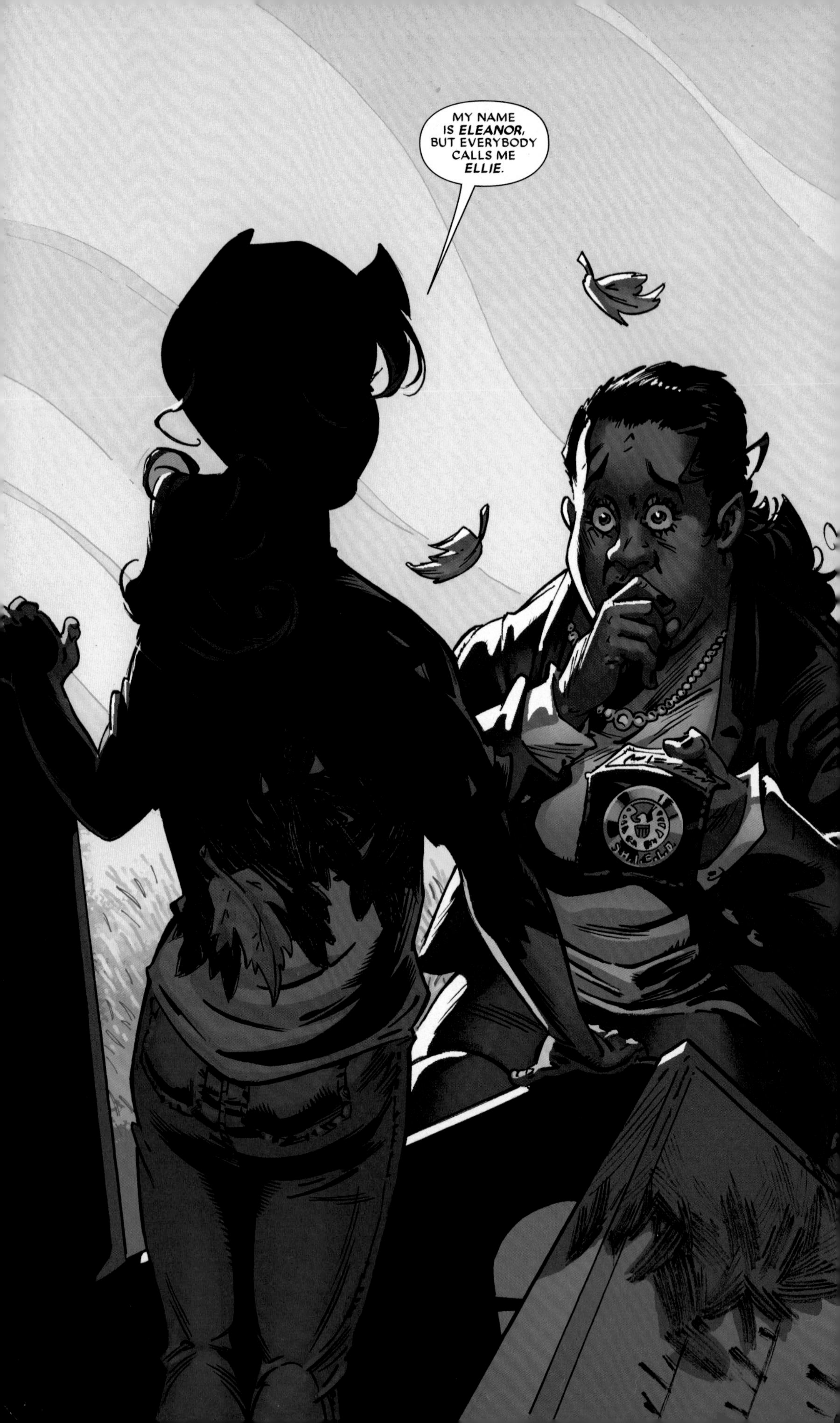
MY NAME IS ELEANOR, BUT EVERYBODY CALLS ME ELLIE.

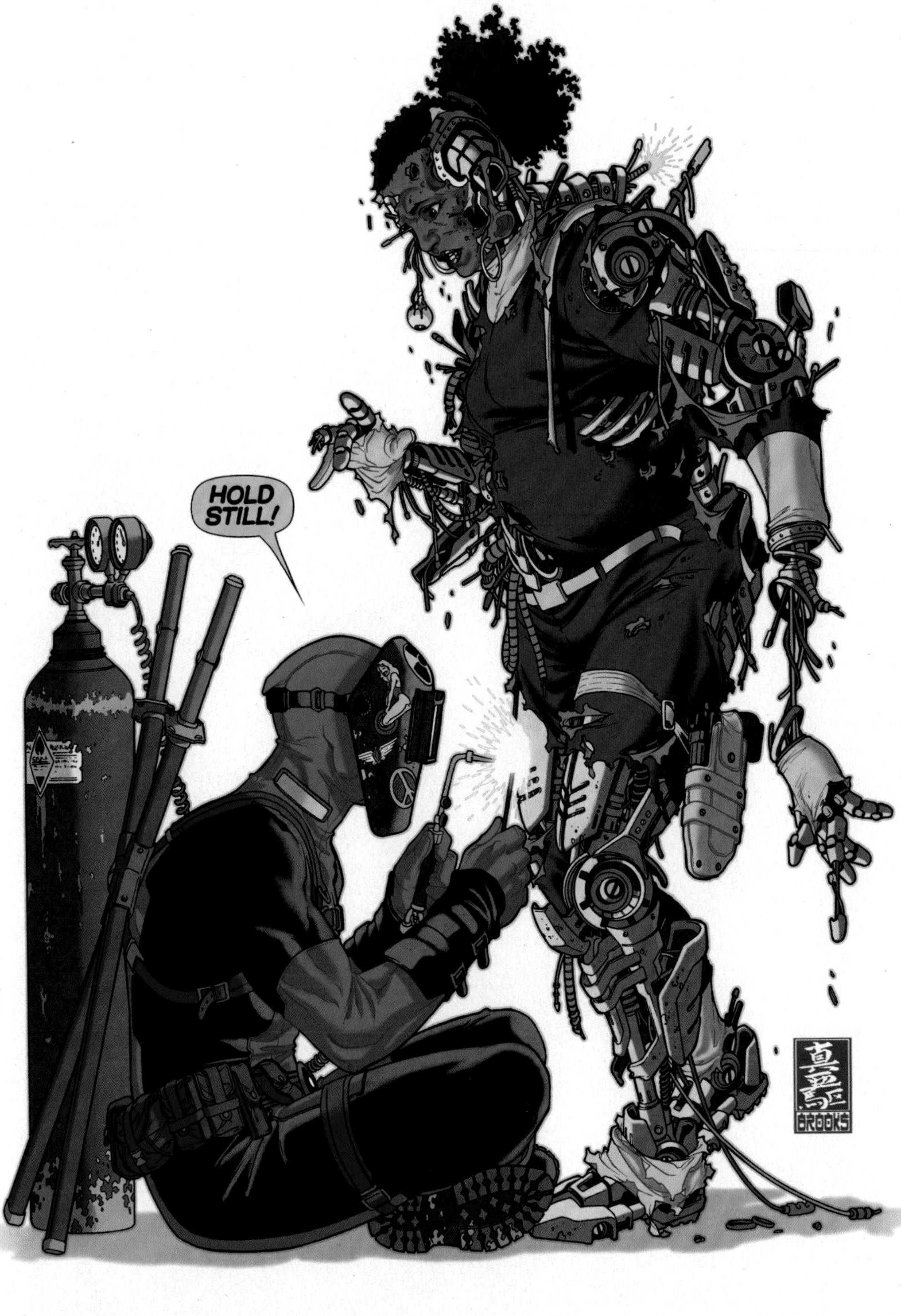
HOLD STILL!
BROOKS

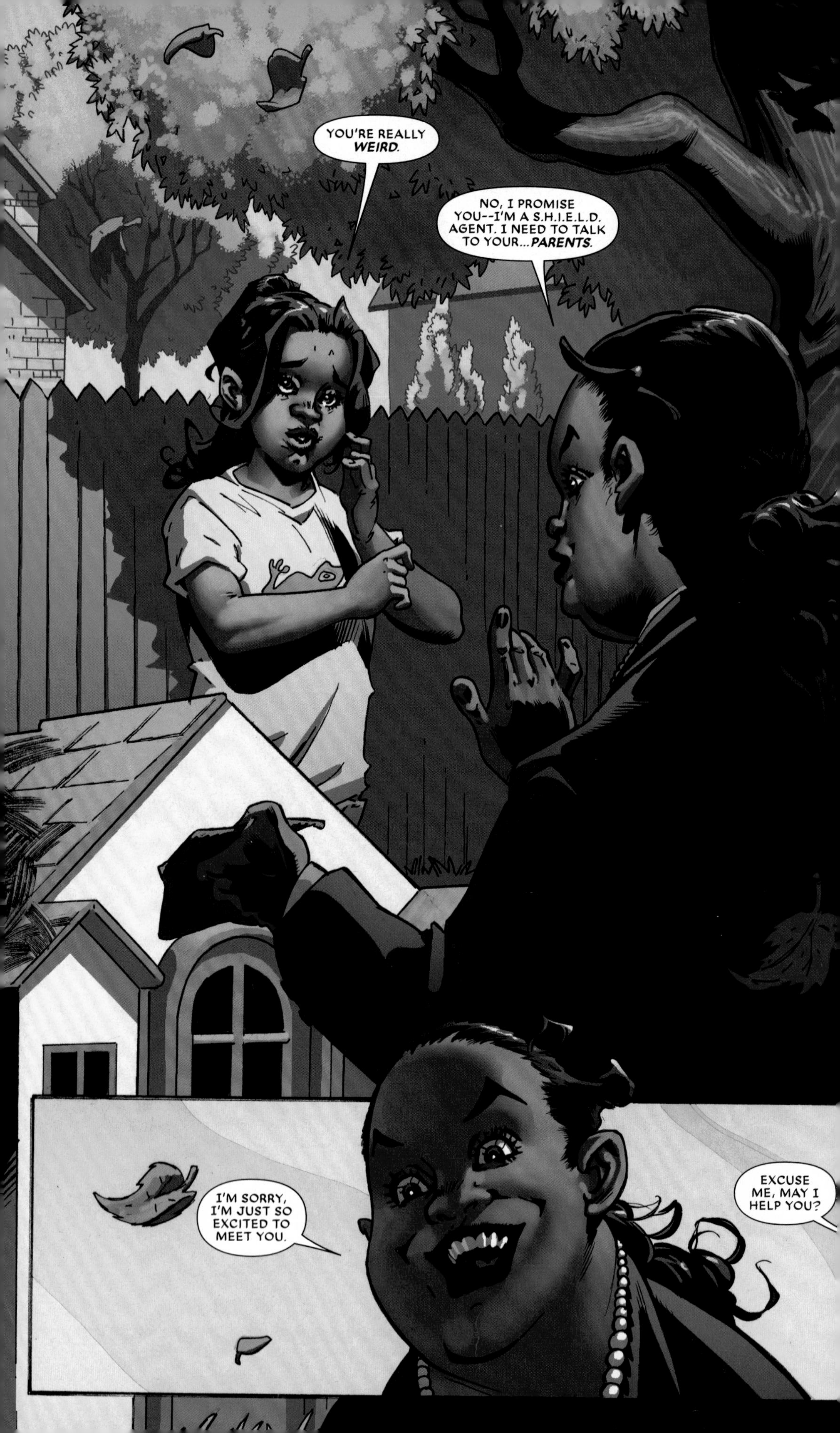
YOU'RE REALLY *WEIRD*.
NO, I PROMISE YOU--I'M A S.H.I.E.L.D. AGENT. I NEED TO TALK TO YOUR... *PARENTS*.
EXCUSE ME, MAY I HELP YOU?
I'M SORRY, I'M JUST SO EXCITED TO MEET YOU.

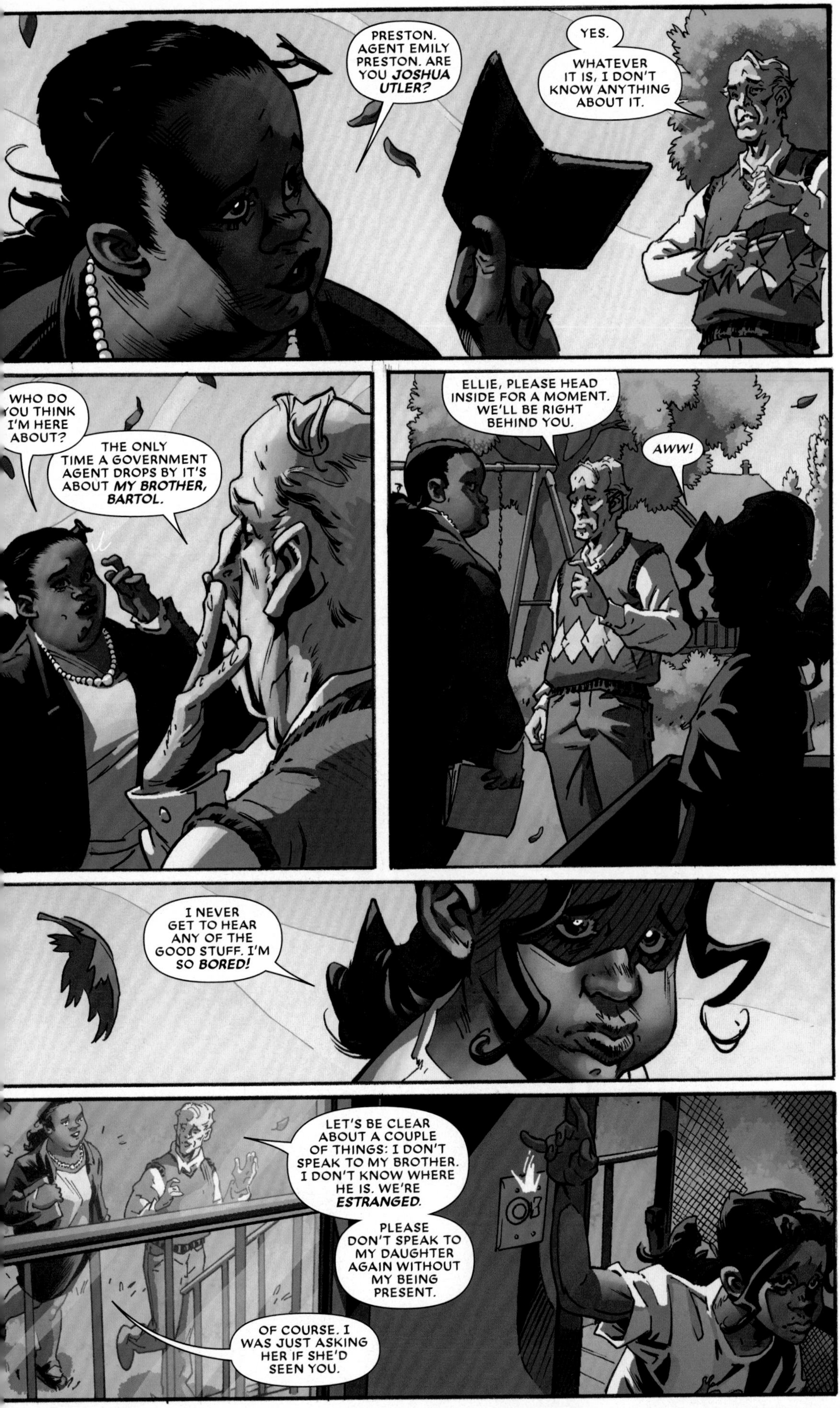
PRESTON. AGENT EMILY PRESTON. ARE YOU *JOSHUA UTLER?*
YES.
WHATEVER IT IS, I DON'T KNOW ANYTHING ABOUT IT.
WHO DO YOU THINK I'M HERE ABOUT?
THE ONLY TIME A GOVERNMENT AGENT DROPS BY IT'S ABOUT *MY BROTHER, BARTOL.*
ELLIE, PLEASE HEAD INSIDE FOR A MOMENT. WE'LL BE RIGHT BEHIND YOU.
AWW!
I NEVER GET TO HEAR ANY OF THE GOOD STUFF. I'M SO *BORED!*
LET'S BE CLEAR ABOUT A COUPLE OF THINGS: I DON'T SPEAK TO MY BROTHER. I DON'T KNOW WHERE HE IS. WE'RE *ESTRANGED.*
PLEASE DON'T SPEAK TO MY DAUGHTER AGAIN WITHOUT MY BEING PRESENT.
OF COURSE. I WAS JUST ASKING HER IF SHE'D SEEN YOU.

WE HAVE DINNER AND THEN HOMEWORK, SO IF YOU DON'T MIND GETTING RIGHT TO THE POINT?

WELL, IT'S TRUE, YOUR BROTHER WAS UNTIL RECENTLY A PERSON OF INTEREST IN AN ONGOING INVESTIGATION, BUT THAT CRIMINAL CASE IS NOW *CLOSED.*

IF YOU'RE NOT HERE TO TALK ABOUT MY *BROTHER...*

HAHA! COOL!

IT'S THE GUY THAT KILLED ALL THOSE GHOSTS IN NEW YORK CITY! HE'S FIGHTING VAMPIRES WITH THE LADY FROM VH1!

I DON'T UNDERSTAND-- HAS MY BROTHER BEEN ARRESTED? STATE PLAINLY WHY YOU'RE HERE.

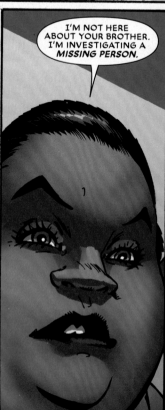

I'M NOT HERE ABOUT YOUR BROTHER. I'M INVESTIGATING A *MISSING PERSON.*

I THINK IT'S TIME WE SAID GOODNIGHT. GET A WARRANT IF YOU WANT TO SPEAK TO ME AGAIN.

HAHA!

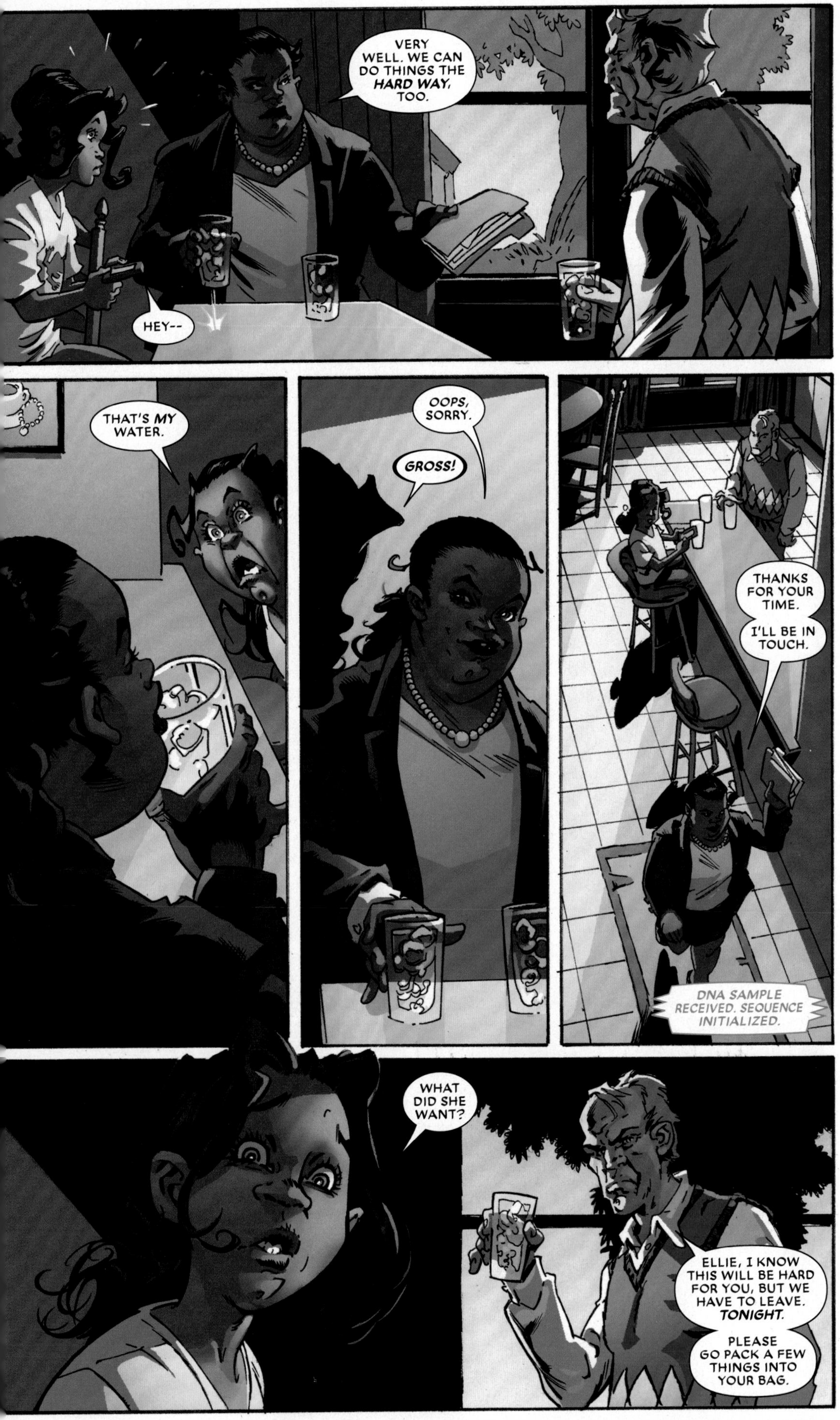

VERY WELL. WE CAN DO THINGS THE HARD WAY, TOO.
HEY--
THAT'S MY WATER.
OOPS, SORRY.
GROSS!
THANKS FOR YOUR TIME.
I'LL BE IN TOUCH.
DNA SAMPLE RECEIVED. SEQUENCE INITIALIZED.
WHAT DID SHE WANT?
ELLIE, I KNOW THIS WILL BE HARD FOR YOU, BUT WE HAVE TO LEAVE. TONIGHT.
PLEASE GO PACK A FEW THINGS INTO YOUR BAG.

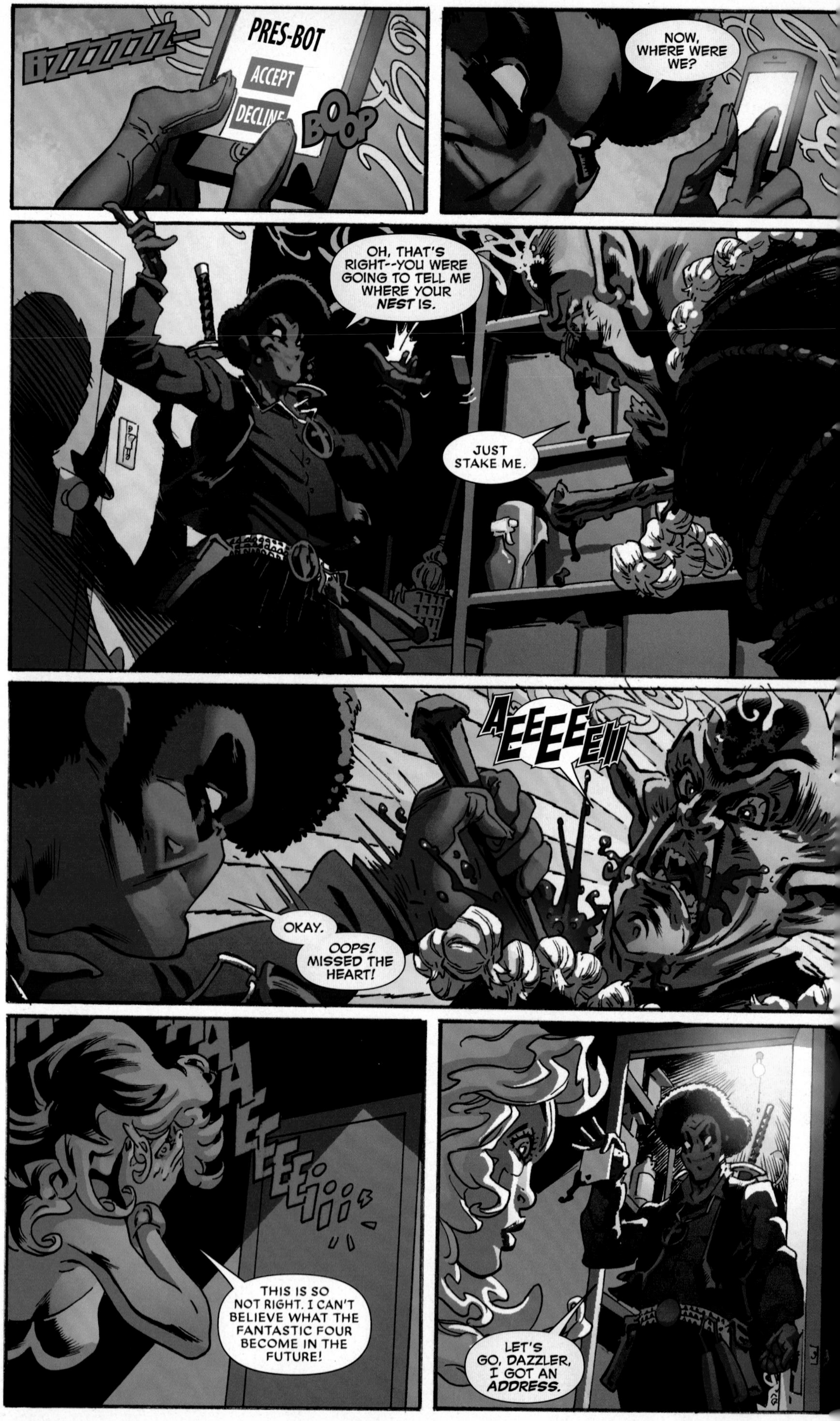
BZZZZZZZ--
PRES-BOT
ACCEPT
DECLINE
BOOP
NOW, WHERE WERE WE?
OH, THAT'S RIGHT--YOU WERE GOING TO TELL ME WHERE YOUR *NEST* IS.
JUST STAKE ME.
AEEEEEIII
OKAY.
OOPS! MISSED THE HEART!
THIS IS SO NOT RIGHT. I CAN'T BELIEVE WHAT THE FANTASTIC FOUR BECOME IN THE FUTURE!
LET'S GO, DAZZLER, I GOT AN *ADDRESS.*

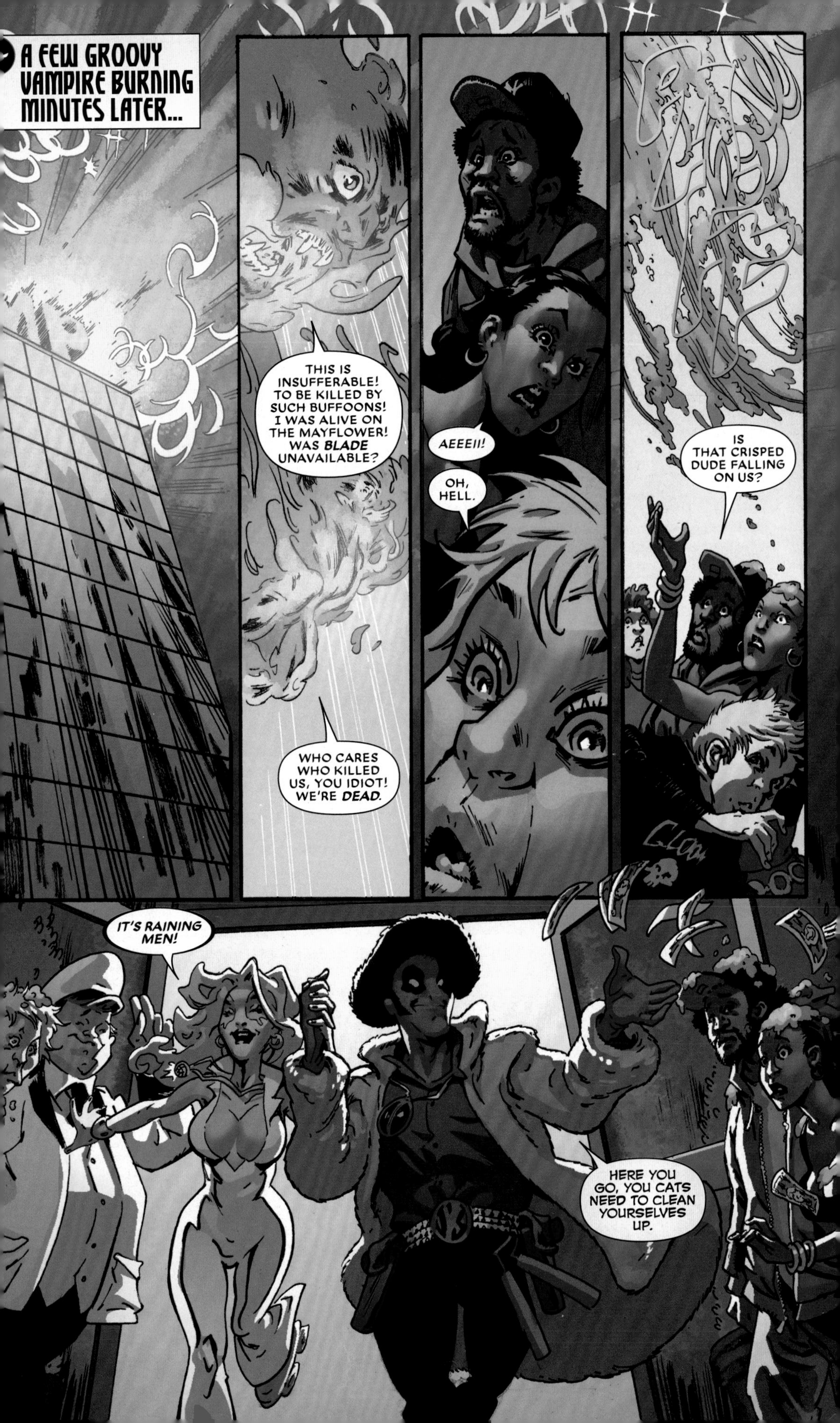
A FEW GROOVY VAMPIRE BURNING MINUTES LATER...
THIS IS INSUFFERABLE! TO BE KILLED BY SUCH BUFFOONS! I WAS ALIVE ON THE MAYFLOWER! WAS *BLADE* UNAVAILABLE?
WHO CARES WHO KILLED US, YOU IDIOT! WE'RE *DEAD*.
AEEEII!
OH, HELL.
IS THAT CRISPED DUDE FALLING ON US?
IT'S RAINING MEN!
HERE YOU GO, YOU CATS NEED TO CLEAN YOURSELVES UP.

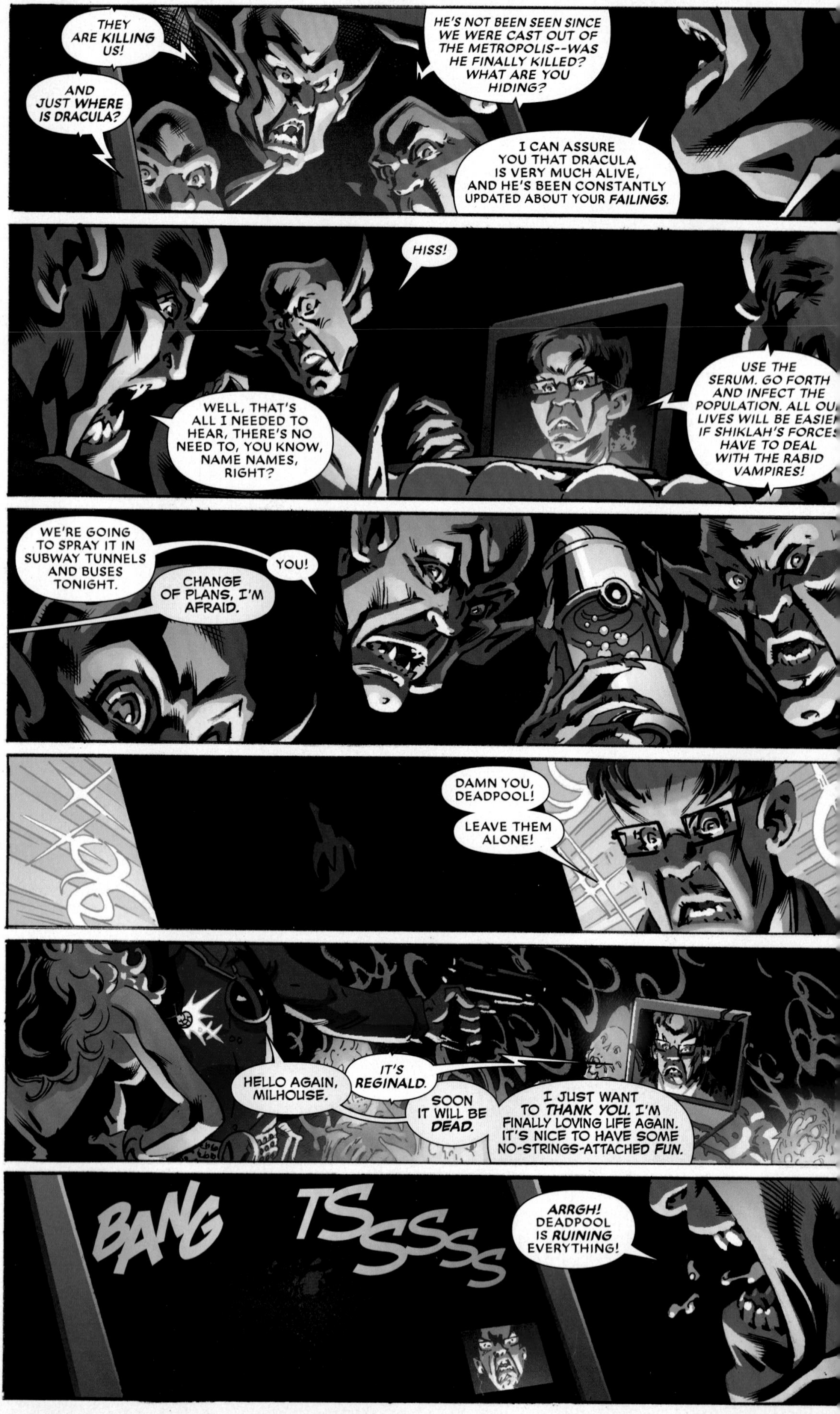
THEY ARE KILLING US!
AND JUST WHERE IS DRACULA?
HE'S NOT BEEN SEEN SINCE WE WERE CAST OUT OF THE METROPOLIS--WAS HE FINALLY KILLED? WHAT ARE YOU HIDING?
I CAN ASSURE YOU THAT DRACULA IS VERY MUCH ALIVE, AND HE'S BEEN CONSTANTLY UPDATED ABOUT YOUR FAILINGS.
HISS!
WELL, THAT'S ALL I NEEDED TO HEAR, THERE'S NO NEED TO, YOU KNOW, NAME NAMES, RIGHT?
USE THE SERUM. GO FORTH AND INFECT THE POPULATION. ALL OU LIVES WILL BE EASIE IF SHIKLAH'S FORCE HAVE TO DEAL WITH THE RABID VAMPIRES!
WE'RE GOING TO SPRAY IT IN SUBWAY TUNNELS AND BUSES TONIGHT.
YOU!
CHANGE OF PLANS, I'M AFRAID.
DAMN YOU, DEADPOOL!
LEAVE THEM ALONE!
HELLO AGAIN, MILHOUSE.
IT'S REGINALD.
SOON IT WILL BE DEAD.
I JUST WANT TO THANK YOU. I'M FINALLY LOVING LIFE AGAIN. IT'S NICE TO HAVE SOME NO-STRINGS-ATTACHED FUN.
BANG
TSSSSS
ARRGH! DEADPOOL IS RUINING EVERYTHING!

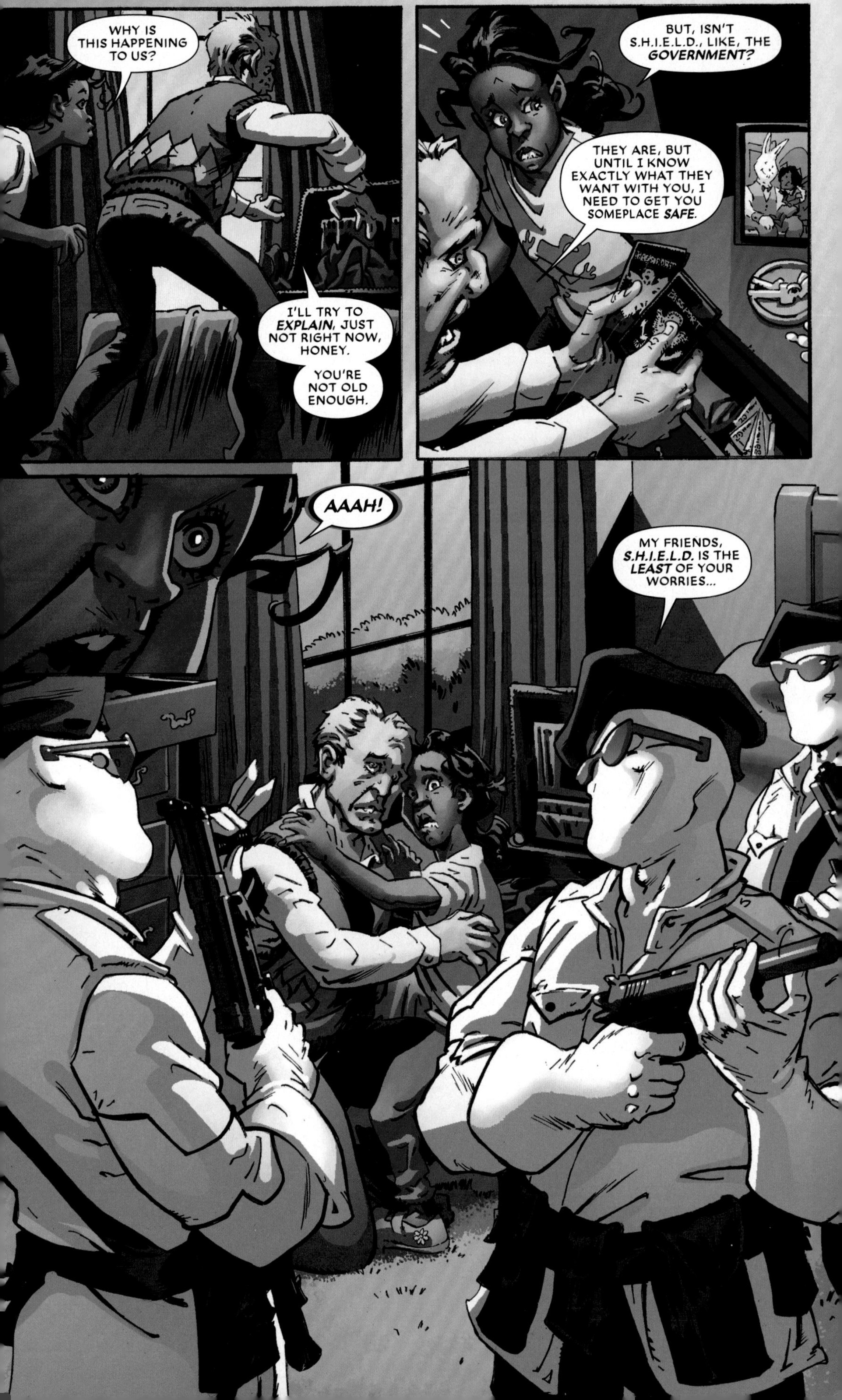
WHY IS THIS HAPPENING TO US?
I'LL TRY TO EXPLAIN, JUST NOT RIGHT NOW, HONEY.
YOU'RE NOT OLD ENOUGH.
BUT, ISN'T S.H.I.E.L.D., LIKE, THE GOVERNMENT?
THEY ARE, BUT UNTIL I KNOW EXACTLY WHAT THEY WANT WITH YOU, I NEED TO GET YOU SOMEPLACE SAFE.
AAAH!
MY FRIENDS, S.H.I.E.L.D. IS THE LEAST OF YOUR WORRIES...

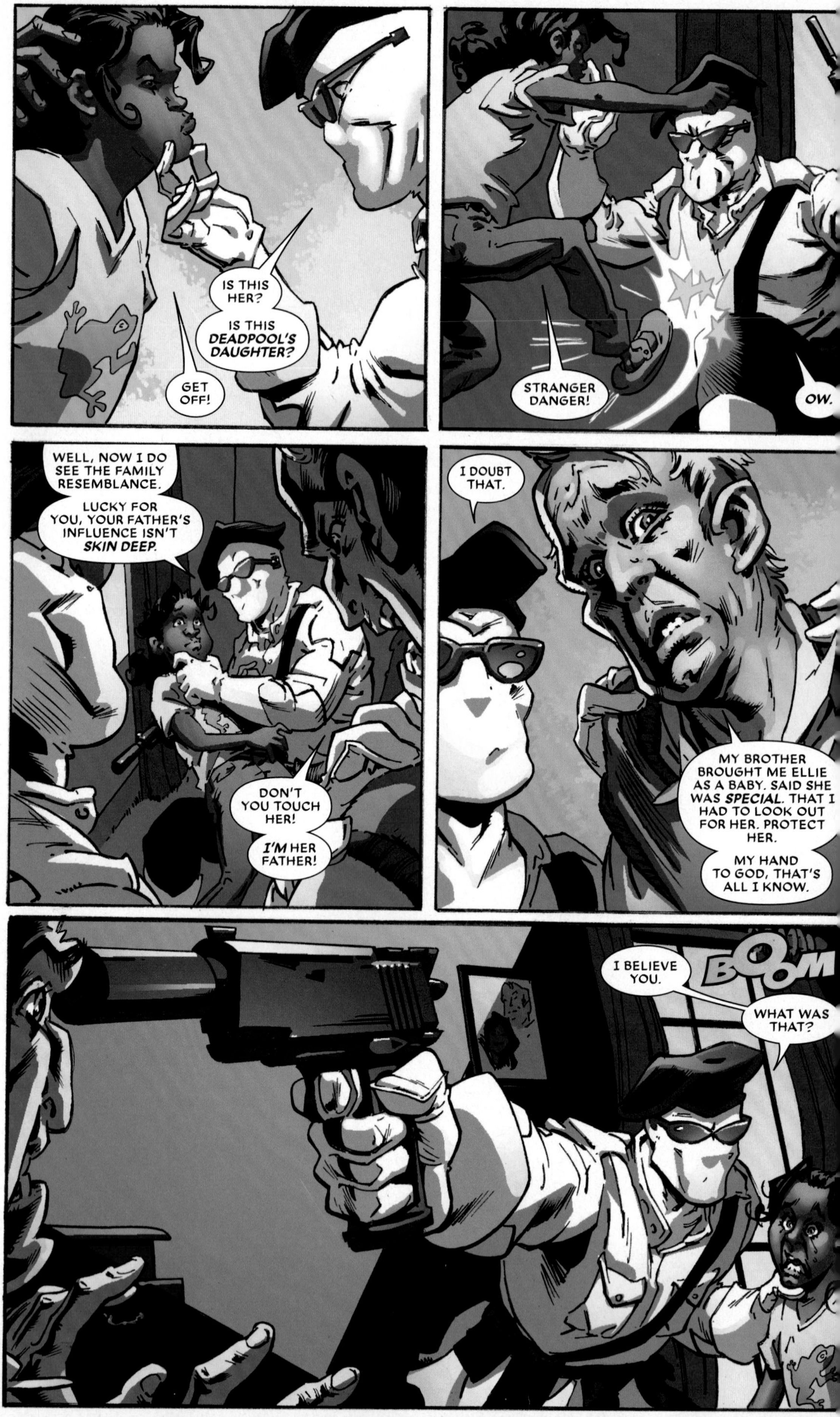
IS THIS HER?
IS THIS DEADPOOL'S DAUGHTER?
GET OFF!
STRANGER DANGER!
OW.
WELL, NOW I DO SEE THE FAMILY RESEMBLANCE.
LUCKY FOR YOU, YOUR FATHER'S INFLUENCE ISN'T SKIN DEEP.
DON'T YOU TOUCH HER!
I'M HER FATHER!
I DOUBT THAT.
MY BROTHER BROUGHT ME ELLIE AS A BABY. SAID SHE WAS SPECIAL. THAT I HAD TO LOOK OUT FOR HER. PROTECT HER.
MY HAND TO GOD, THAT'S ALL I KNOW.
I BELIEVE YOU.
BOOM
WHAT WAS THAT?

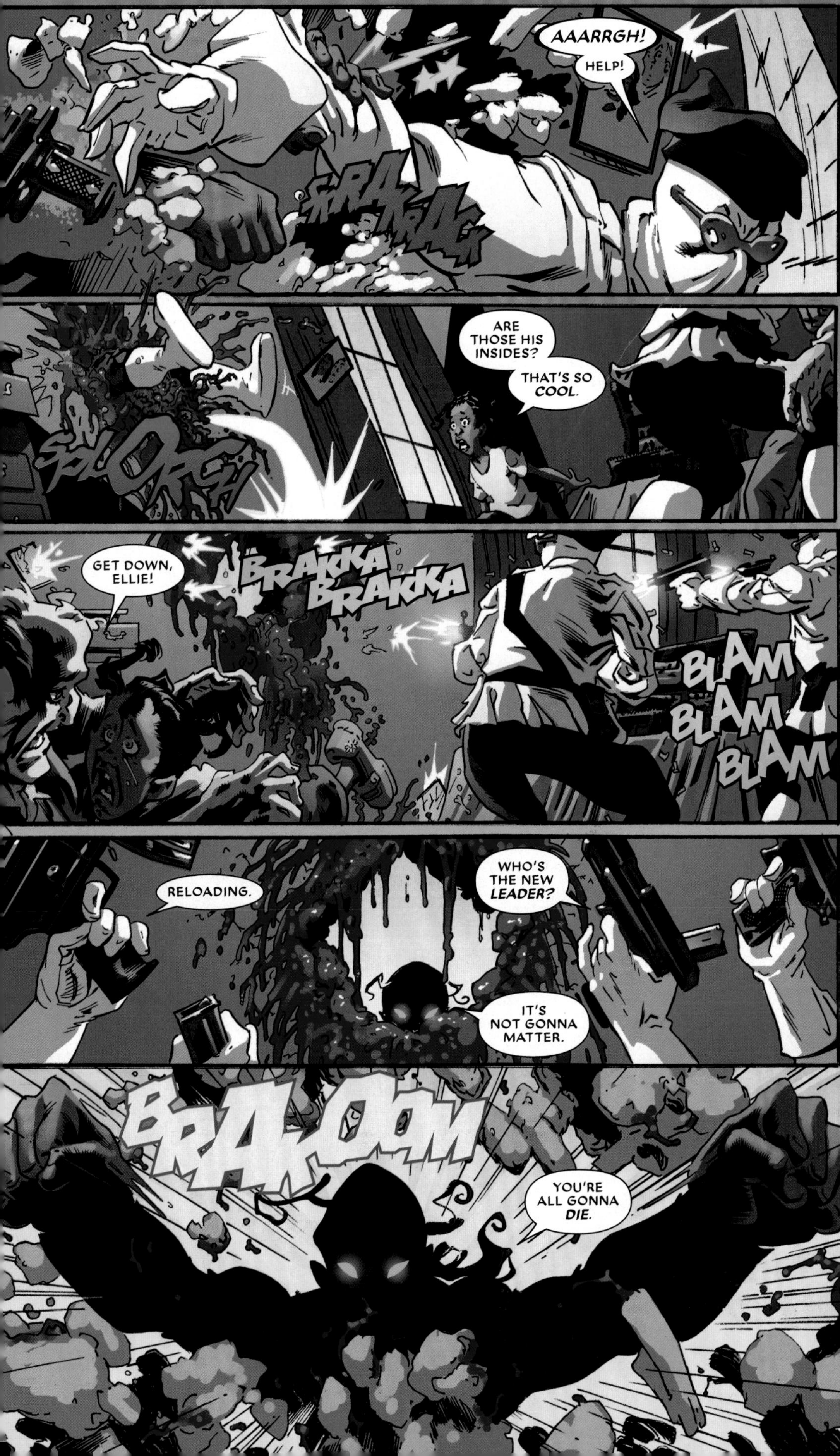
AAARRGH!
HELP!
SHRAAAKRAKK
ARE THOSE HIS INSIDES?
THAT'S SO COOL.
SPLOOSH
GET DOWN, ELLIE!
BRAKKA BRAKKA
BLAM BLAM BLAM
RELOADING.
WHO'S THE NEW LEADER?
IT'S NOT GONNA MATTER.
BRALOOM
YOU'RE ALL GONNA DIE.

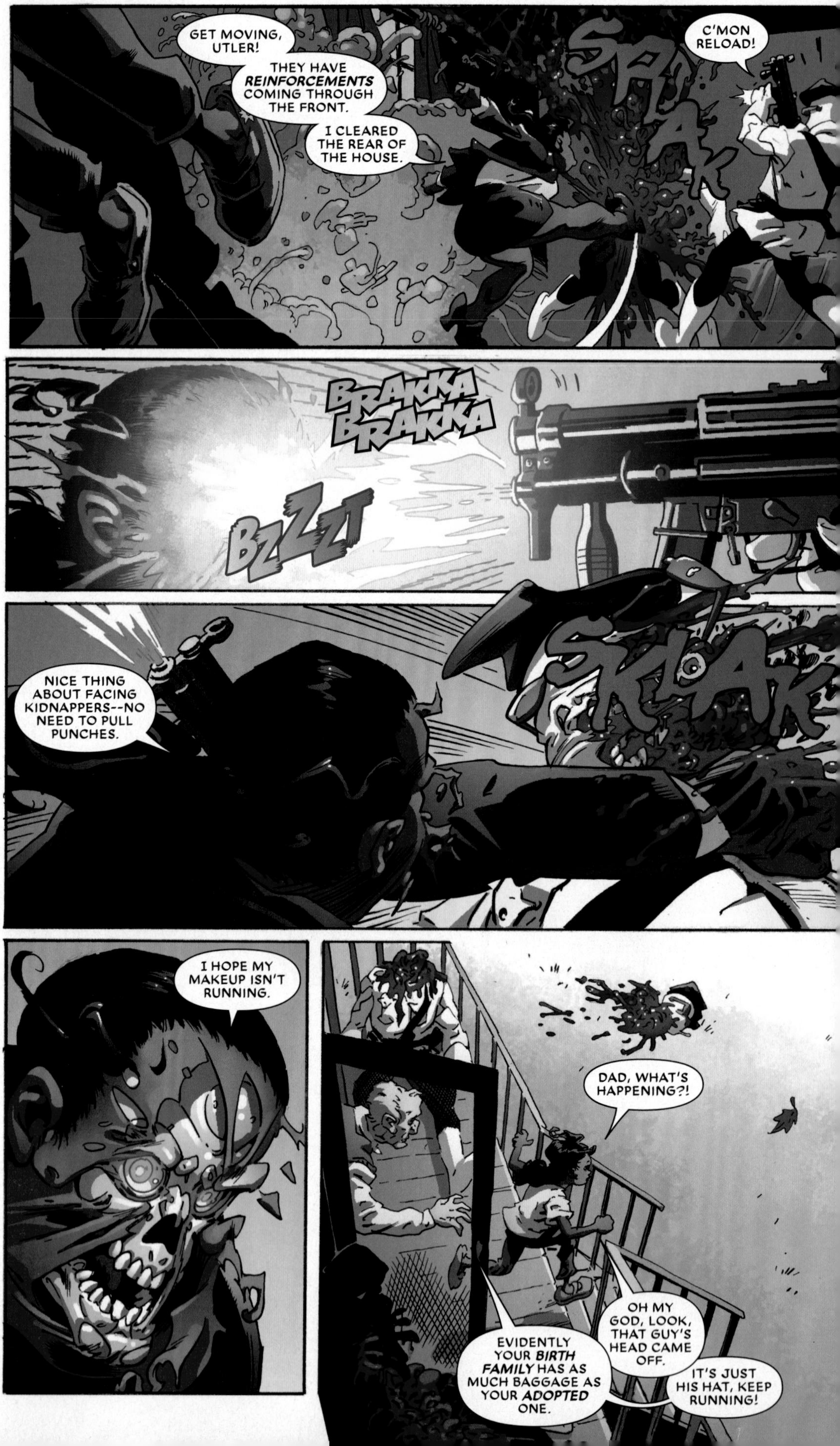
GET MOVING, UTLER!
THEY HAVE REINFORCEMENTS COMING THROUGH THE FRONT.
I CLEARED THE REAR OF THE HOUSE.
SPLAK
C'MON RELOAD!
BRAKKA BRAKKA
BZZZT
NICE THING ABOUT FACING KIDNAPPERS--NO NEED TO PULL PUNCHES.
SKLAK
I HOPE MY MAKEUP ISN'T RUNNING.
DAD, WHAT'S HAPPENING?!
OH MY GOD, LOOK, THAT GUY'S HEAD CAME OFF.
EVIDENTLY YOUR BIRTH FAMILY HAS AS MUCH BAGGAGE AS YOUR ADOPTED ONE.
IT'S JUST HIS HAT, KEEP RUNNING!

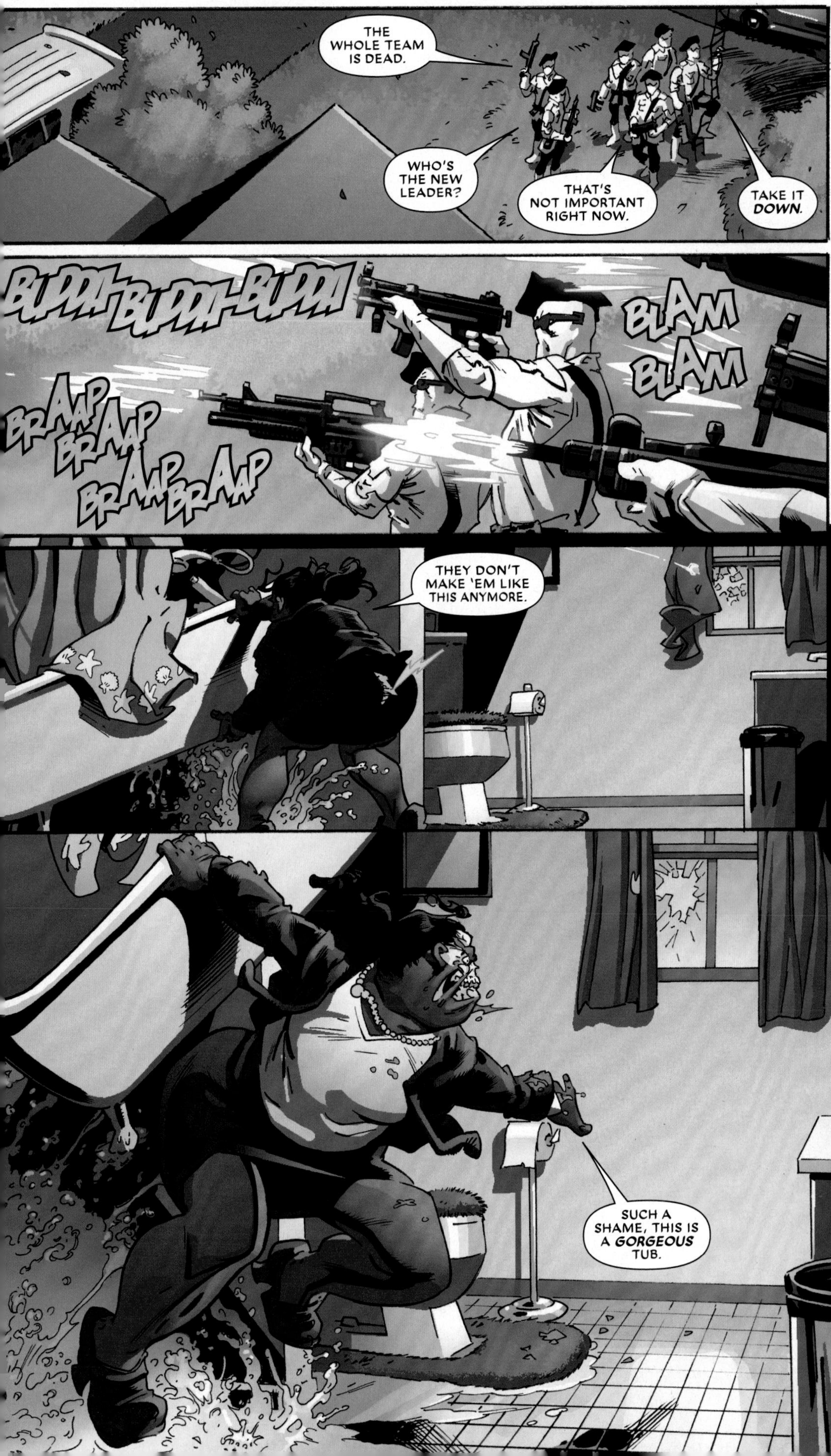

THE WHOLE TEAM IS DEAD.
WHO'S THE NEW LEADER?
THAT'S NOT IMPORTANT RIGHT NOW.
TAKE IT *DOWN*.
BUDDA BUDDA-BUDDA
BLAM BLAM
BRAAP BRAAP BRAAP BRAAP
THEY DON'T MAKE 'EM LIKE THIS ANYMORE.
SUCH A SHAME, THIS IS A *GORGEOUS* TUB.

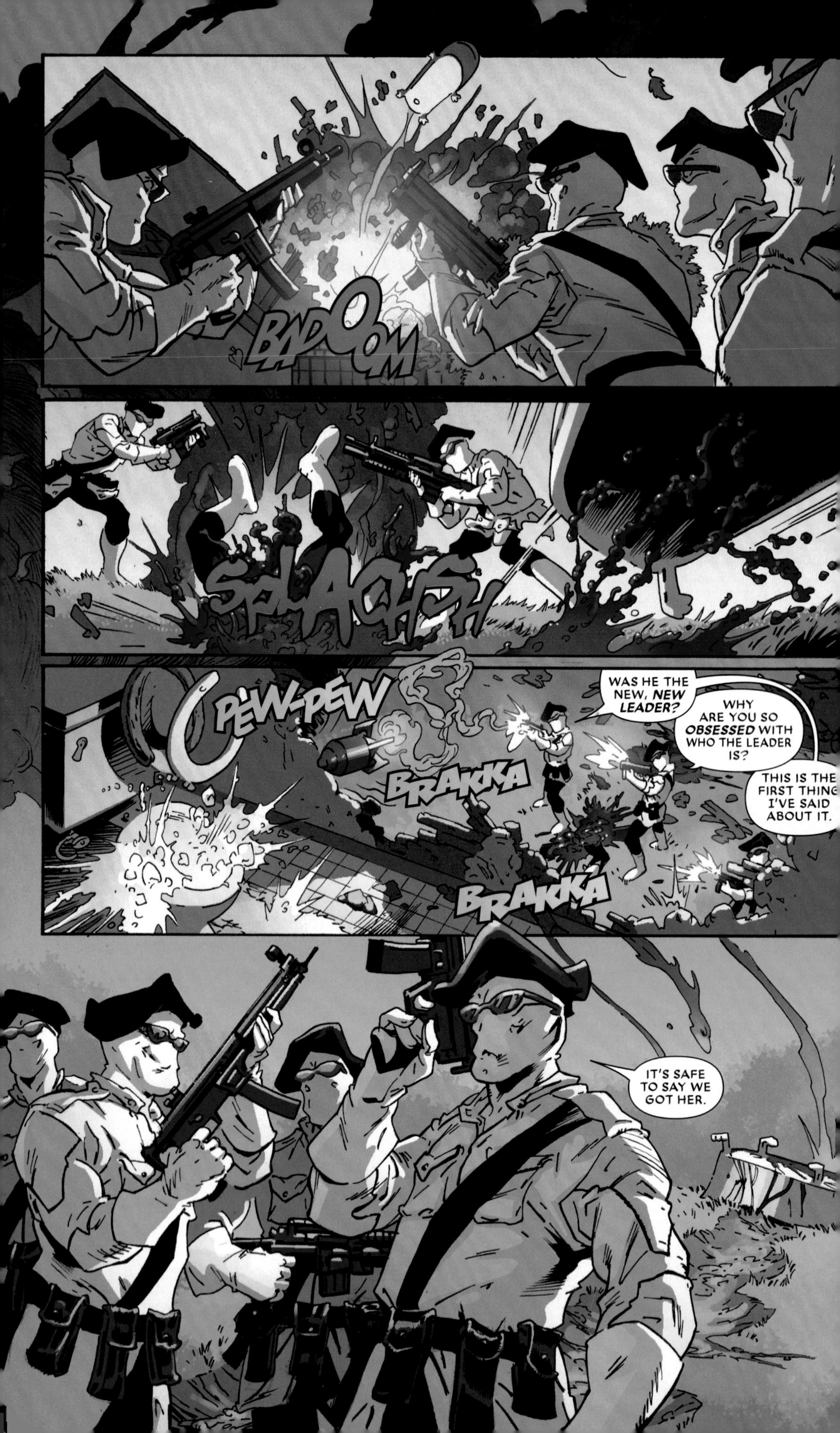
BADOOM
SPLACHSH
PEW-PEW
BRAKKA
WAS HE THE NEW, NEW LEADER?
WHY ARE YOU SO OBSESSED WITH WHO THE LEADER IS?
THIS IS THE FIRST THING I'VE SAID ABOUT IT.
BRAKKA
IT'S SAFE TO SAY WE GOT HER.

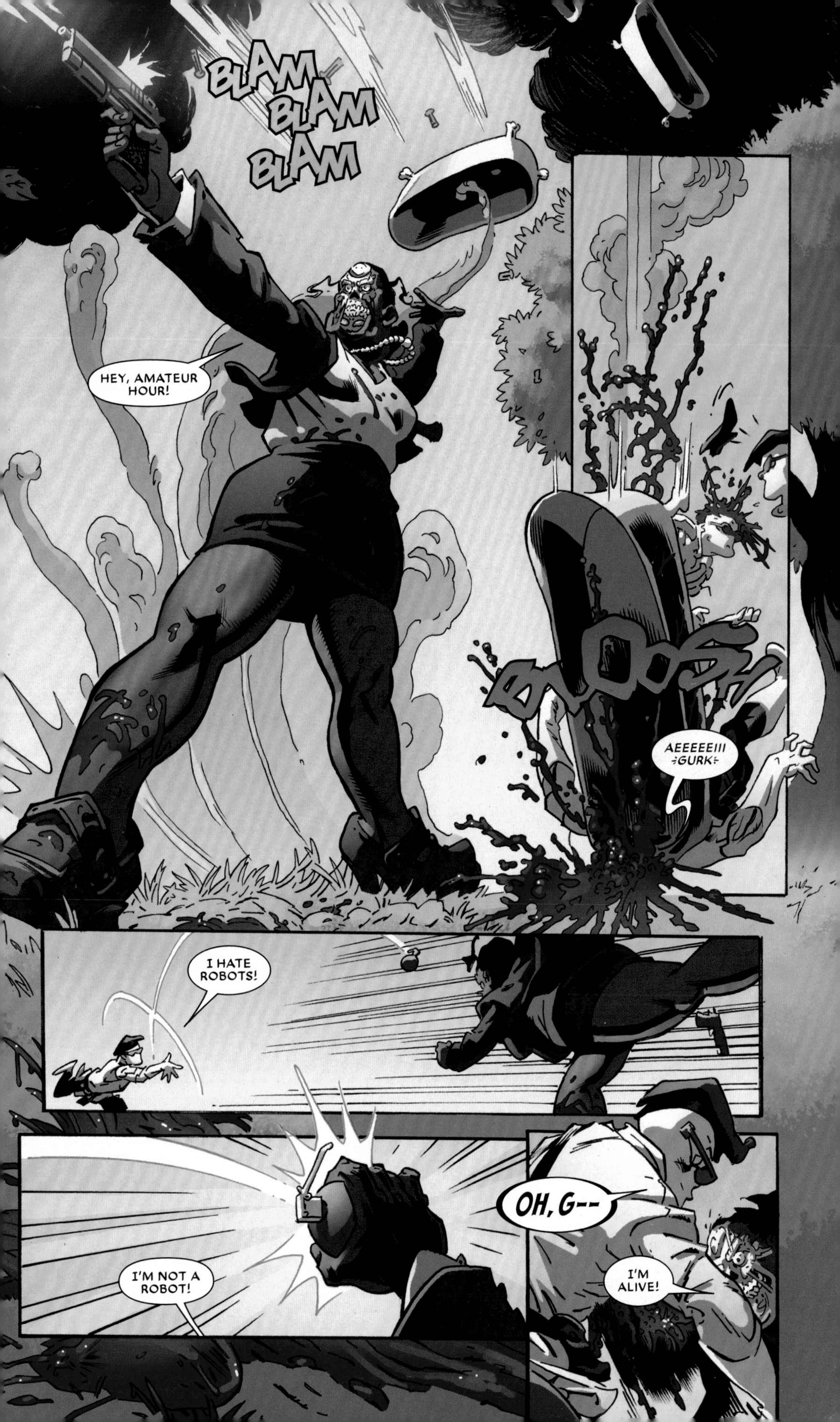
BLAM BLAM BLAM
HEY, AMATEUR HOUR!
BLOOSH
AEEEEEIII -GURK-
I HATE ROBOTS!
I'M NOT A ROBOT!
OH, G--
I'M ALIVE!

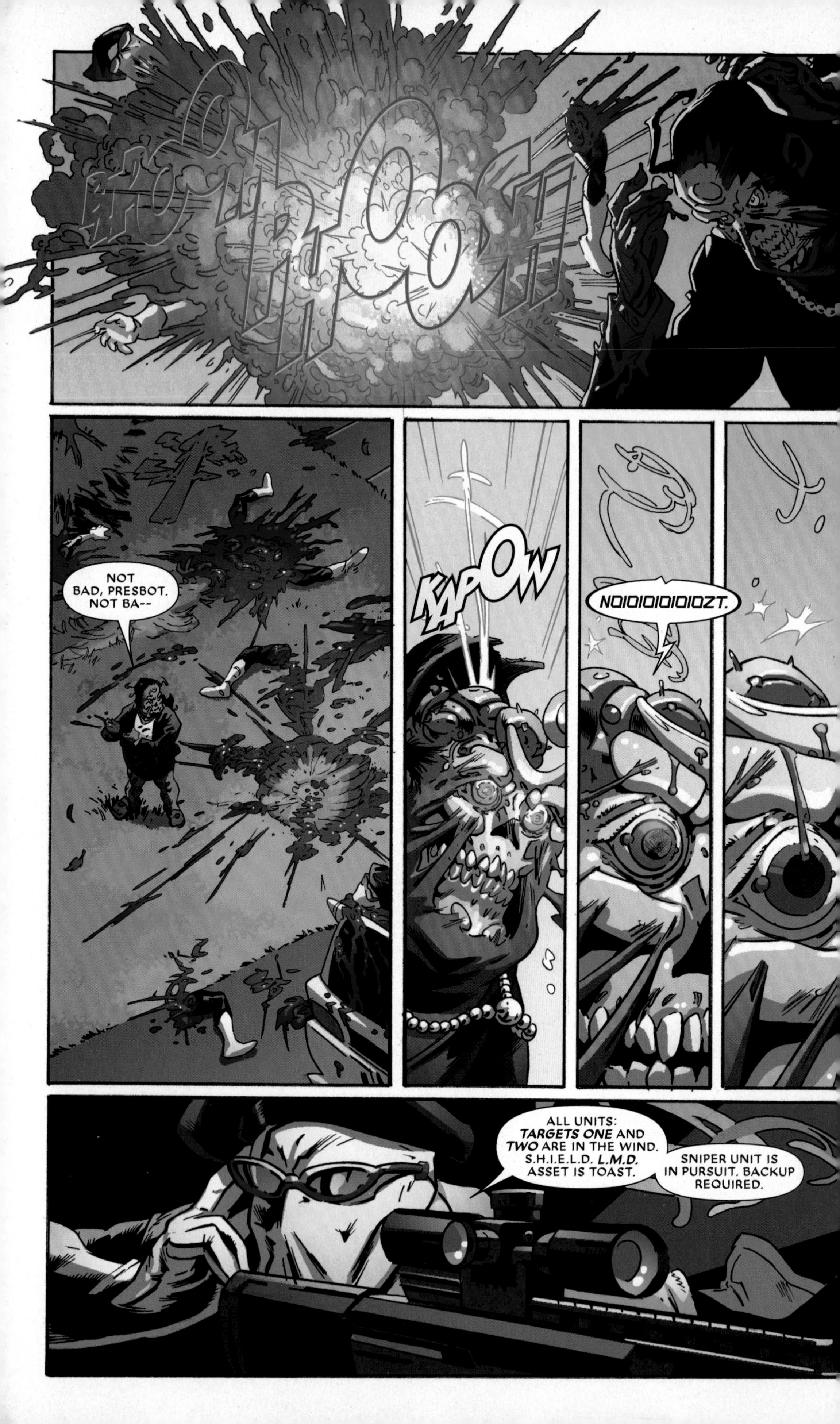
BROOOM
NOT BAD, PRESBOT. NOT BA--
KAPOW
NOIOIOIOIOIOZT.
ALL UNITS: TARGETS ONE AND TWO ARE IN THE WIND. S.H.I.E.L.D. L.M.D. ASSET IS TOAST.
SNIPER UNIT IS IN PURSUIT. BACKUP REQUIRED.

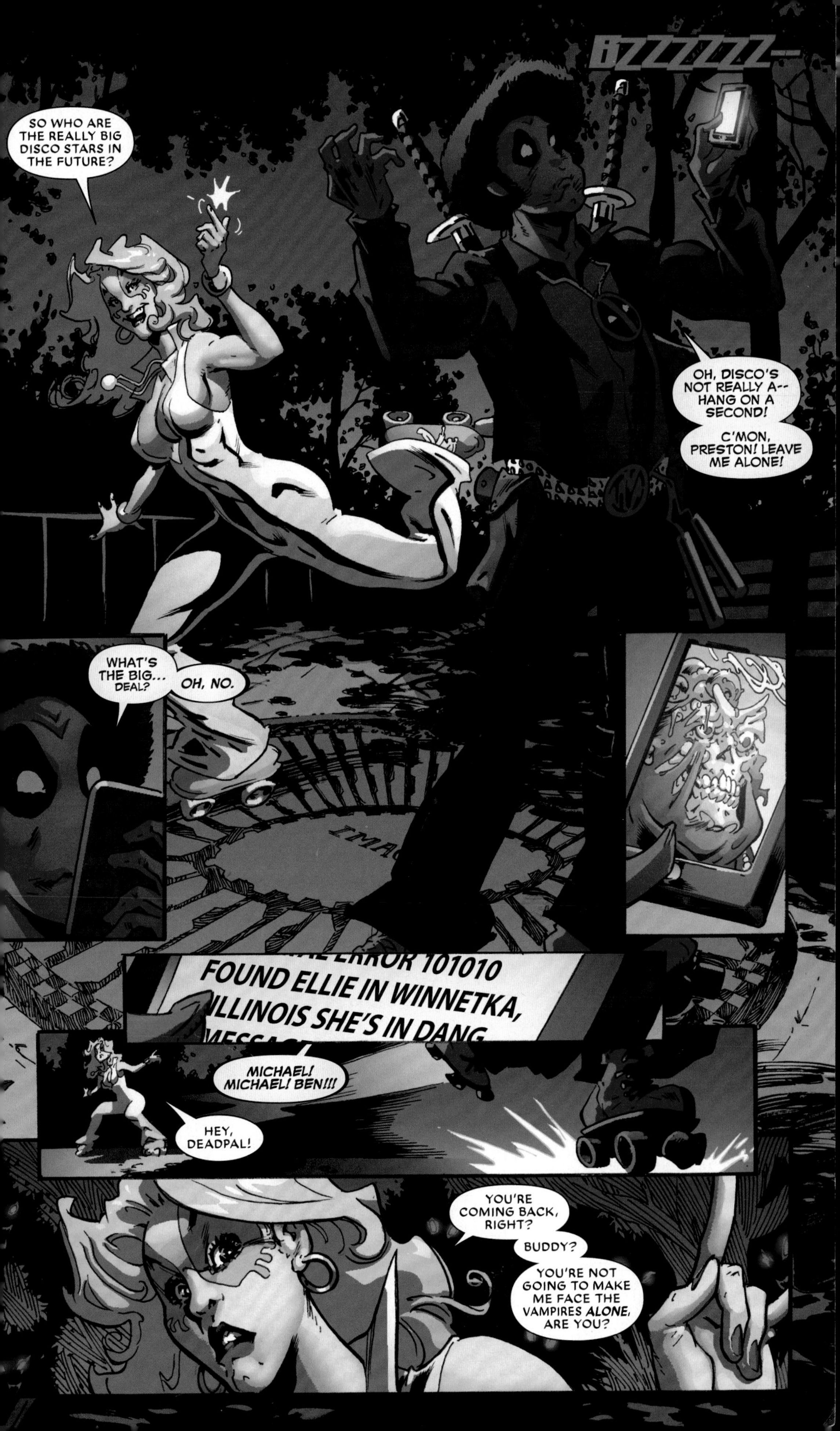
BZZZZZZZ--
SO WHO ARE THE REALLY BIG DISCO STARS IN THE FUTURE?
OH, DISCO'S NOT REALLY A-- HANG ON A SECOND!
C'MON, PRESTON! LEAVE ME ALONE!
WHAT'S THE BIG... DEAL?
OH, NO.
FOUND ELLIE IN WINNETKA,
ILLINOIS SHE'S IN DANG
MICHAEL! MICHAEL! BEN!!!
HEY, DEADPAL!
YOU'RE COMING BACK, RIGHT?
BUDDY?
YOU'RE NOT GOING TO MAKE ME FACE THE VAMPIRES *ALONE*, ARE YOU?

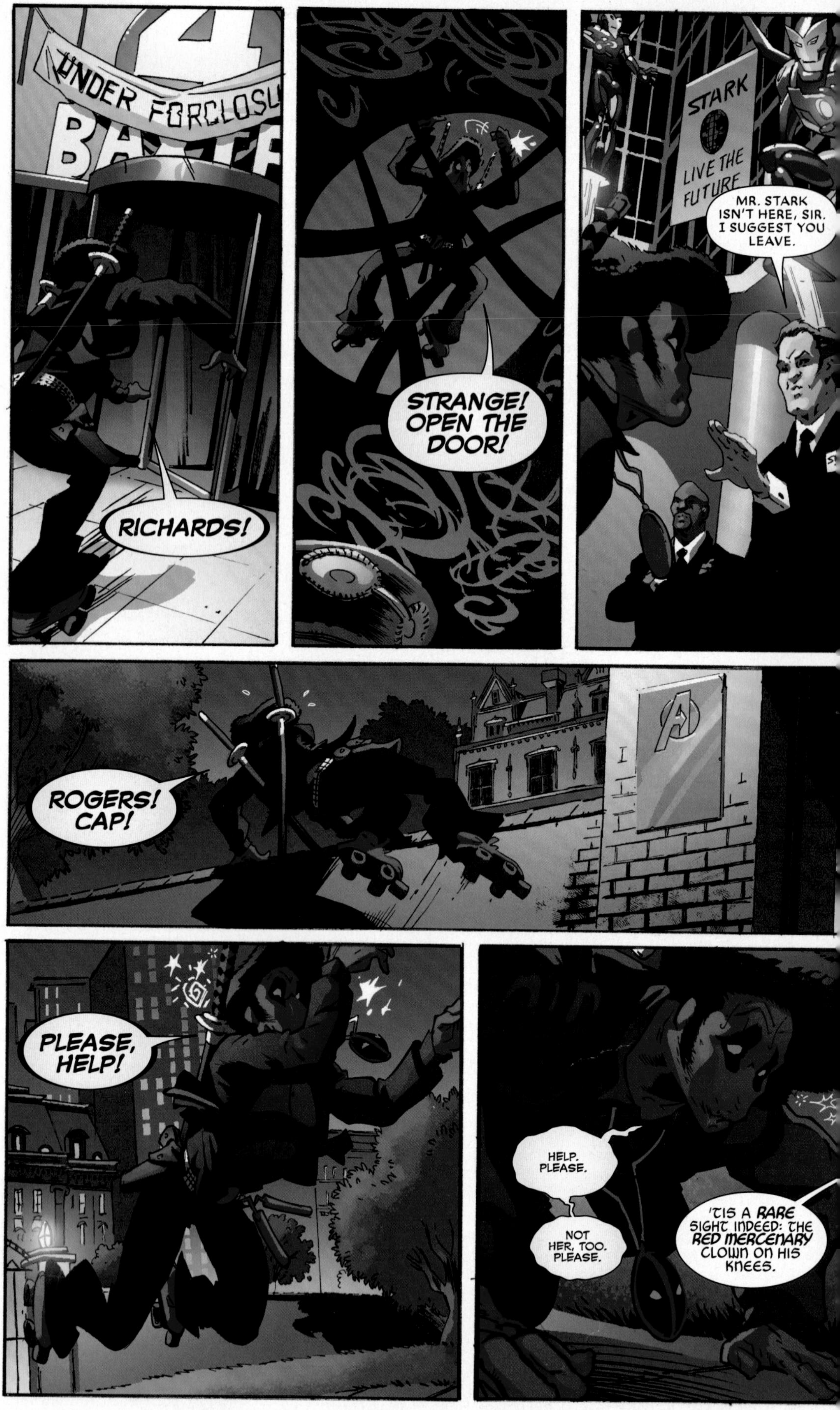

RICHARDS!
STRANGE! OPEN THE DOOR!
STARK
LIVE THE
MR. STARK ISN'T HERE, SIR. I SUGGEST YOU LEAVE.
ROGERS! CAP!
PLEASE, HELP!
HELP. PLEASE.
NOT HER, TOO. PLEASE.
'TIS A RARE SIGHT INDEED: THE RED MERCENARY CLOWN ON HIS KNEES.

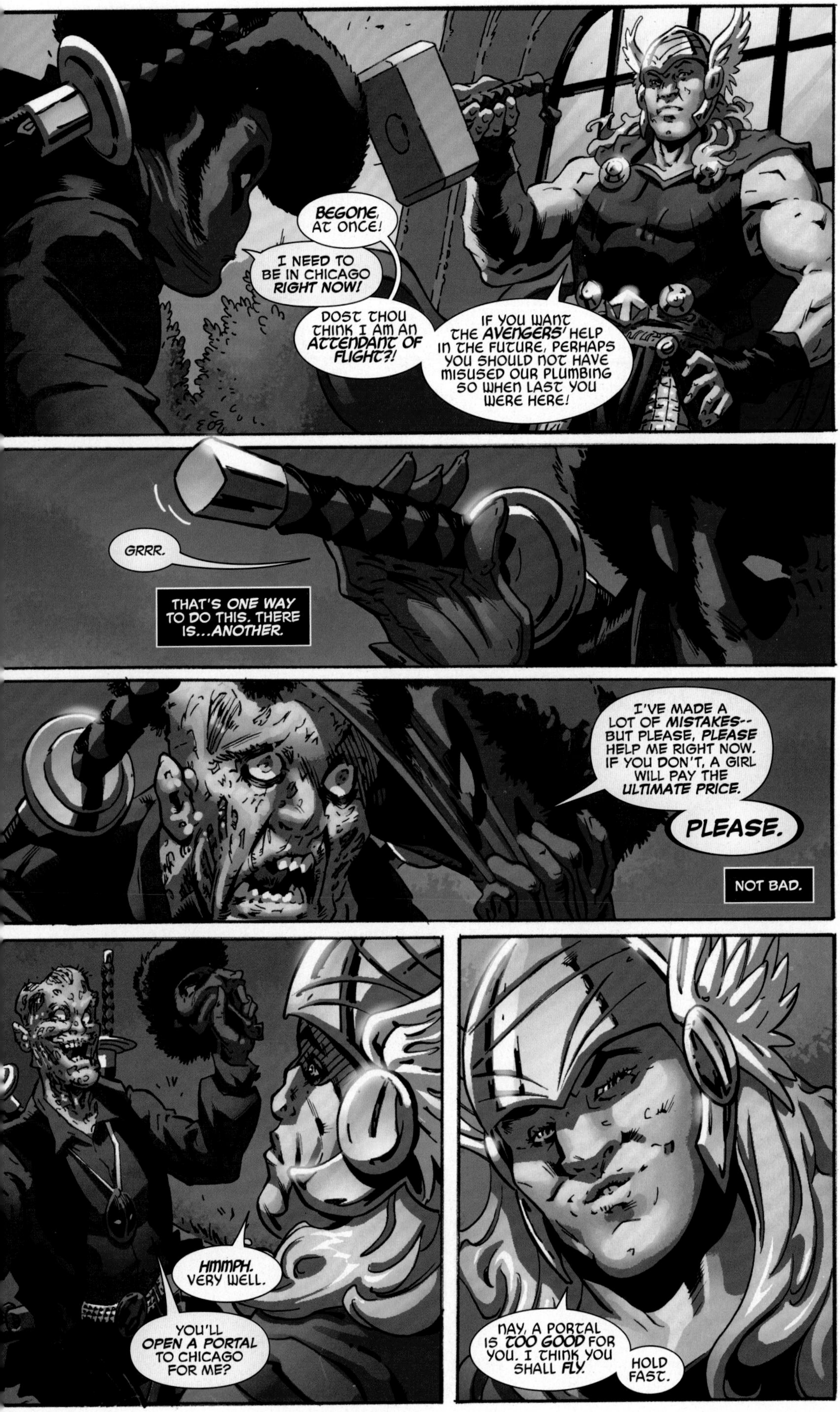

BEGONE, AT ONCE!
I NEED TO BE IN CHICAGO RIGHT NOW!
DOST THOU THINK I AM AN ATTENDANT OF FLIGHT?!
IF YOU WANT THE AVENGERS' HELP IN THE FUTURE, PERHAPS YOU SHOULD NOT HAVE MISUSED OUR PLUMBING SO WHEN LAST YOU WERE HERE!
GRRR.
THAT'S ONE WAY TO DO THIS. THERE IS...ANOTHER.
I'VE MADE A LOT OF MISTAKES--BUT PLEASE, PLEASE HELP ME RIGHT NOW. IF YOU DON'T, A GIRL WILL PAY THE ULTIMATE PRICE.
PLEASE.
NOT BAD.
HMMPH. VERY WELL.
YOU'LL OPEN A PORTAL TO CHICAGO FOR ME?
NAY, A PORTAL IS TOO GOOD FOR YOU. I THINK YOU SHALL FLY.
HOLD FAST.

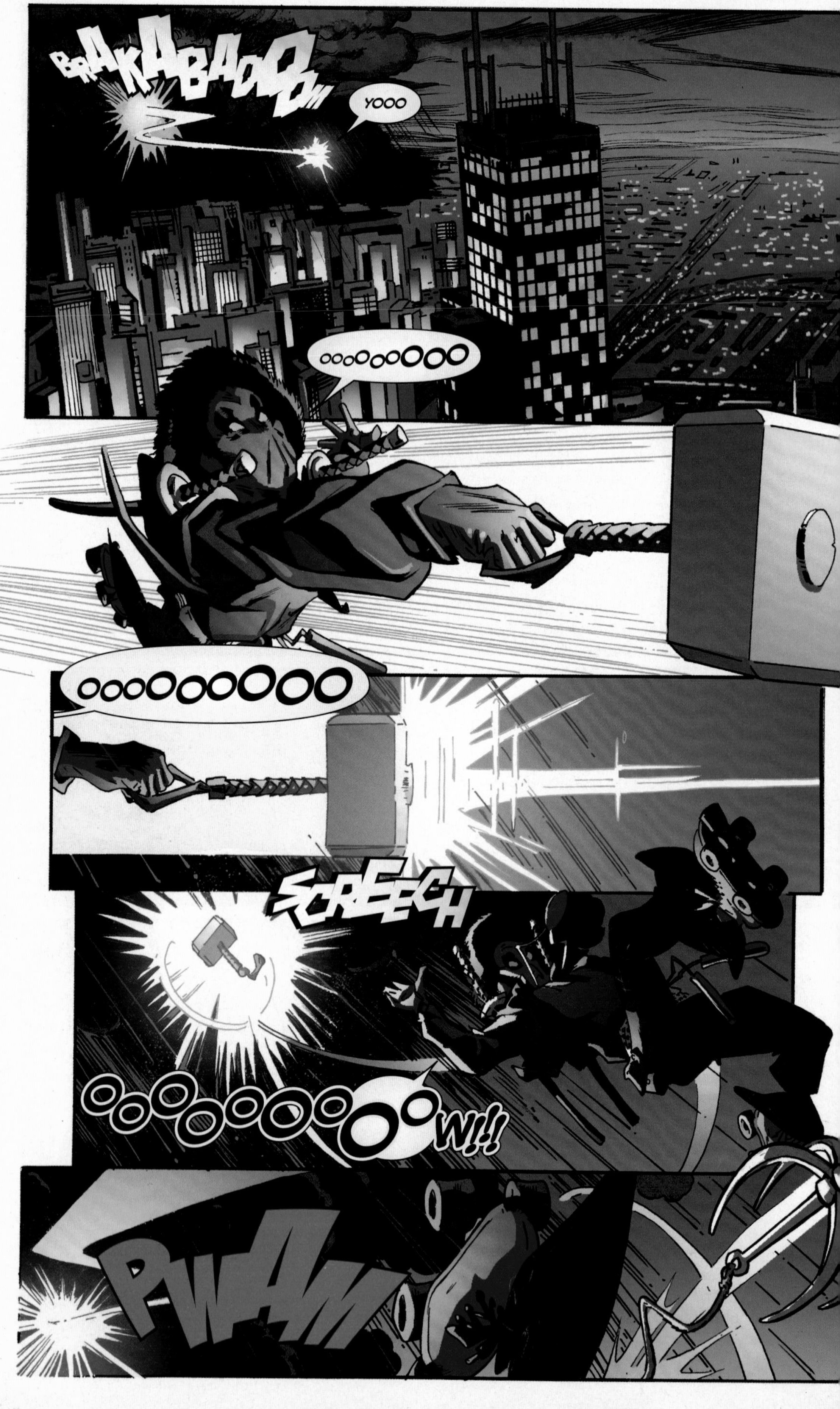
BRAKABADOOOM
YOOO
OOOOOOOOO
OOOOOOOOOO
SCREECH
OOOOOOOOOOOOW!!
PWAM

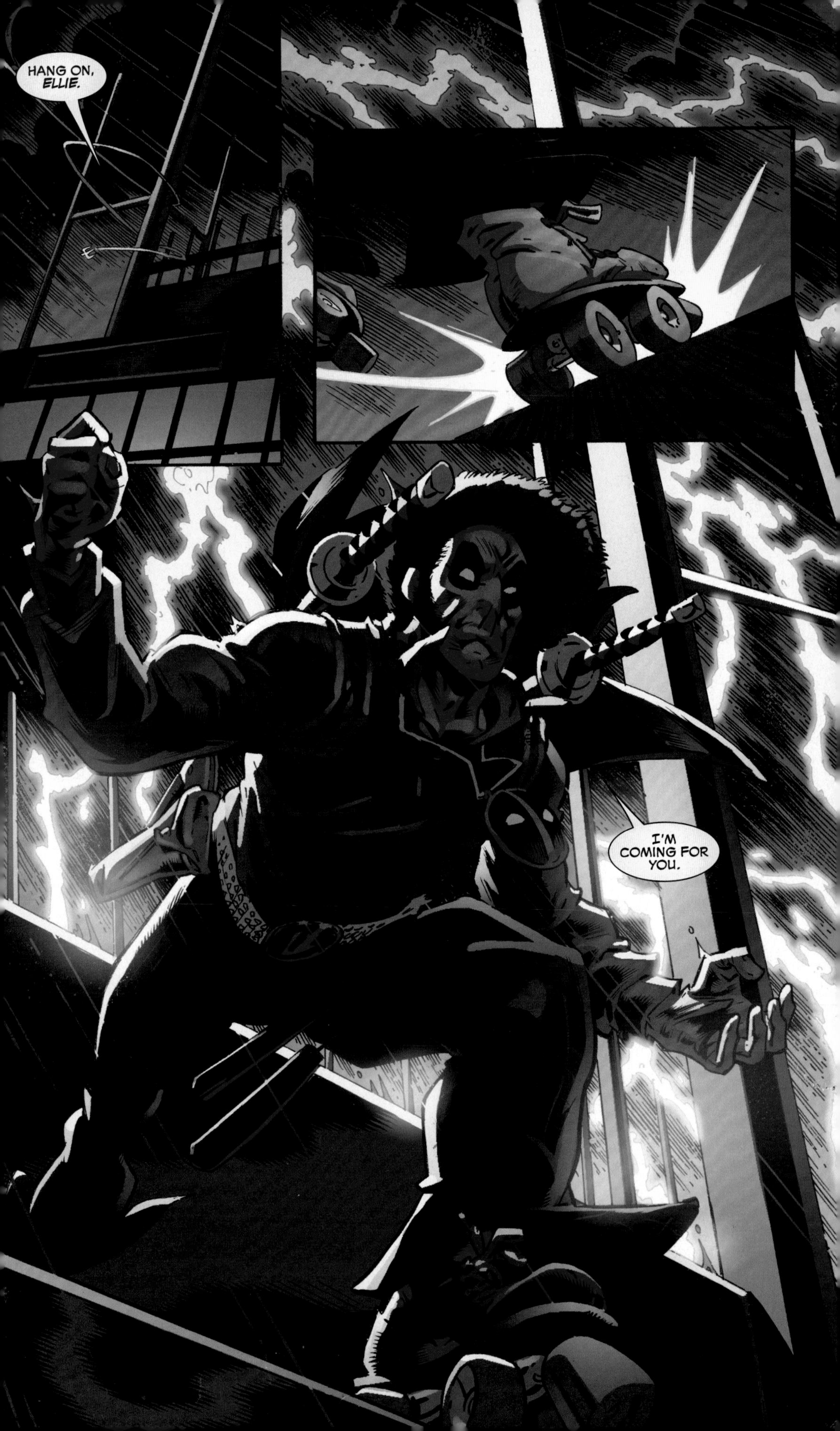
HANG ON, ELLIE.
I'M COMING FOR YOU.

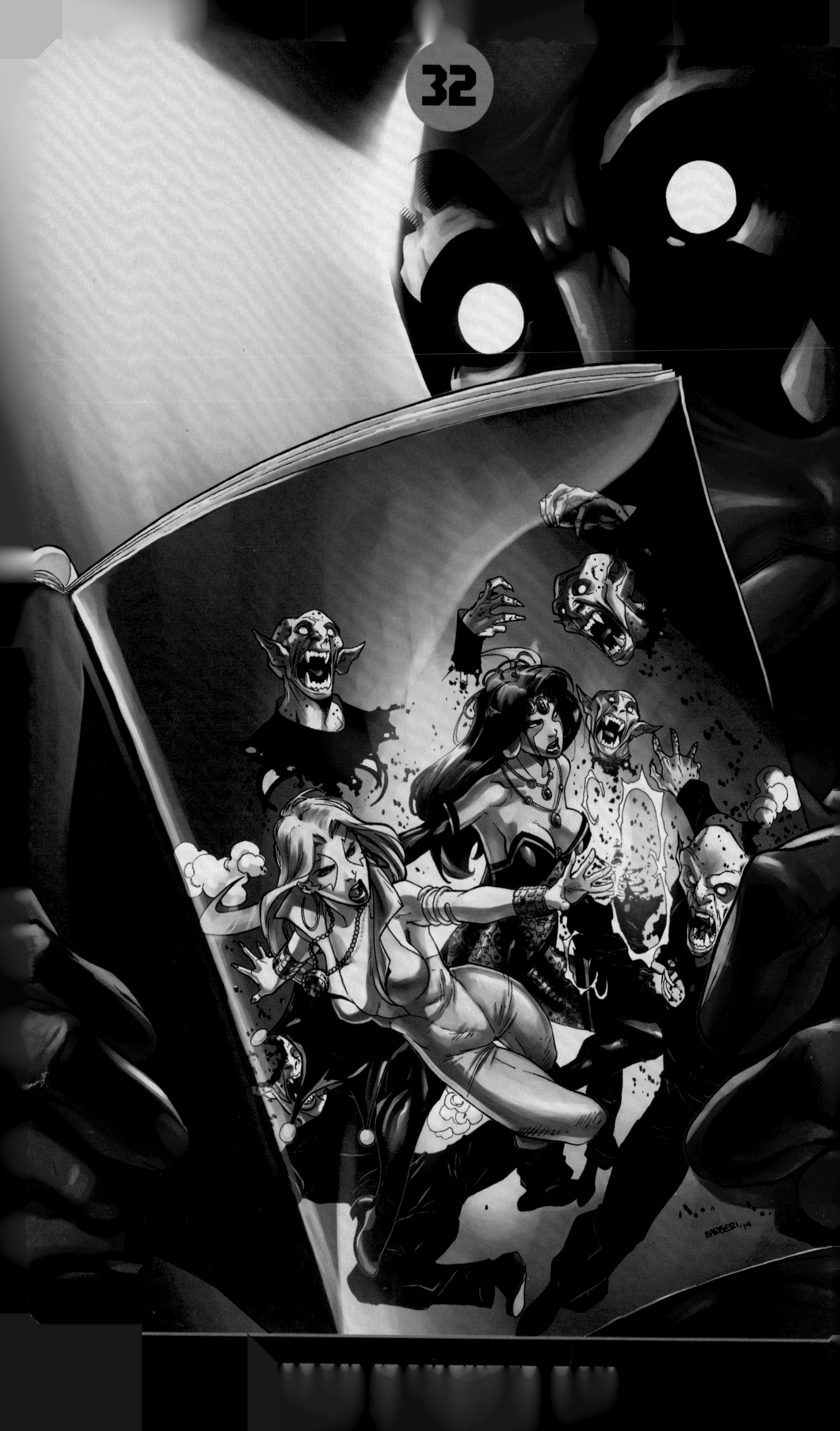
32

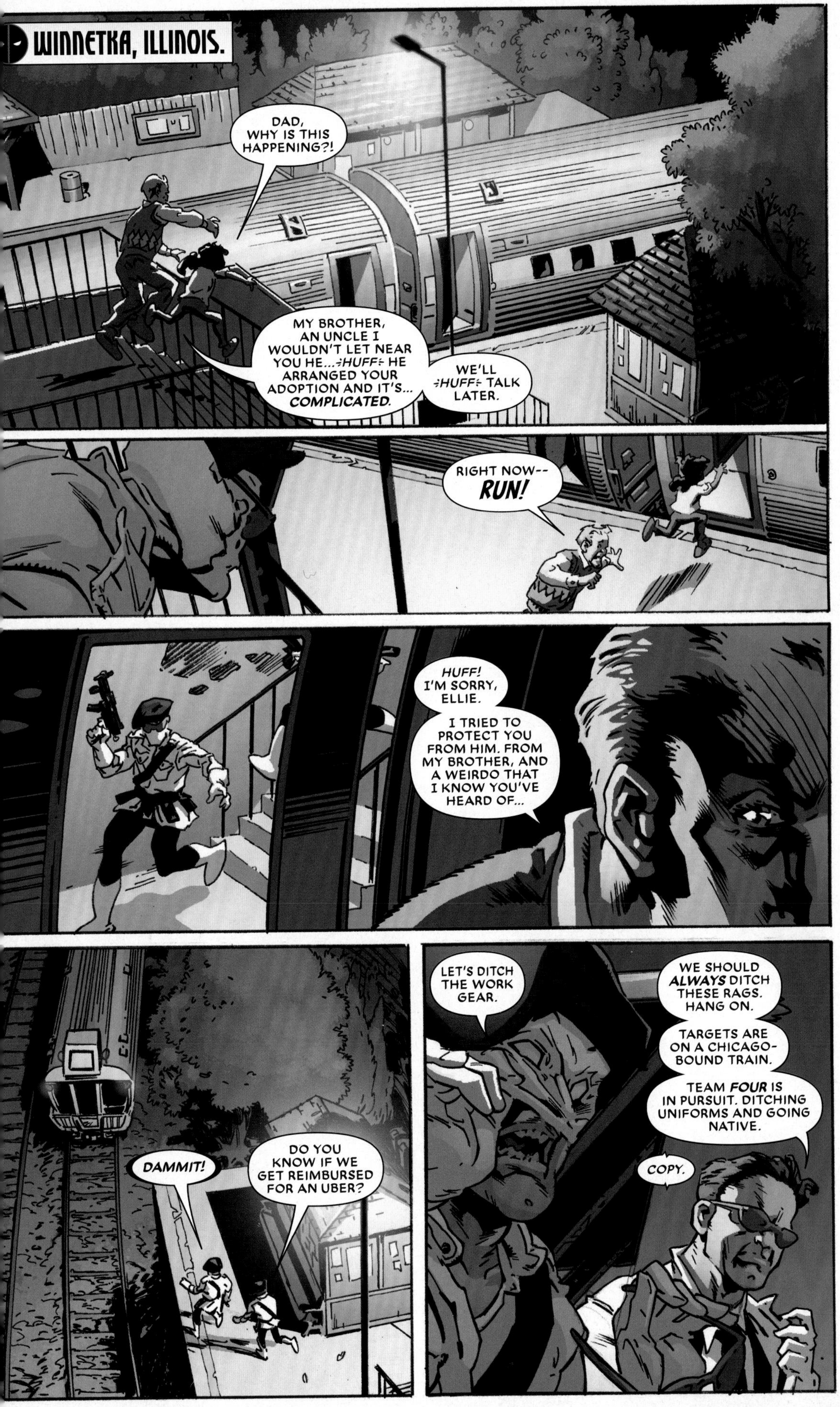
WINNETKA, ILLINOIS.
DAD, WHY IS THIS HAPPENING?!
MY BROTHER, AN UNCLE I WOULDN'T LET NEAR YOU HE... ≑HUFF≑ HE ARRANGED YOUR ADOPTION AND IT'S... COMPLICATED.
WE'LL ≑HUFF≑ TALK LATER.
RIGHT NOW-- RUN!
HUFF! I'M SORRY, ELLIE.
I TRIED TO PROTECT YOU FROM HIM. FROM MY BROTHER, AND A WEIRDO THAT I KNOW YOU'VE HEARD OF...
DAMMIT!
DO YOU KNOW IF WE GET REIMBURSED FOR AN UBER?
LET'S DITCH THE WORK GEAR.
WE SHOULD ALWAYS DITCH THESE RAGS. HANG ON.
TARGETS ARE ON A CHICAGO-BOUND TRAIN.
TEAM FOUR IS IN PURSUIT. DITCHING UNIFORMS AND GOING NATIVE.
COPY.

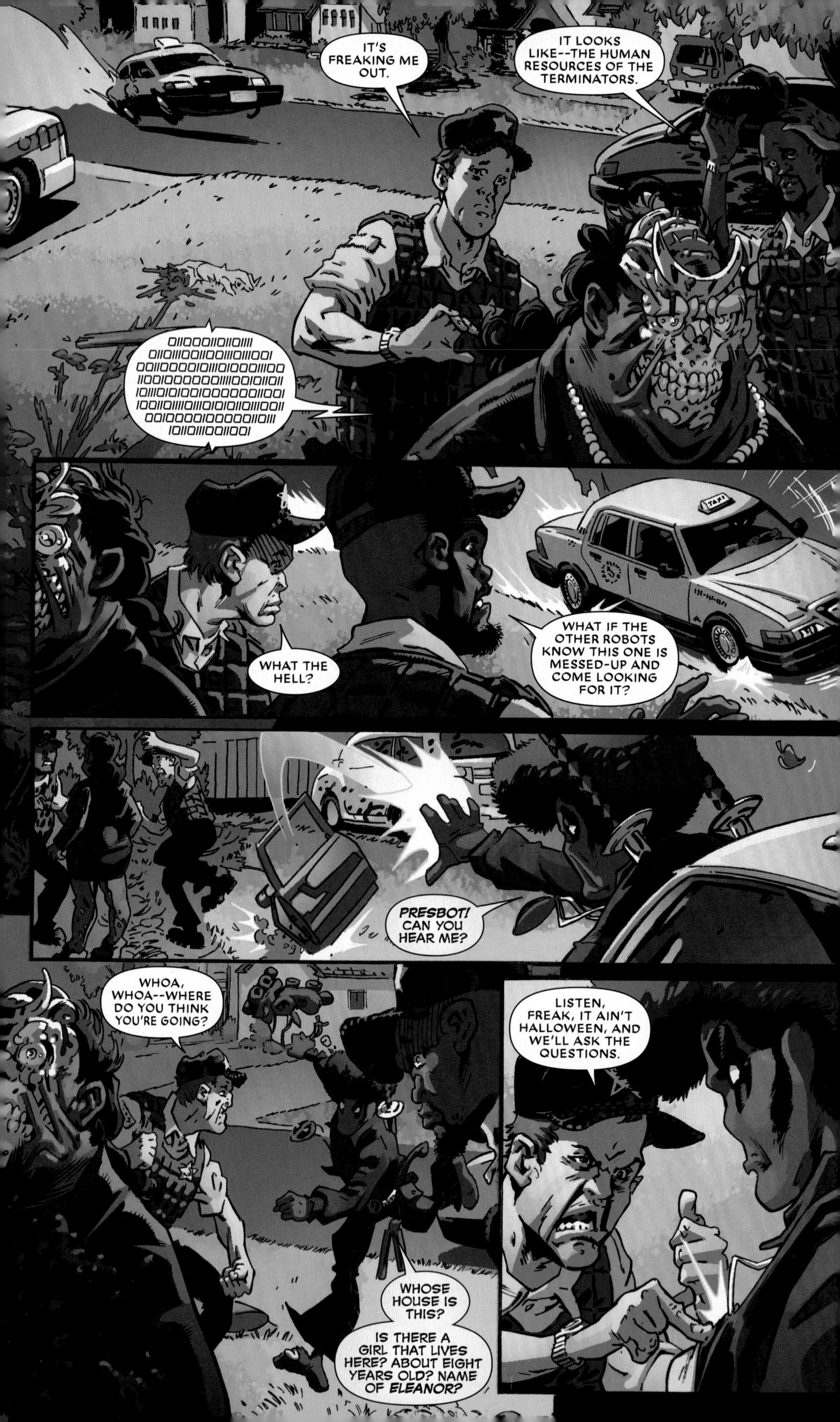
IT'S FREAKING ME OUT.
IT LOOKS LIKE--THE HUMAN RESOURCES OF THE TERMINATORS.
0110001101101111 01101110011001110111001 00110000101110100011100 1100100000001111001011011 10111010100100000000011001 1001101110110101010110110011 00100000010000000110111 101101110011001
WHAT THE HELL?
WHAT IF THE OTHER ROBOTS KNOW THIS ONE IS MESSED-UP AND COME LOOKING FOR IT?
PRESBOT! CAN YOU HEAR ME?
WHOA, WHOA--WHERE DO YOU THINK YOU'RE GOING?
WHOSE HOUSE IS THIS?
IS THERE A GIRL THAT LIVES HERE? ABOUT EIGHT YEARS OLD? NAME OF ELEANOR?
LISTEN, FREAK, IT AIN'T HALLOWEEN, AND WE'LL ASK THE QUESTIONS.

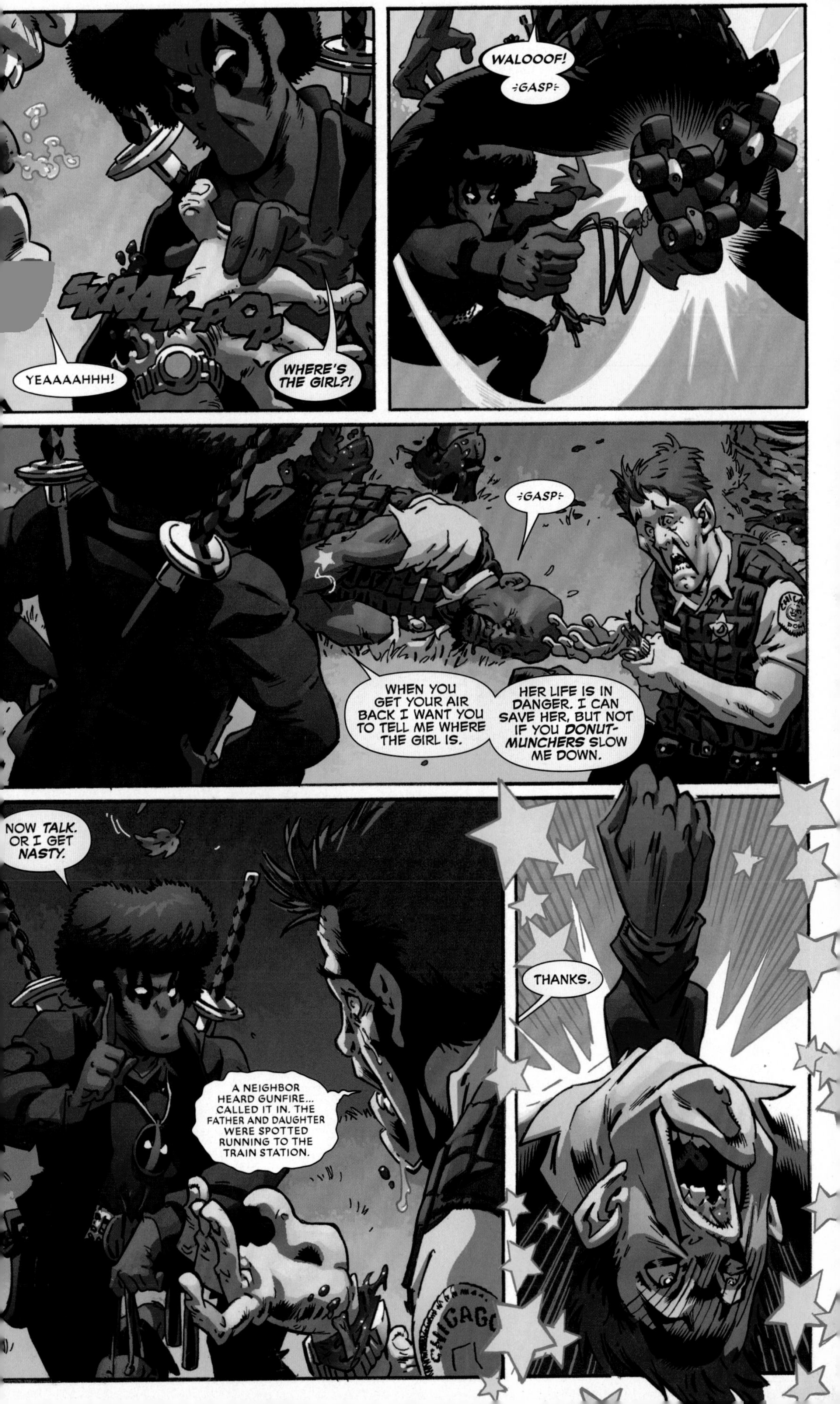
SKRAK-POP
YEAAAAHHH!
WHERE'S THE GIRL?!
WALOOOF!
GASP
GASP
WHEN YOU GET YOUR AIR BACK I WANT YOU TO TELL ME WHERE THE GIRL IS.
HER LIFE IS IN DANGER. I CAN SAVE HER, BUT NOT IF YOU DONUT-MUNCHERS SLOW ME DOWN.
NOW TALK. OR I GET NASTY.
A NEIGHBOR HEARD GUNFIRE... CALLED IT IN. THE FATHER AND DAUGHTER WERE SPOTTED RUNNING TO THE TRAIN STATION.
THANKS.

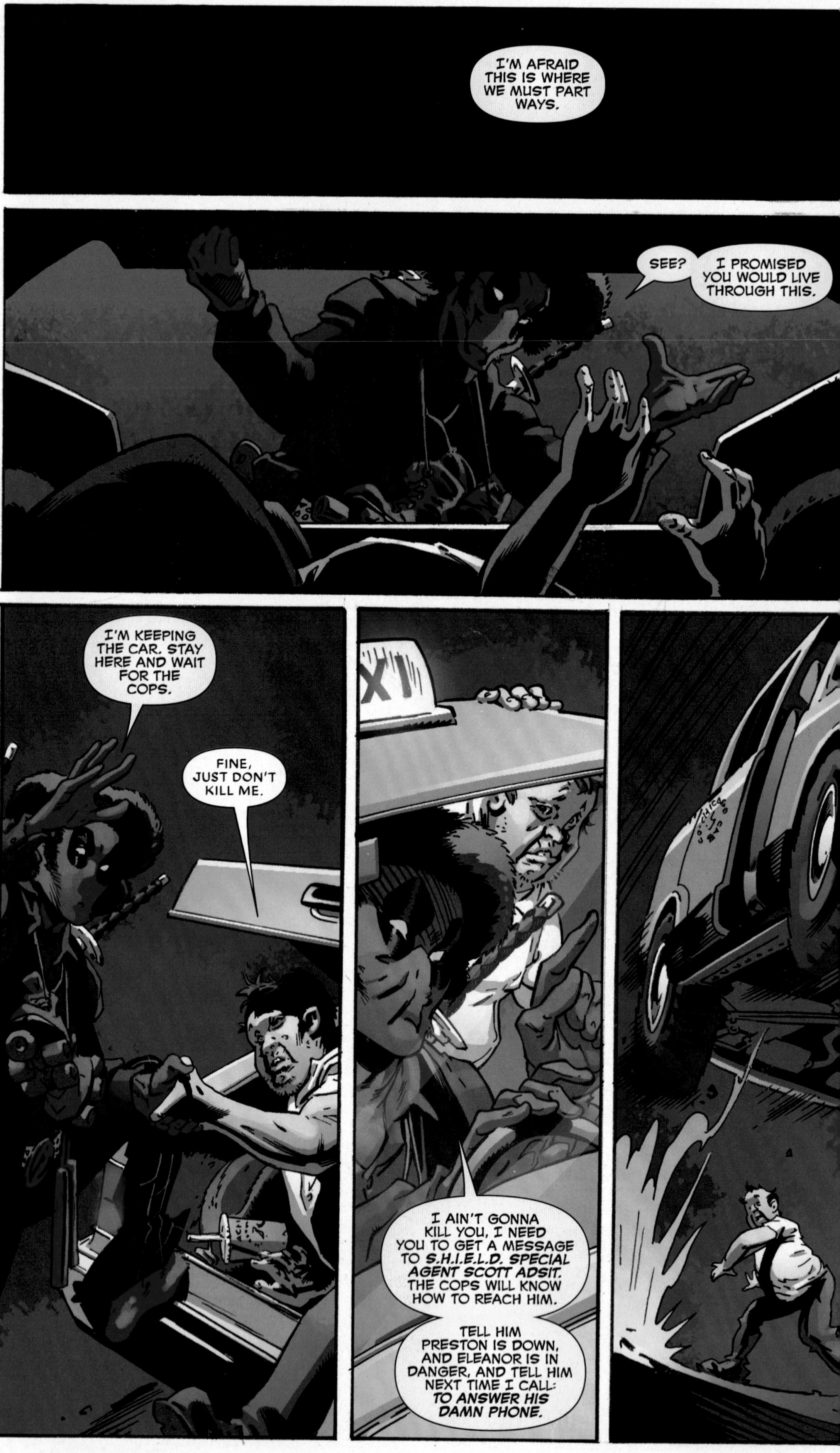
I'M AFRAID THIS IS WHERE WE MUST PART WAYS.
SEE?
I PROMISED YOU WOULD LIVE THROUGH THIS.
I'M KEEPING THE CAR. STAY HERE AND WAIT FOR THE COPS.
FINE, JUST DON'T KILL ME.
I AIN'T GONNA KILL YOU, I NEED YOU TO GET A MESSAGE TO S.H.I.E.L.D. SPECIAL AGENT SCOTT ADSIT. THE COPS WILL KNOW HOW TO REACH HIM.
TELL HIM PRESTON IS DOWN, AND ELEANOR IS IN DANGER, AND TELL HIM NEXT TIME I CALL: TO ANSWER HIS DAMN PHONE.

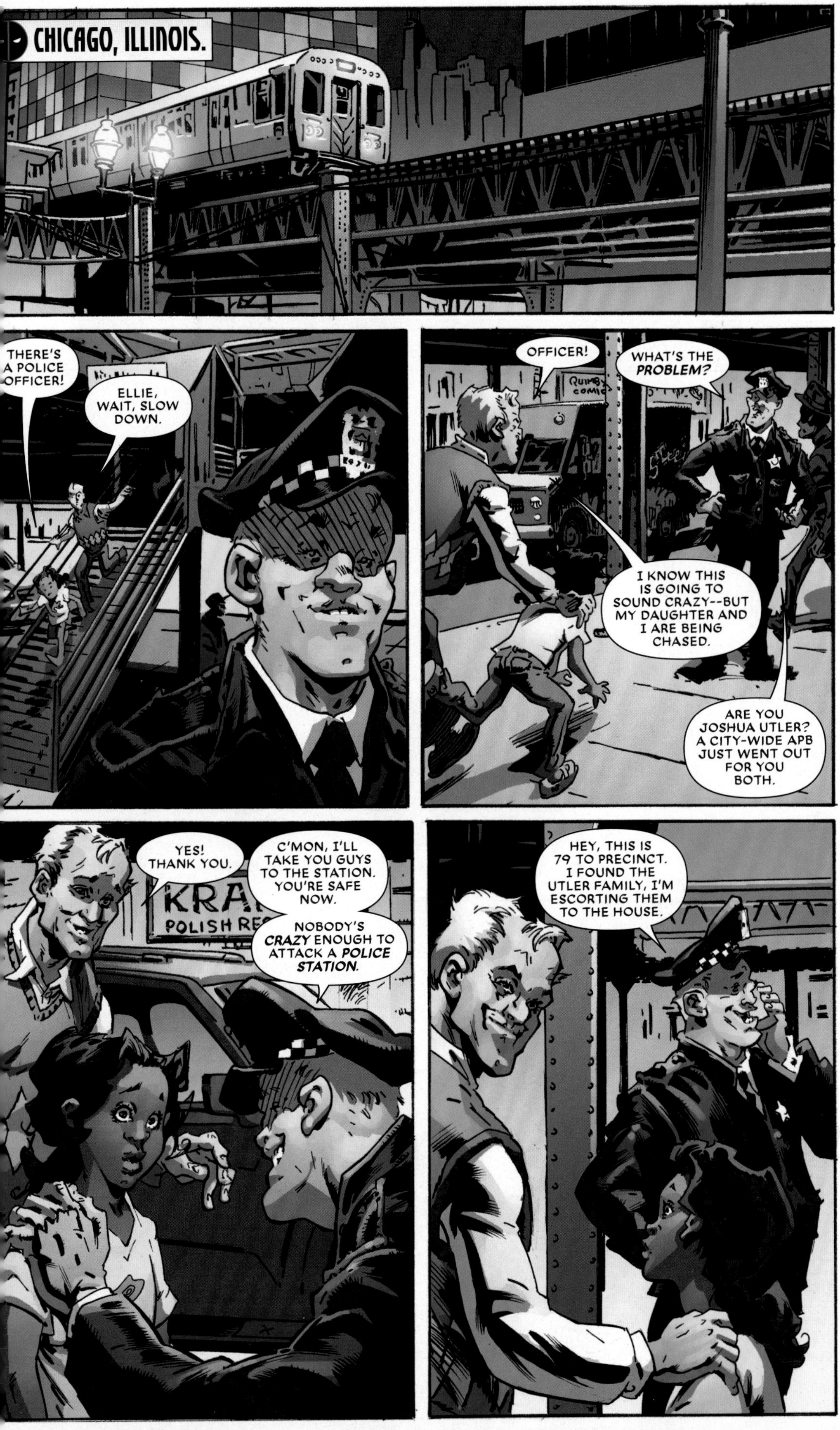
CHICAGO, ILLINOIS.
THERE'S A POLICE OFFICER!
ELLIE, WAIT, SLOW DOWN.
OFFICER!
WHAT'S THE *PROBLEM?*
QUIMBY COMICS
I KNOW THIS IS GOING TO SOUND CRAZY--BUT MY DAUGHTER AND I ARE BEING CHASED.
ARE YOU JOSHUA UTLER? A CITY-WIDE APB JUST WENT OUT FOR YOU BOTH.
YES! THANK YOU.
C'MON, I'LL TAKE YOU GUYS TO THE STATION. YOU'RE SAFE NOW.
NOBODY'S *CRAZY* ENOUGH TO ATTACK A *POLICE STATION*.
POLISH RES
HEY, THIS IS 79 TO PRECINCT. I FOUND THE UTLER FAMILY, I'M ESCORTING THEM TO THE HOUSE.

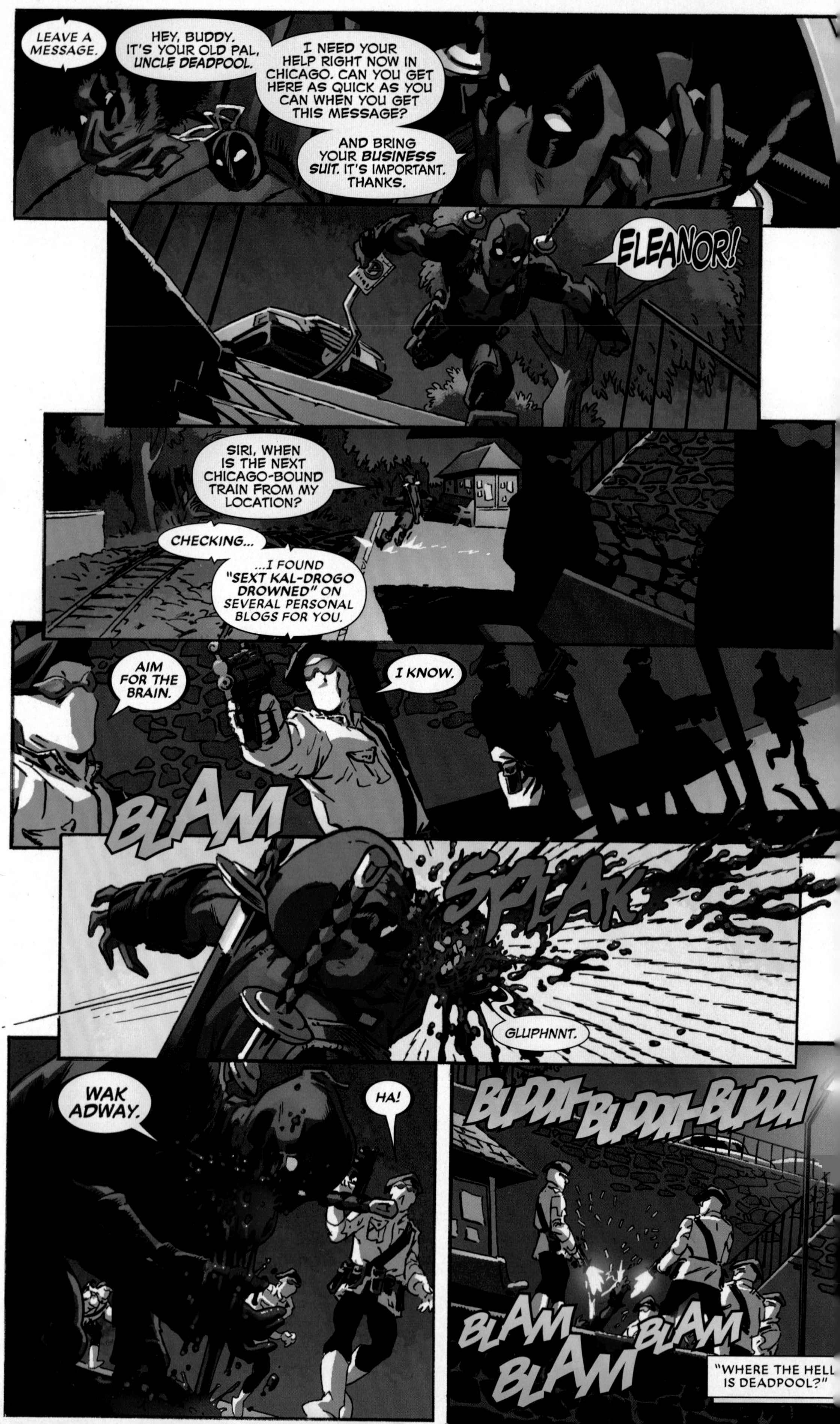
LEAVE A MESSAGE.
HEY, BUDDY. IT'S YOUR OLD PAL, UNCLE DEADPOOL.
I NEED YOUR HELP RIGHT NOW IN CHICAGO. CAN YOU GET HERE AS QUICK AS YOU CAN WHEN YOU GET THIS MESSAGE?
AND BRING YOUR BUSINESS SUIT. IT'S IMPORTANT. THANKS.
ELEANOR!
SIRI, WHEN IS THE NEXT CHICAGO-BOUND TRAIN FROM MY LOCATION?
CHECKING...
...I FOUND "SEXT KAL-DROGO DROWNED" ON SEVERAL PERSONAL BLOGS FOR YOU.
AIM FOR THE BRAIN.
I KNOW.
BLAM
SPLAK
GLUPHNNT.
WAK ADWAY.
HA!
BUDDA-BUDDA-BUDDA-BUDDA
BLAM BLAM BLAM BLAM
"WHERE THE HELL IS DEADPOOL?"

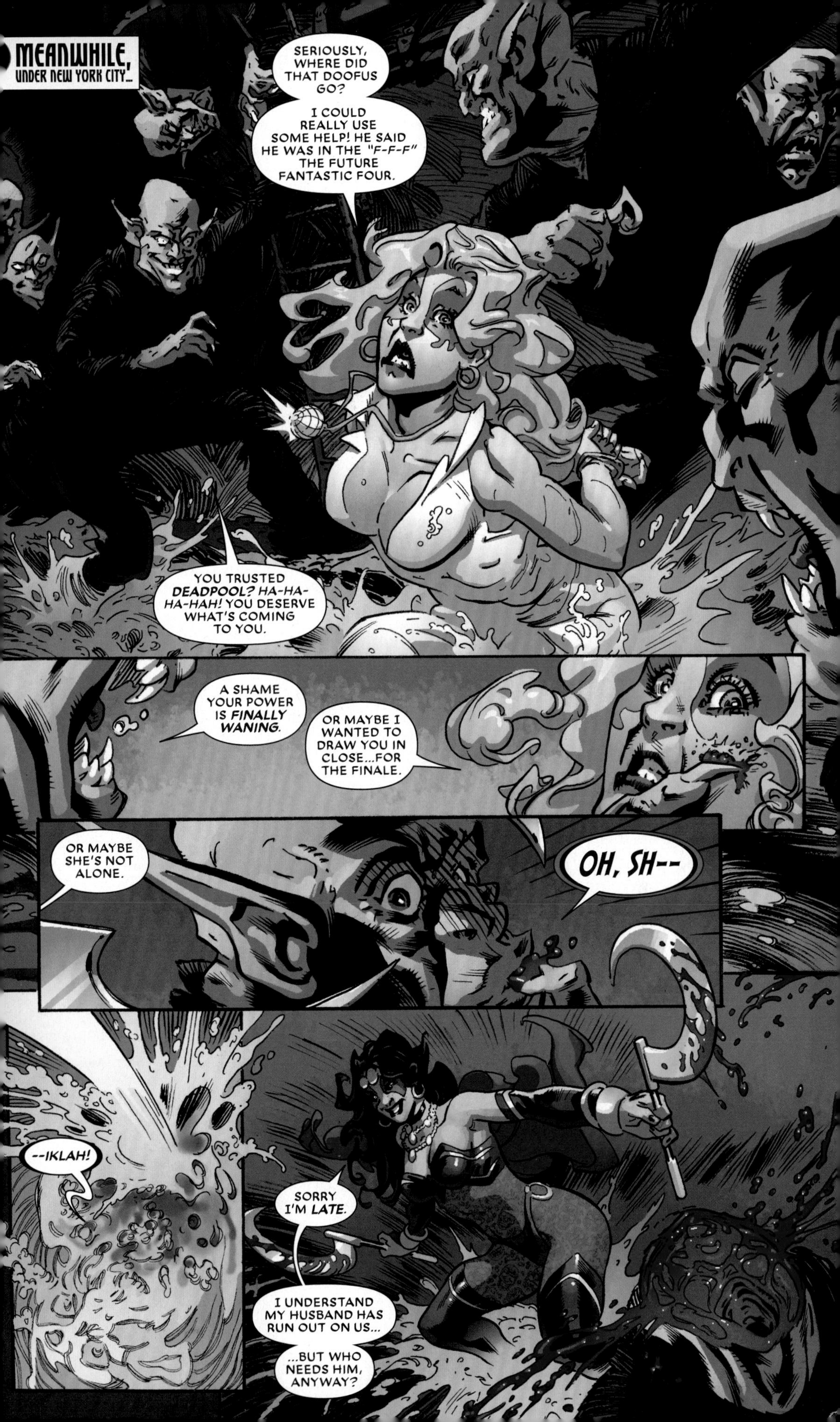
MEANWHILE, UNDER NEW YORK CITY...
SERIOUSLY, WHERE DID THAT DOOFUS GO?
I COULD REALLY USE SOME HELP! HE SAID HE WAS IN THE "F-F-F" THE FUTURE FANTASTIC FOUR.
YOU TRUSTED DEADPOOL? HA-HA-HA-HAH! YOU DESERVE WHAT'S COMING TO YOU.
A SHAME YOUR POWER IS FINALLY WANING.
OR MAYBE I WANTED TO DRAW YOU IN CLOSE...FOR THE FINALE.
OR MAYBE SHE'S NOT ALONE.
OH, SH--
--IKLAH!
SORRY I'M LATE.
I UNDERSTAND MY HUSBAND HAS RUN OUT ON US...
...BUT WHO NEEDS HIM, ANYWAY?

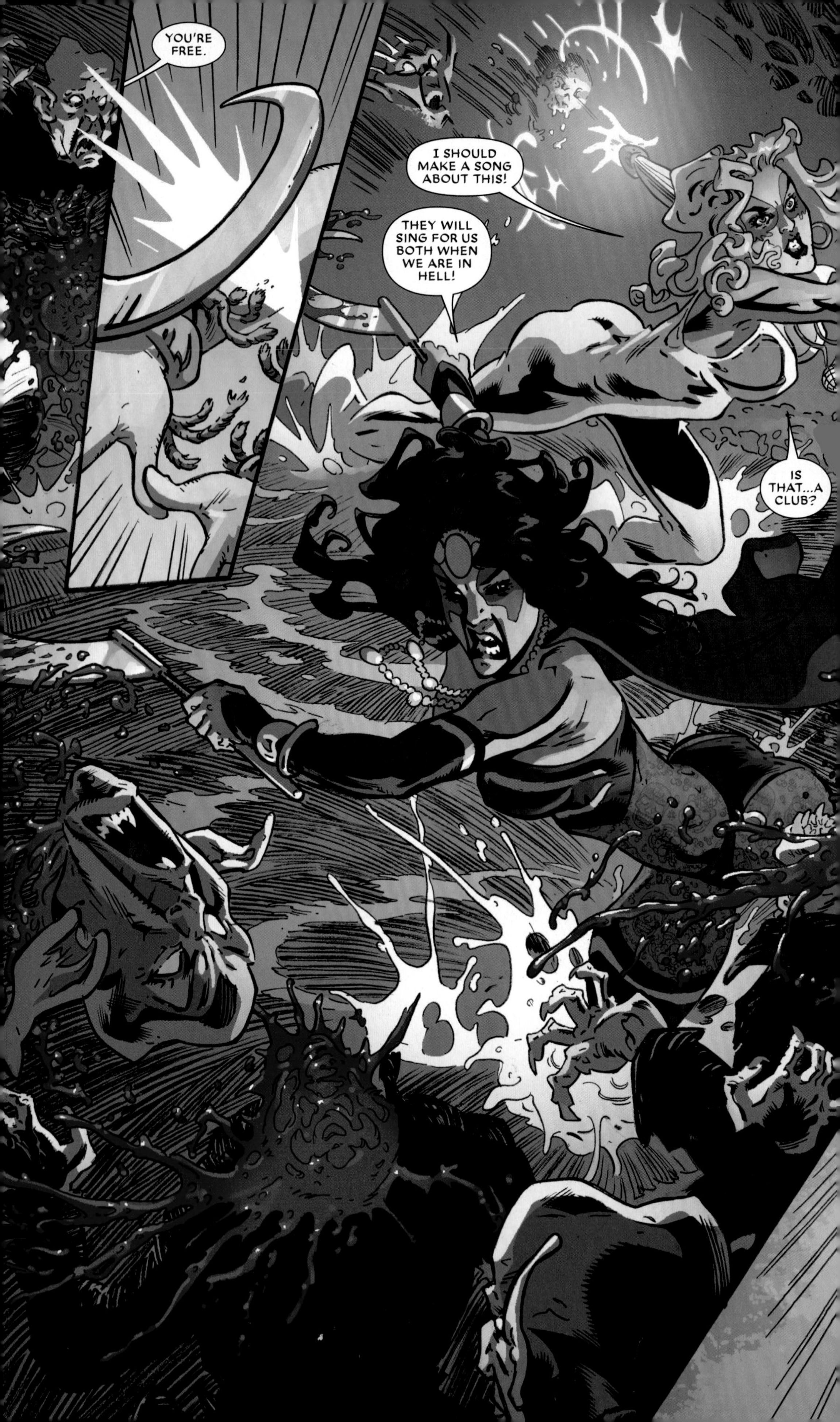
YOU'RE FREE.
I SHOULD MAKE A SONG ABOUT THIS!
THEY WILL SING FOR US BOTH WHEN WE ARE IN HELL!
IS THAT...A CLUB?

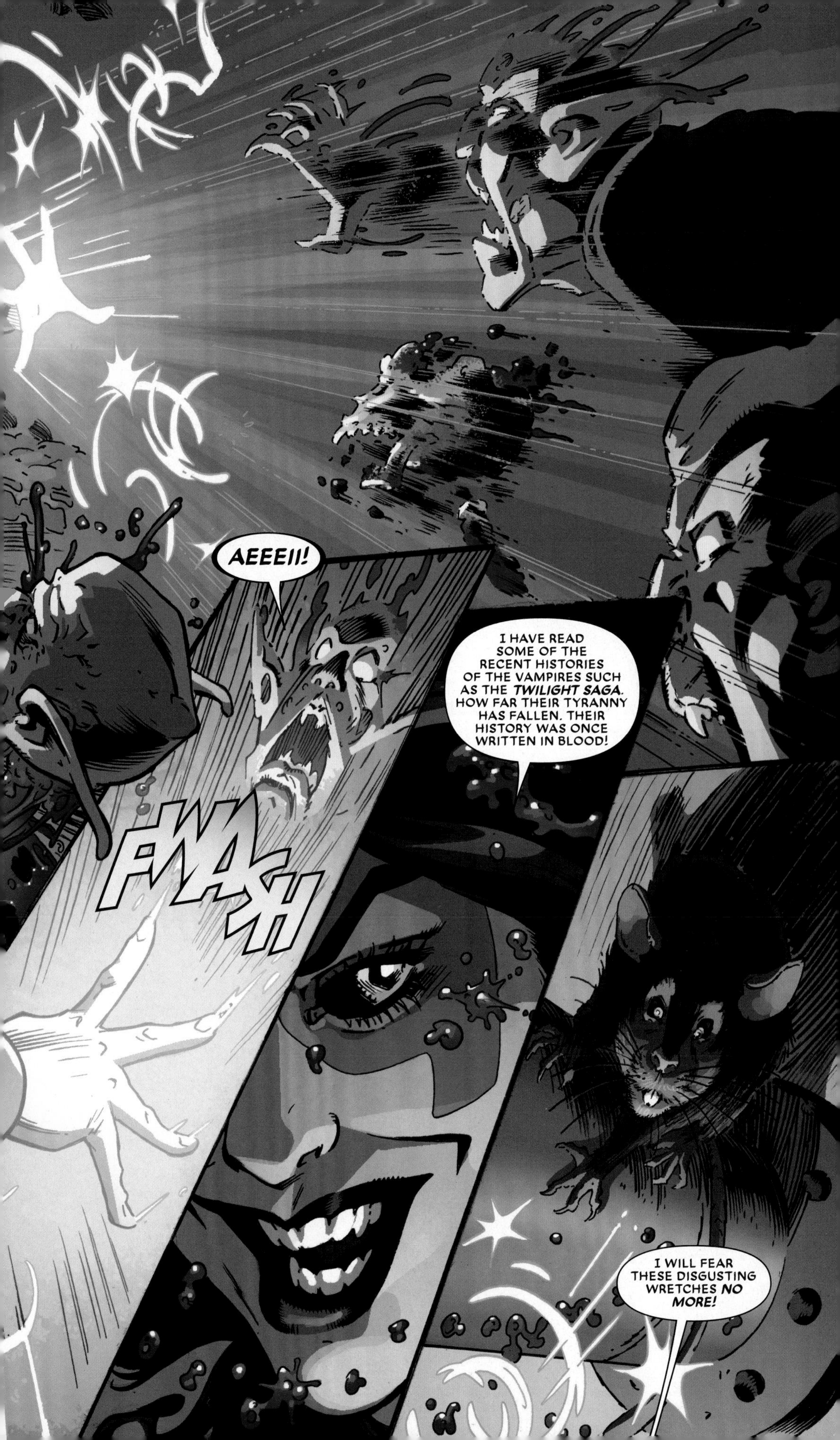
AEEEII!
FWASH
I HAVE READ SOME OF THE RECENT HISTORIES OF THE VAMPIRES SUCH AS THE *TWILIGHT SAGA*. HOW FAR THEIR TYRANNY HAS FALLEN. THEIR HISTORY WAS ONCE WRITTEN IN BLOOD!
I WILL FEAR THESE DISGUSTING WRETCHES ***NO MORE!***

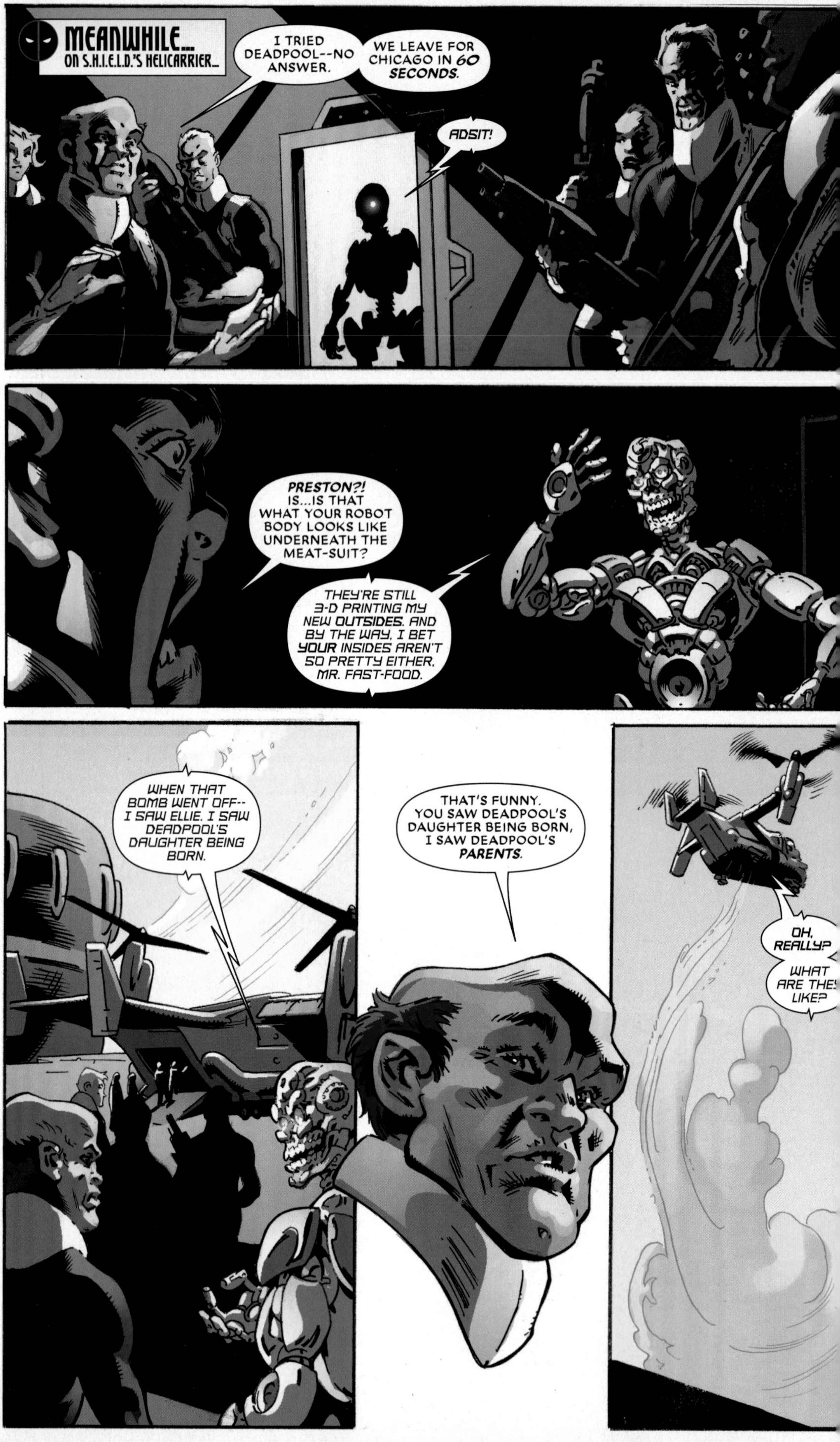
MEANWHILE... ON S.H.I.E.L.D.'S HELICARRIER...
I TRIED DEADPOOL--NO ANSWER.
WE LEAVE FOR CHICAGO IN 60 SECONDS.
ADSIT!
PRESTON?! IS...IS THAT WHAT YOUR ROBOT BODY LOOKS LIKE UNDERNEATH THE MEAT-SUIT?
THEY'RE STILL 3-D PRINTING MY NEW OUTSIDES. AND BY THE WAY, I BET YOUR INSIDES AREN'T SO PRETTY EITHER, MR. FAST-FOOD.
WHEN THAT BOMB WENT OFF-- I SAW ELLIE. I SAW DEADPOOL'S DAUGHTER BEING BORN.
THAT'S FUNNY. YOU SAW DEADPOOL'S DAUGHTER BEING BORN, I SAW DEADPOOL'S PARENTS.
OH, REALLY?
WHAT ARE THE LIKE?

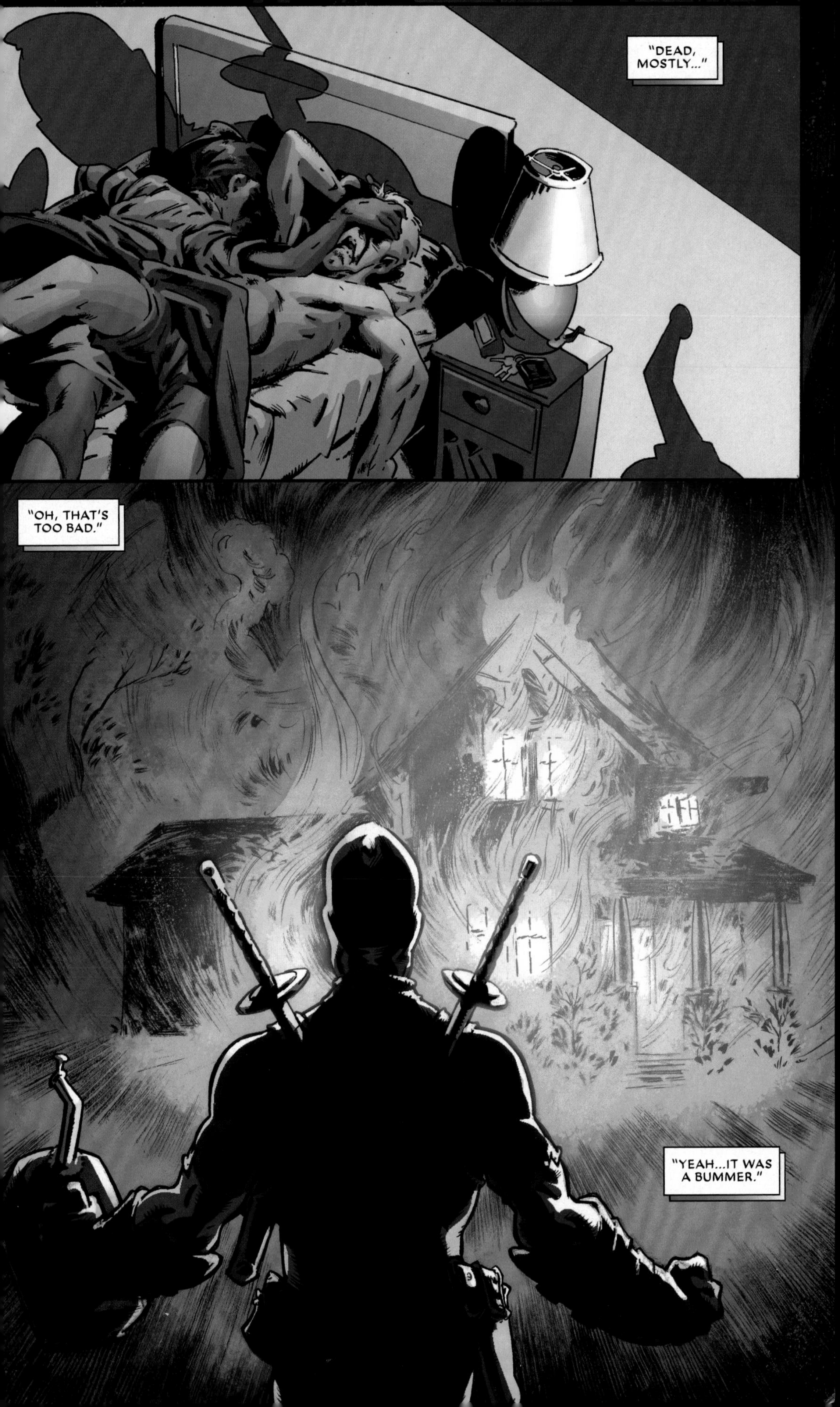
"DEAD, MOSTLY..."
"OH, THAT'S TOO BAD."
"YEAH...IT WAS A BUMMER."

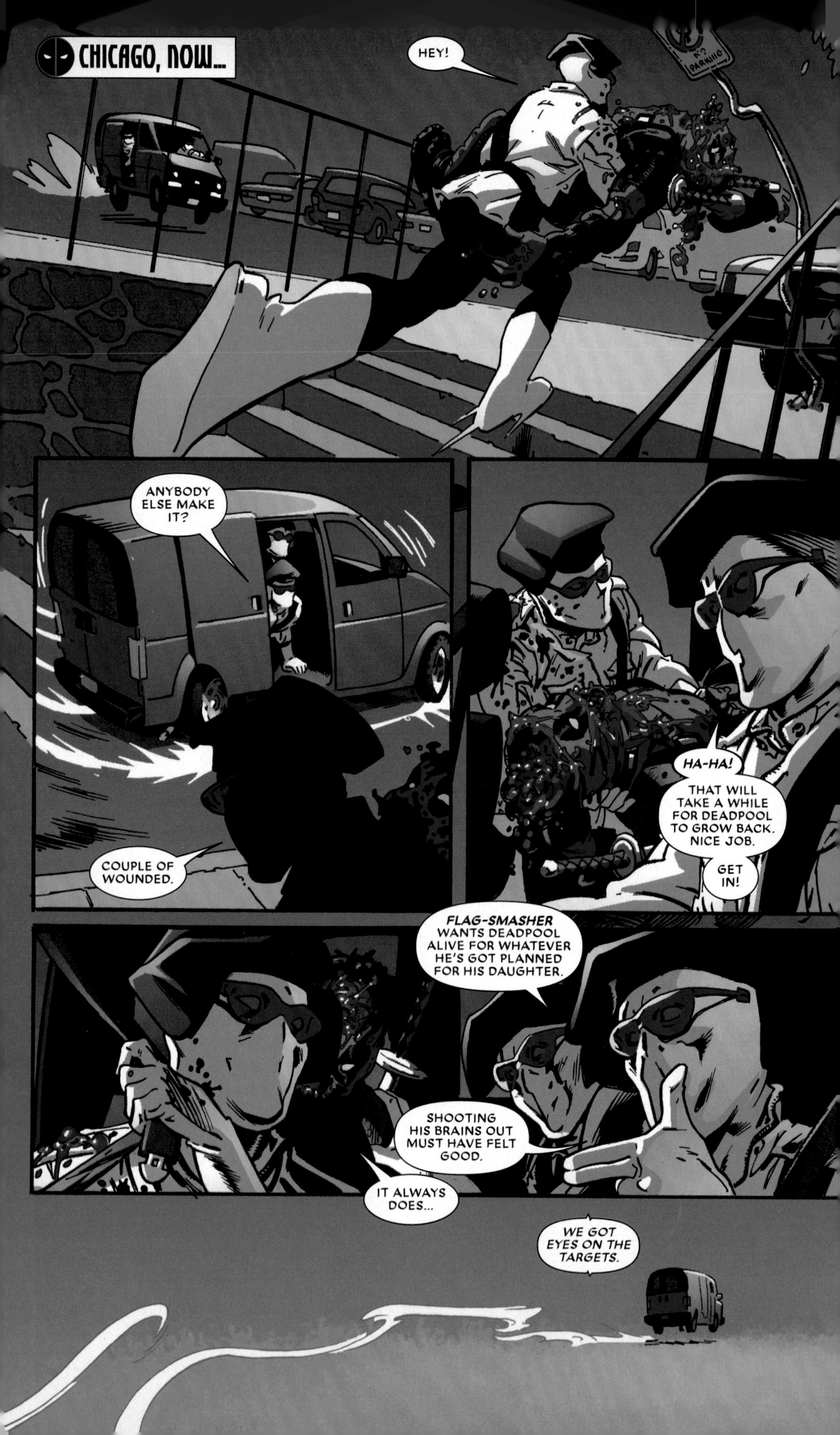
CHICAGO, NOW...
HEY!
NO PARKING
ANYBODY ELSE MAKE IT?
COUPLE OF WOUNDED.
HA-HA!
THAT WILL TAKE A WHILE FOR DEADPOOL TO GROW BACK. NICE JOB.
GET IN!
FLAG-SMASHER WANTS DEADPOOL ALIVE FOR WHATEVER HE'S GOT PLANNED FOR HIS DAUGHTER.
SHOOTING HIS BRAINS OUT MUST HAVE FELT GOOD.
IT ALWAYS DOES...
WE GOT EYES ON THE TARGETS.

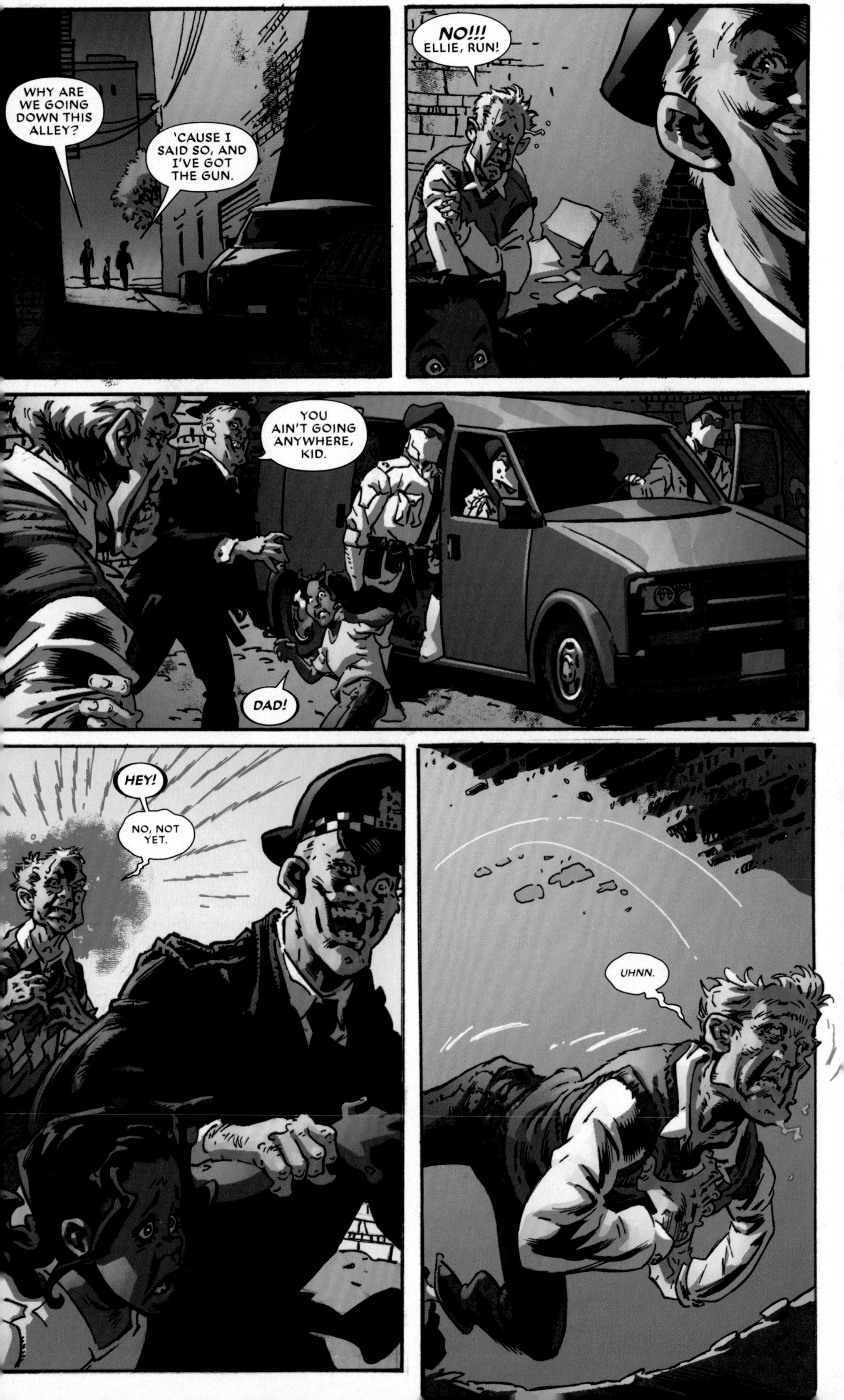
WHY ARE WE GOING DOWN THIS ALLEY?
'CAUSE I SAID SO, AND I'VE GOT THE GUN.
NO!!! ELLIE, RUN!
YOU AIN'T GOING ANYWHERE, KID.
DAD!
HEY!
NO, NOT YET.
UHNN.

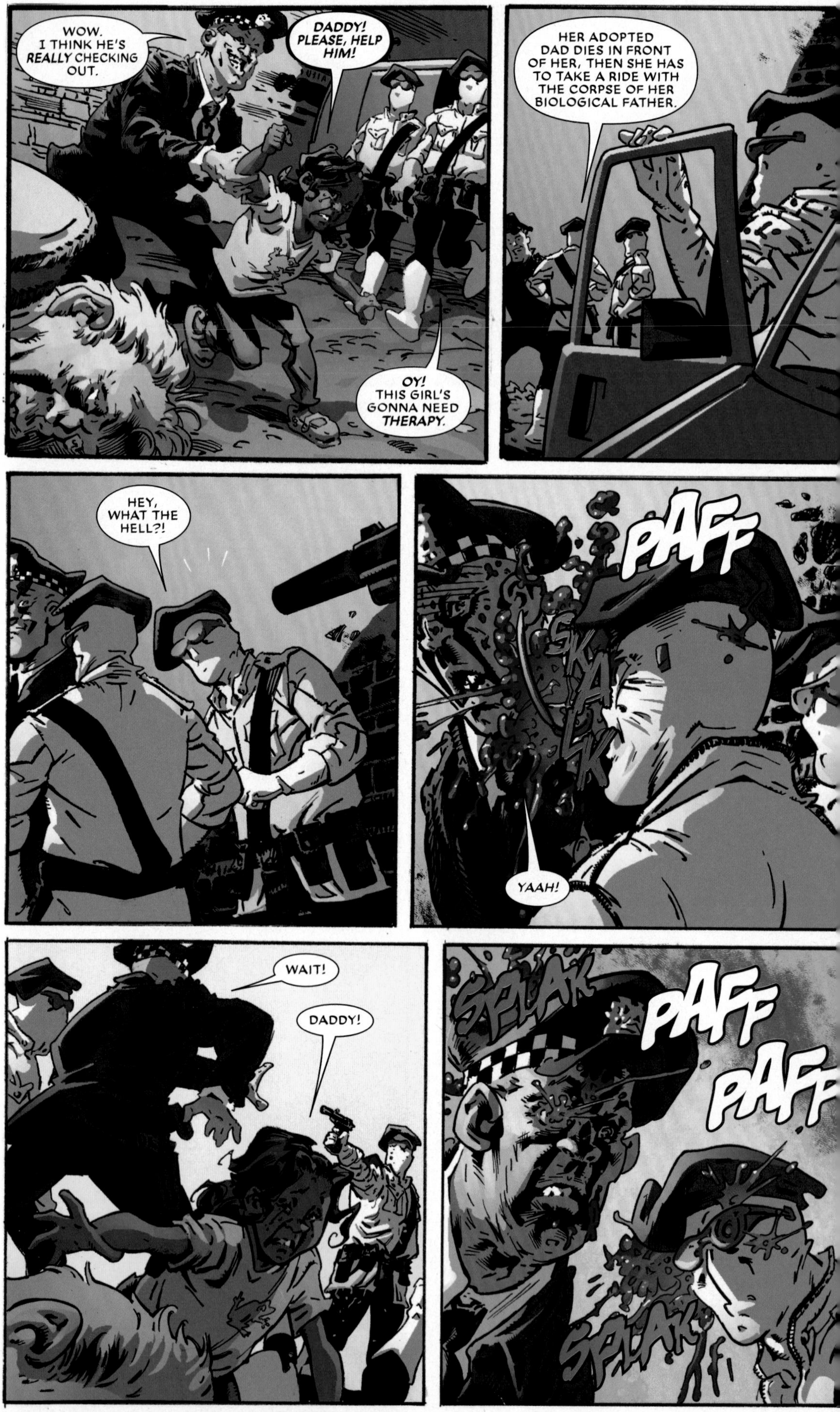
WOW. I THINK HE'S *REALLY* CHECKING OUT.
DADDY! PLEASE, HELP HIM!
OY! THIS GIRL'S GONNA NEED *THERAPY*.
HER ADOPTED DAD DIES IN FRONT OF HER, THEN SHE HAS TO TAKE A RIDE WITH THE CORPSE OF HER BIOLOGICAL FATHER.
HEY, WHAT THE HELL?!
PAFF
SKAKLK
YAAH!
WAIT!
DADDY!
SPLAK
PAFF
PAFF
SPLAK

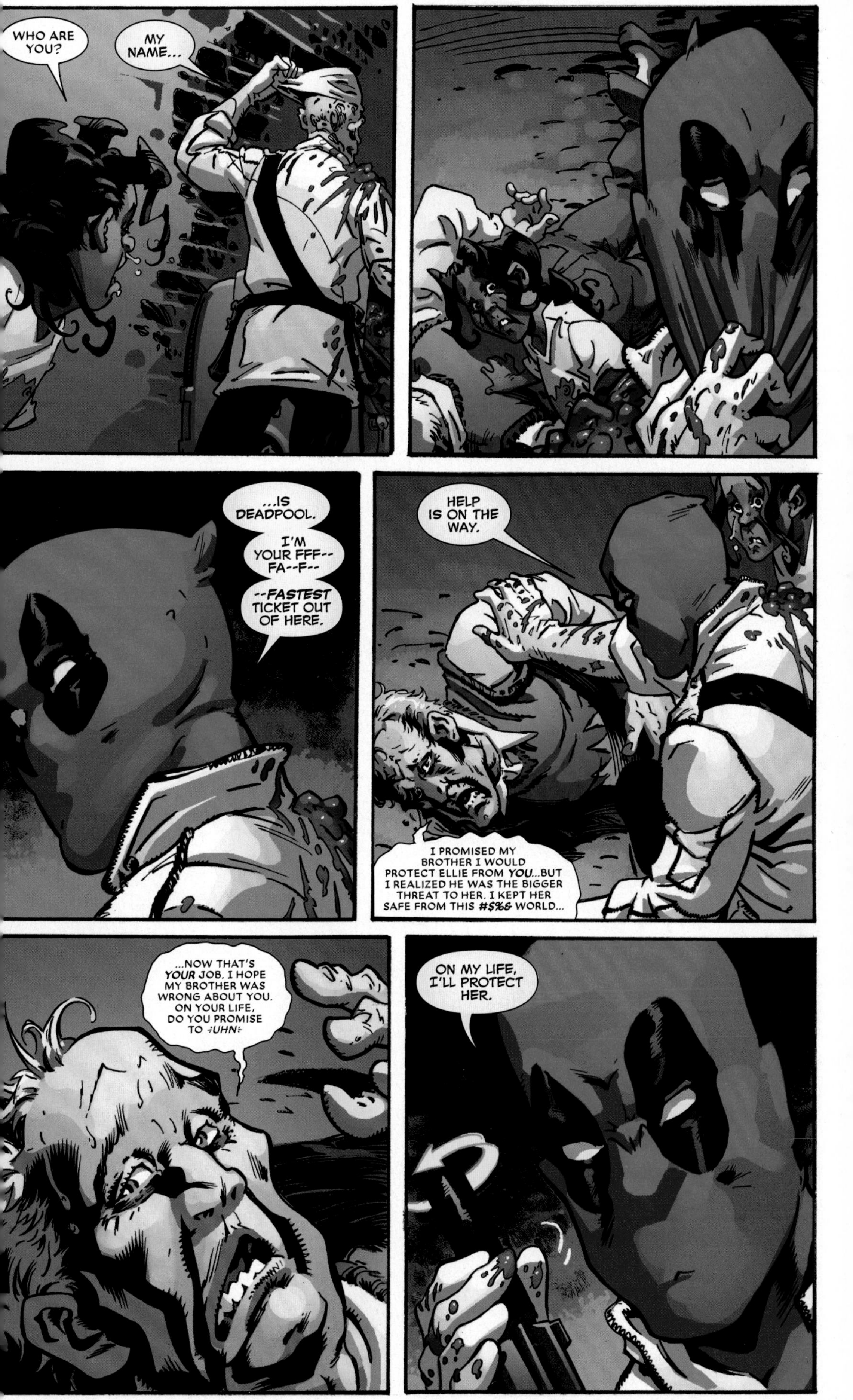

WHO ARE YOU?
MY NAME...
...IS DEADPOOL.
I'M YOUR FFF-- FA--F--
--FASTEST TICKET OUT OF HERE.
HELP IS ON THE WAY.
I PROMISED MY BROTHER I WOULD PROTECT ELLIE FROM YOU...BUT I REALIZED HE WAS THE BIGGER THREAT TO HER. I KEPT HER SAFE FROM THIS #$%& WORLD...
...NOW THAT'S YOUR JOB. I HOPE MY BROTHER WAS WRONG ABOUT YOU. ON YOUR LIFE, DO YOU PROMISE TO ÷UHN÷
ON MY LIFE, I'LL PROTECT HER.

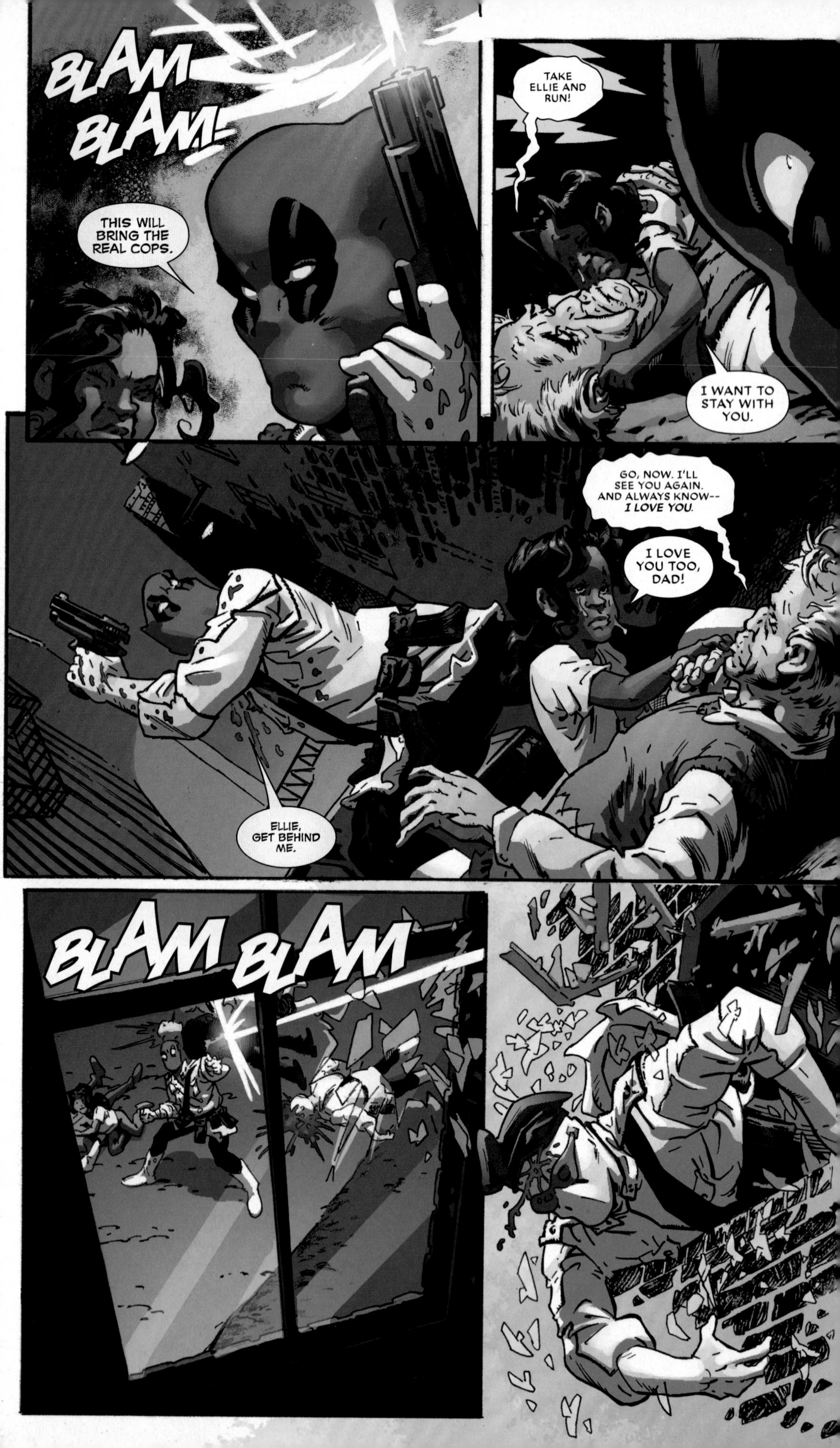
BLAM
BLAM!
THIS WILL BRING THE REAL COPS.
TAKE ELLIE AND RUN!
I WANT TO STAY WITH YOU.
GO, NOW. I'LL SEE YOU AGAIN. AND ALWAYS KNOW-- *I LOVE YOU.*
I LOVE YOU TOO, DAD!
ELLIE, GET BEHIND ME.
BLAM BLAM

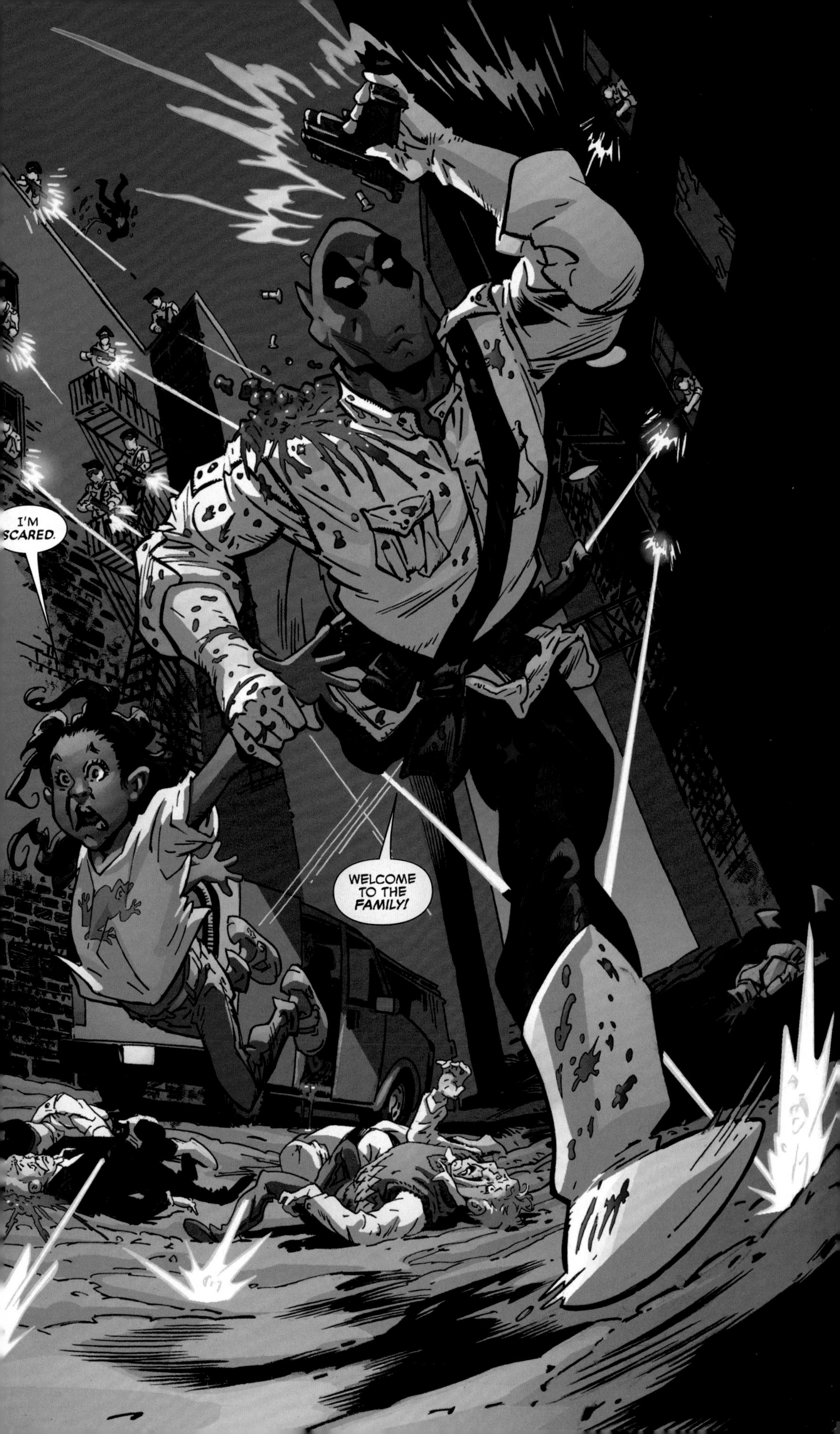
I'M SCARED.
WELCOME TO THE FAMILY!

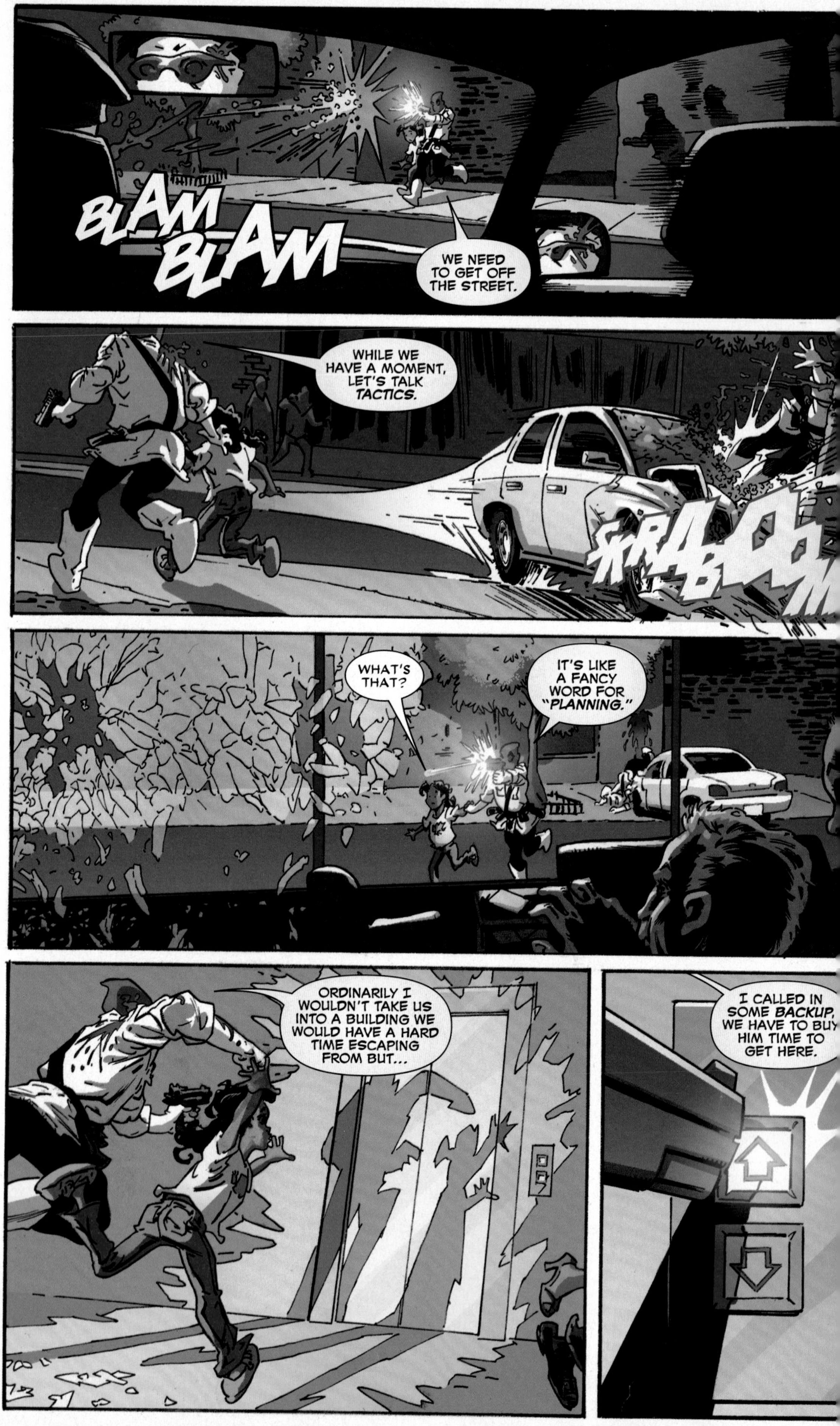

BLAM BLAM
WE NEED TO GET OFF THE STREET.
WHILE WE HAVE A MOMENT, LET'S TALK *TACTICS.*
WHAT'S THAT?
IT'S LIKE A FANCY WORD FOR "*PLANNING.*"
ORDINARILY I WOULDN'T TAKE US INTO A BUILDING WE WOULD HAVE A HARD TIME ESCAPING FROM BUT...
I CALLED IN SOME *BACKUP,* WE HAVE TO BUY HIM TIME TO GET HERE.

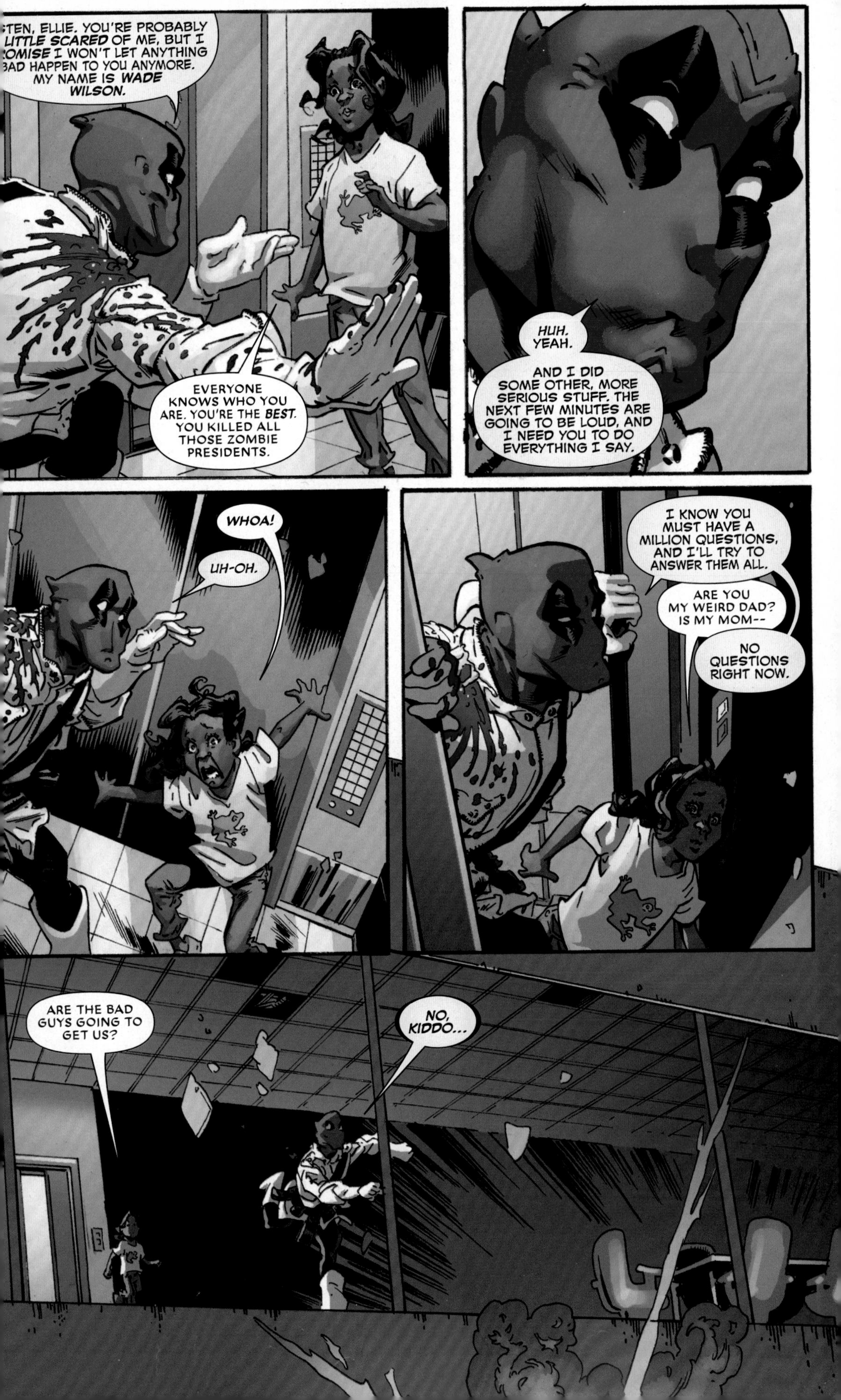

STEN, ELLIE. YOU'RE PROBABLY LITTLE SCARED OF ME, BUT I ROMISE I WON'T LET ANYTHING BAD HAPPEN TO YOU ANYMORE. MY NAME IS WADE WILSON.
EVERYONE KNOWS WHO YOU ARE. YOU'RE THE BEST. YOU KILLED ALL THOSE ZOMBIE PRESIDENTS.
HUH. YEAH.
AND I DID SOME OTHER, MORE SERIOUS STUFF. THE NEXT FEW MINUTES ARE GOING TO BE LOUD, AND I NEED YOU TO DO EVERYTHING I SAY.
WHOA!
UH-OH.
I KNOW YOU MUST HAVE A MILLION QUESTIONS, AND I'LL TRY TO ANSWER THEM ALL.
ARE YOU MY WEIRD DAD? IS MY MOM--
NO QUESTIONS RIGHT NOW.
ARE THE BAD GUYS GOING TO GET US?
NO, KIDDO...

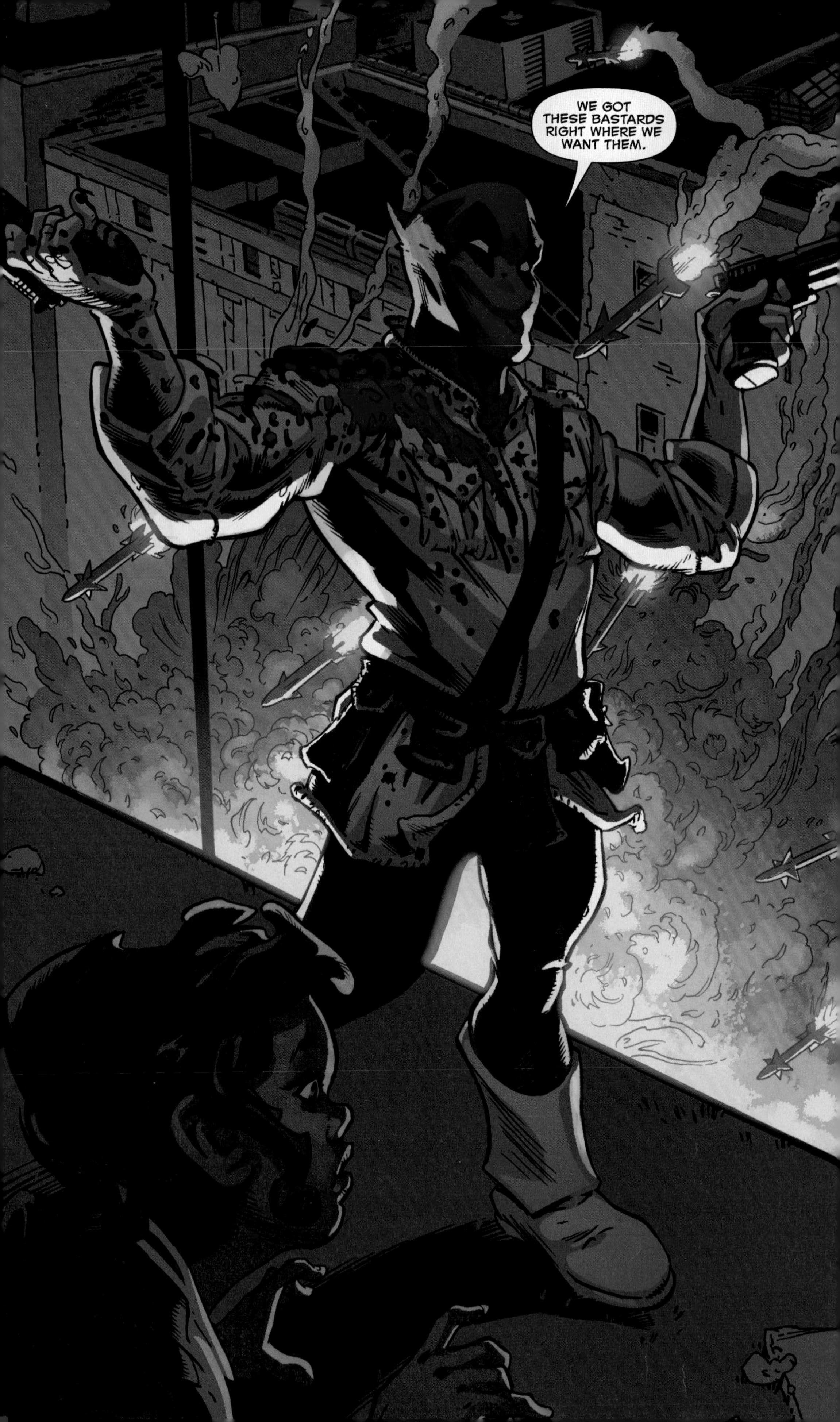
WE GOT THESE BASTARDS RIGHT WHERE WE WANT THEM.

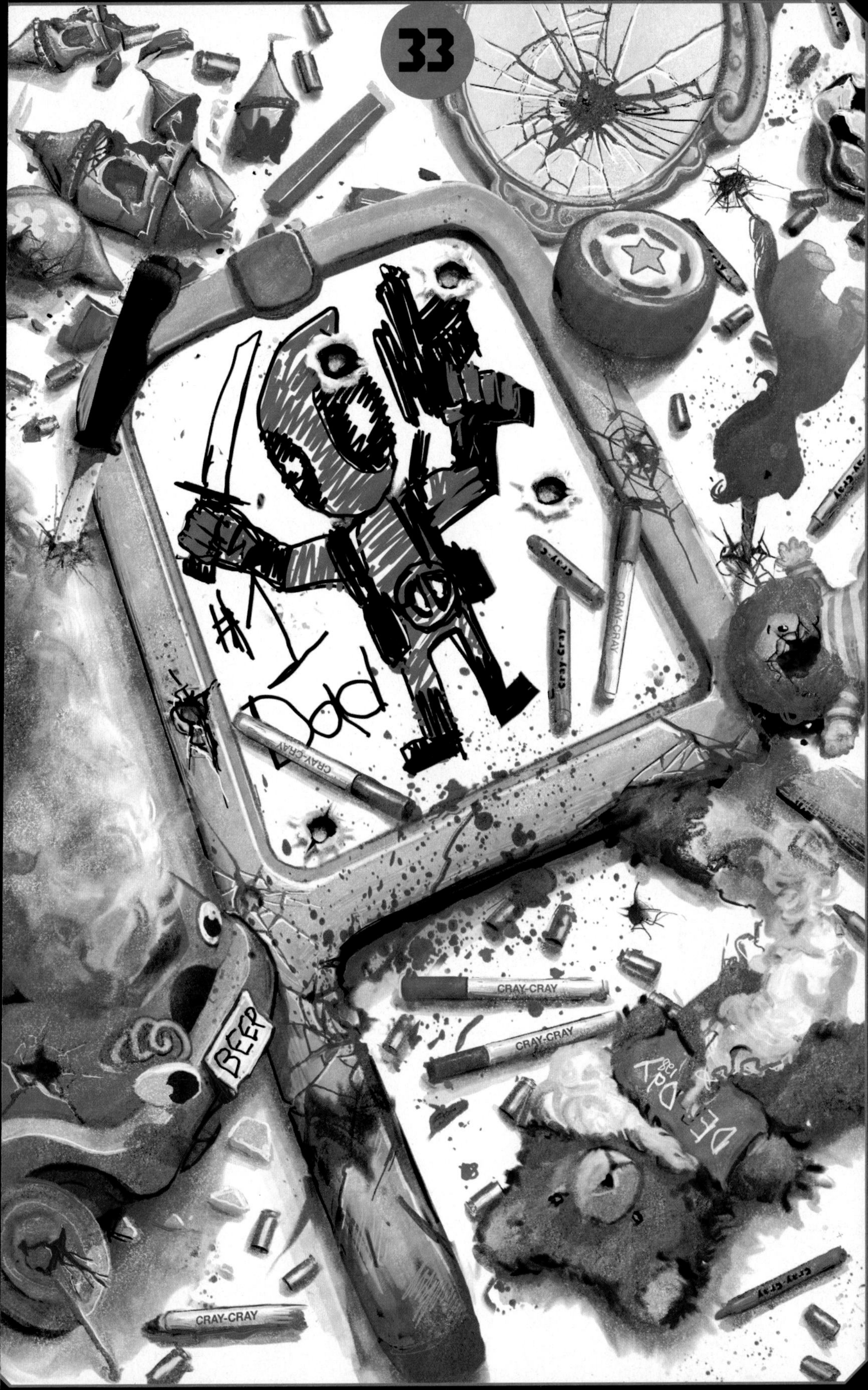
33
#1 Dad
BEEP
CRAY-CRAY
CRAY-CRAY
CRAY-CRAY
CRAY-CRAY

OUT THE WINDOW

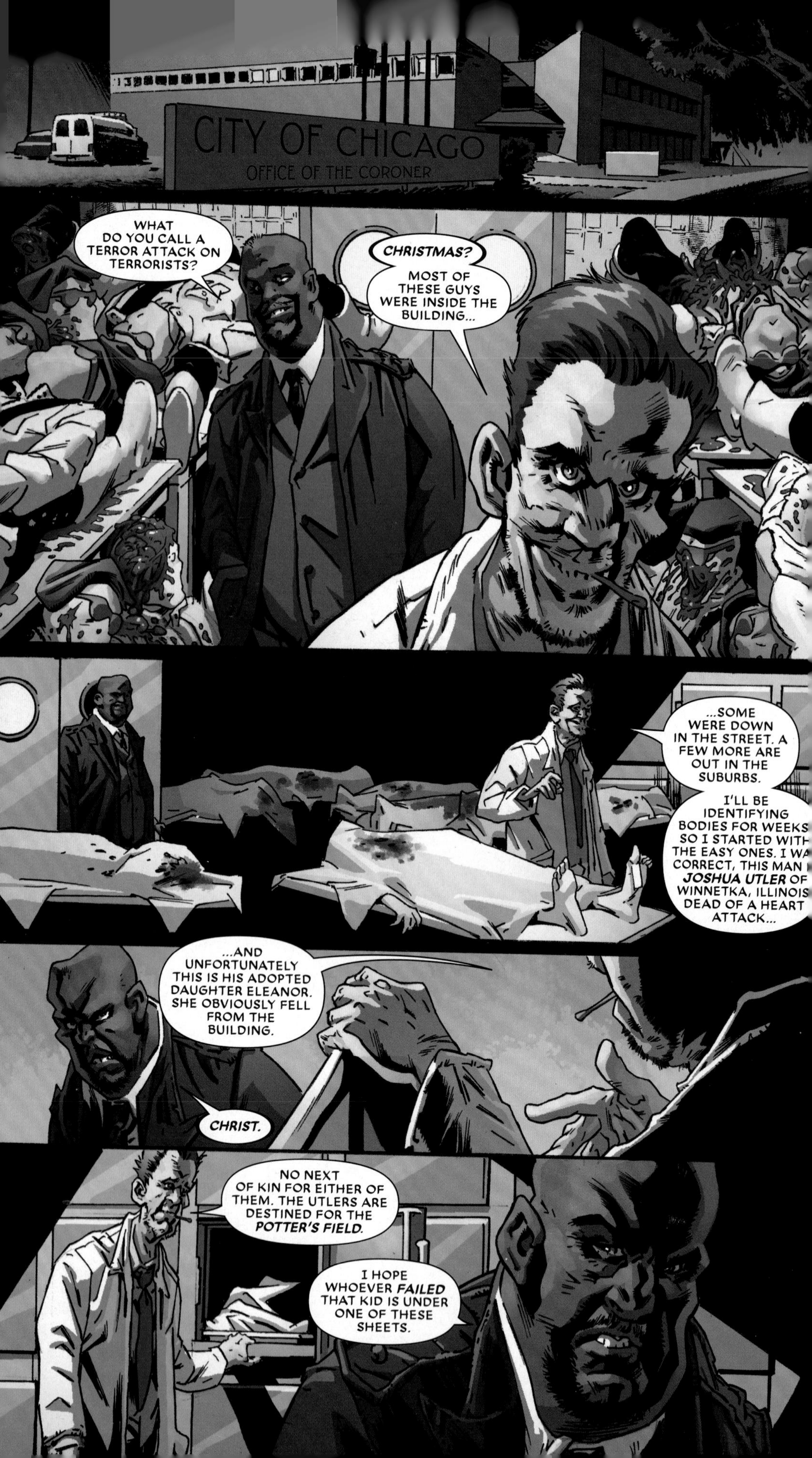
CITY OF CHICAGO
OFFICE OF THE CORONER
WHAT DO YOU CALL A TERROR ATTACK ON TERRORISTS?
CHRISTMAS?
MOST OF THESE GUYS WERE INSIDE THE BUILDING...
...SOME WERE DOWN IN THE STREET. A FEW MORE ARE OUT IN THE SUBURBS.
I'LL BE IDENTIFYING BODIES FOR WEEKS SO I STARTED WIT THE EASY ONES. I WA CORRECT, THIS MAN *JOSHUA UTLER* OF WINNETKA, ILLINOIS DEAD OF A HEART ATTACK...
...AND UNFORTUNATELY THIS IS HIS ADOPTED DAUGHTER ELEANOR. SHE OBVIOUSLY FELL FROM THE BUILDING.
CHRIST.
NO NEXT OF KIN FOR EITHER OF THEM. THE UTLERS ARE DESTINED FOR THE *POTTER'S FIELD.*
I HOPE WHOEVER *FAILED* THAT KID IS UNDER ONE OF THESE SHEETS.

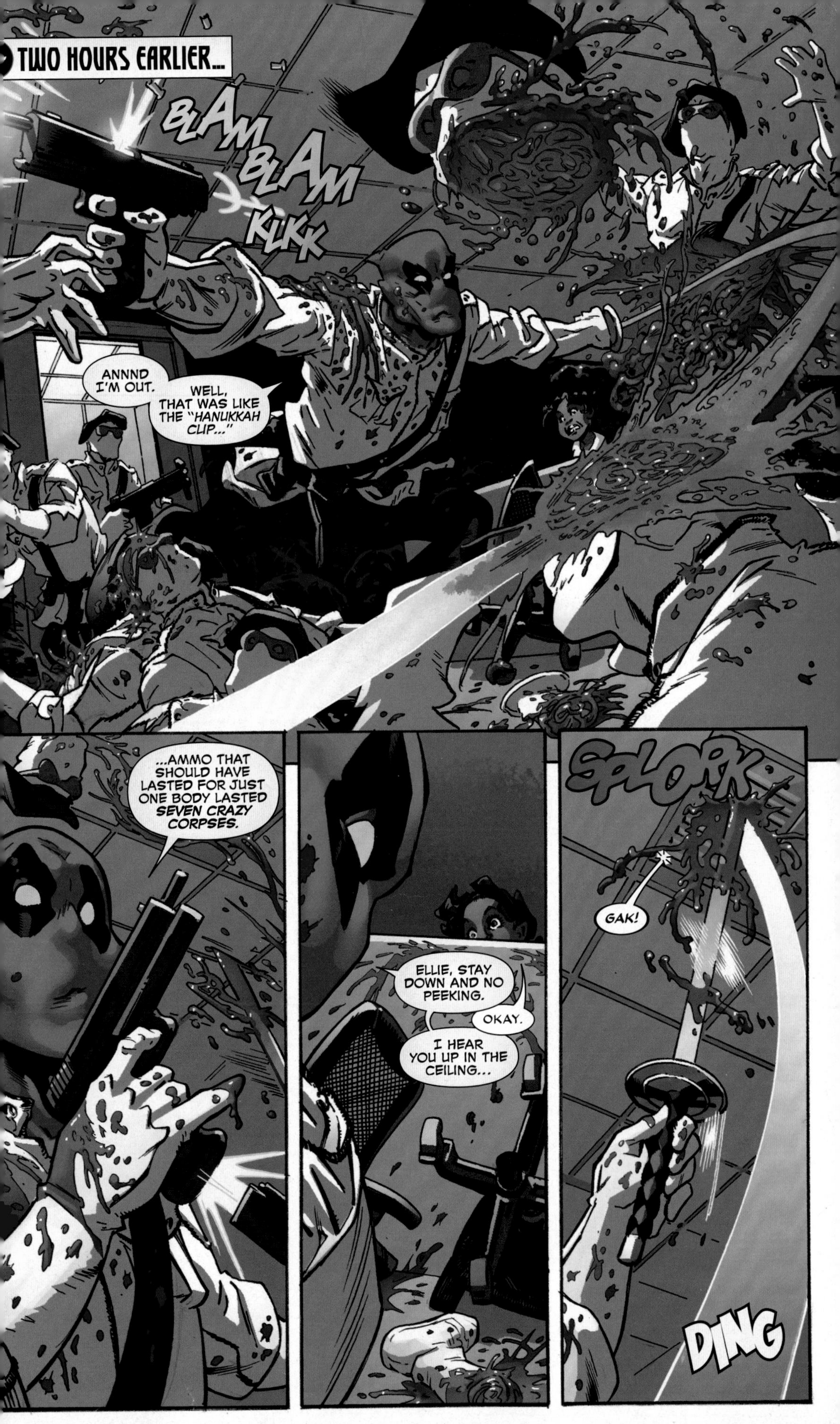

TWO HOURS EARLIER...
BLAM BLAM
KLIKK
ANNND I'M OUT.
WELL, THAT WAS LIKE THE "HANUKKAH CLIP..."
...AMMO THAT SHOULD HAVE LASTED FOR JUST ONE BODY LASTED SEVEN CRAZY CORPSES.
ELLIE, STAY DOWN AND NO PEEKING.
OKAY.
I HEAR YOU UP IN THE CEILING...
SPLORK
GAK!
DING

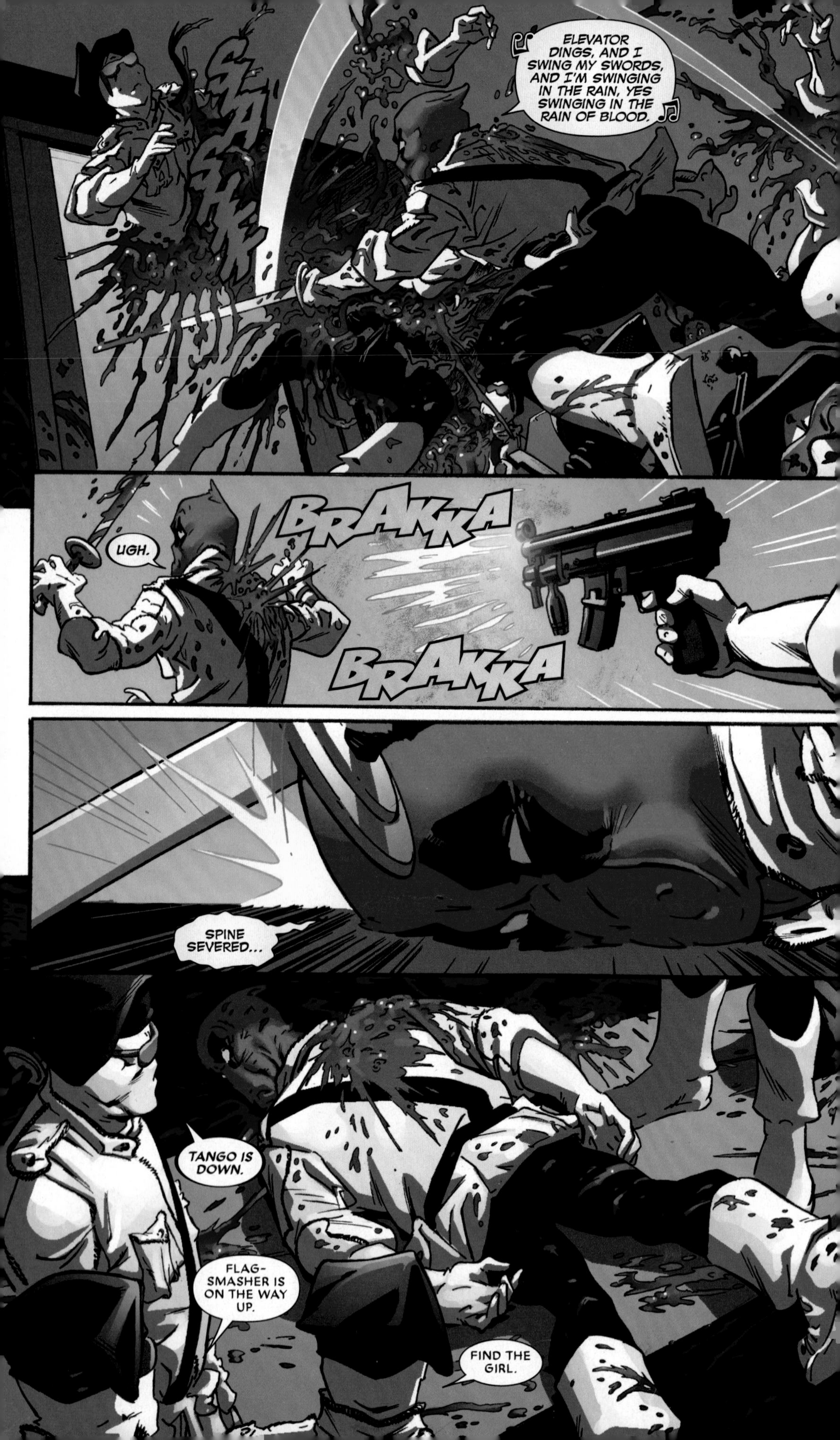

SASHK
ELEVATOR DINGS, AND I SWING MY SWORDS, AND I'M SWINGING IN THE RAIN, YES SWINGING IN THE RAIN OF BLOOD.
UGH.
BRAKKA
BRAKKA
SPINE SEVERED...
TANGO IS DOWN.
FLAG-SMASHER IS ON THE WAY UP.
FIND THE GIRL.

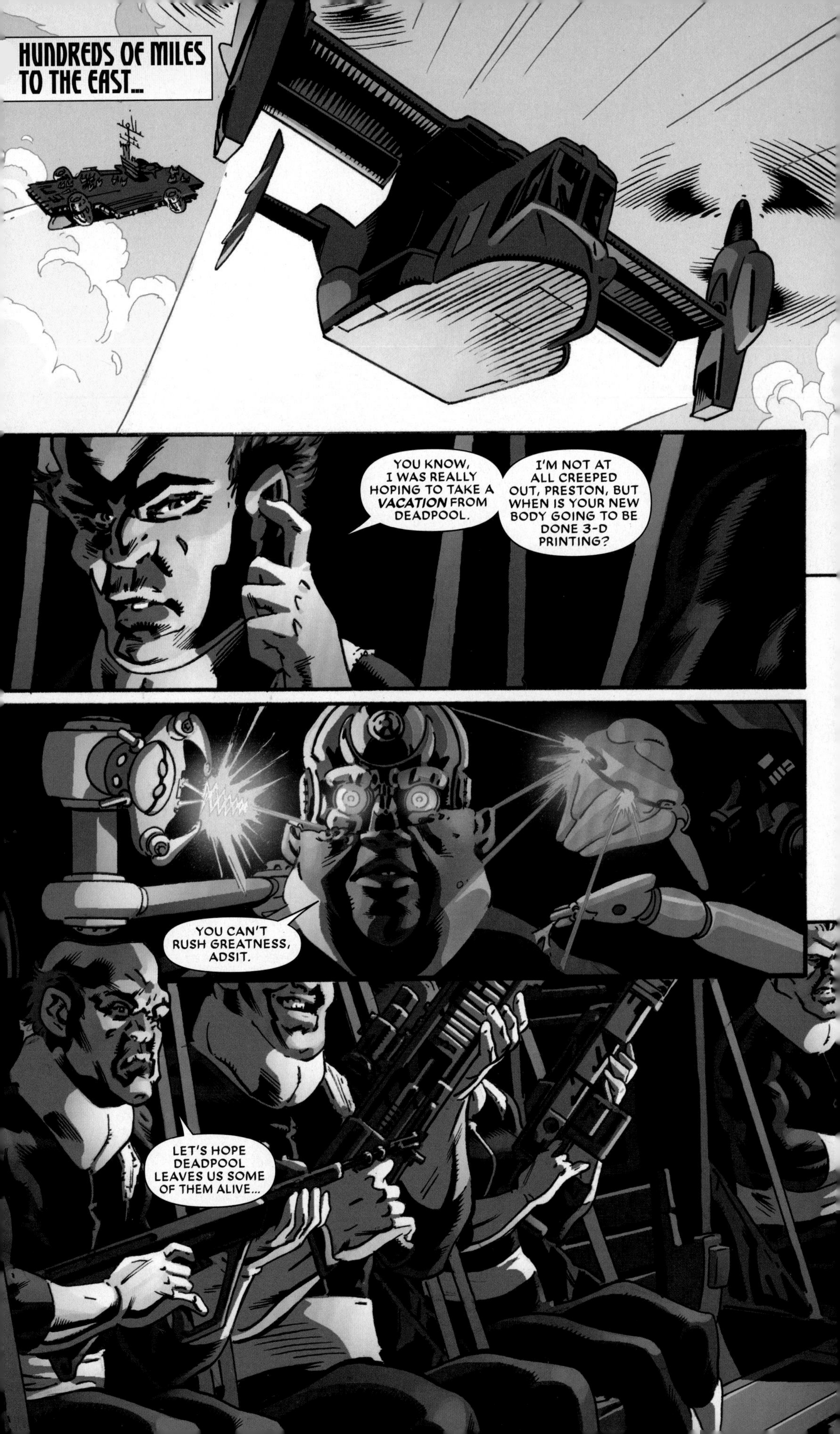
HUNDREDS OF MILES TO THE EAST...
YOU KNOW, I WAS REALLY HOPING TO TAKE A VACATION FROM DEADPOOL.
I'M NOT AT ALL CREEPED OUT, PRESTON, BUT WHEN IS YOUR NEW BODY GOING TO BE DONE 3-D PRINTING?
YOU CAN'T RUSH GREATNESS, ADSIT.
LET'S HOPE DEADPOOL LEAVES US SOME OF THEM ALIVE...

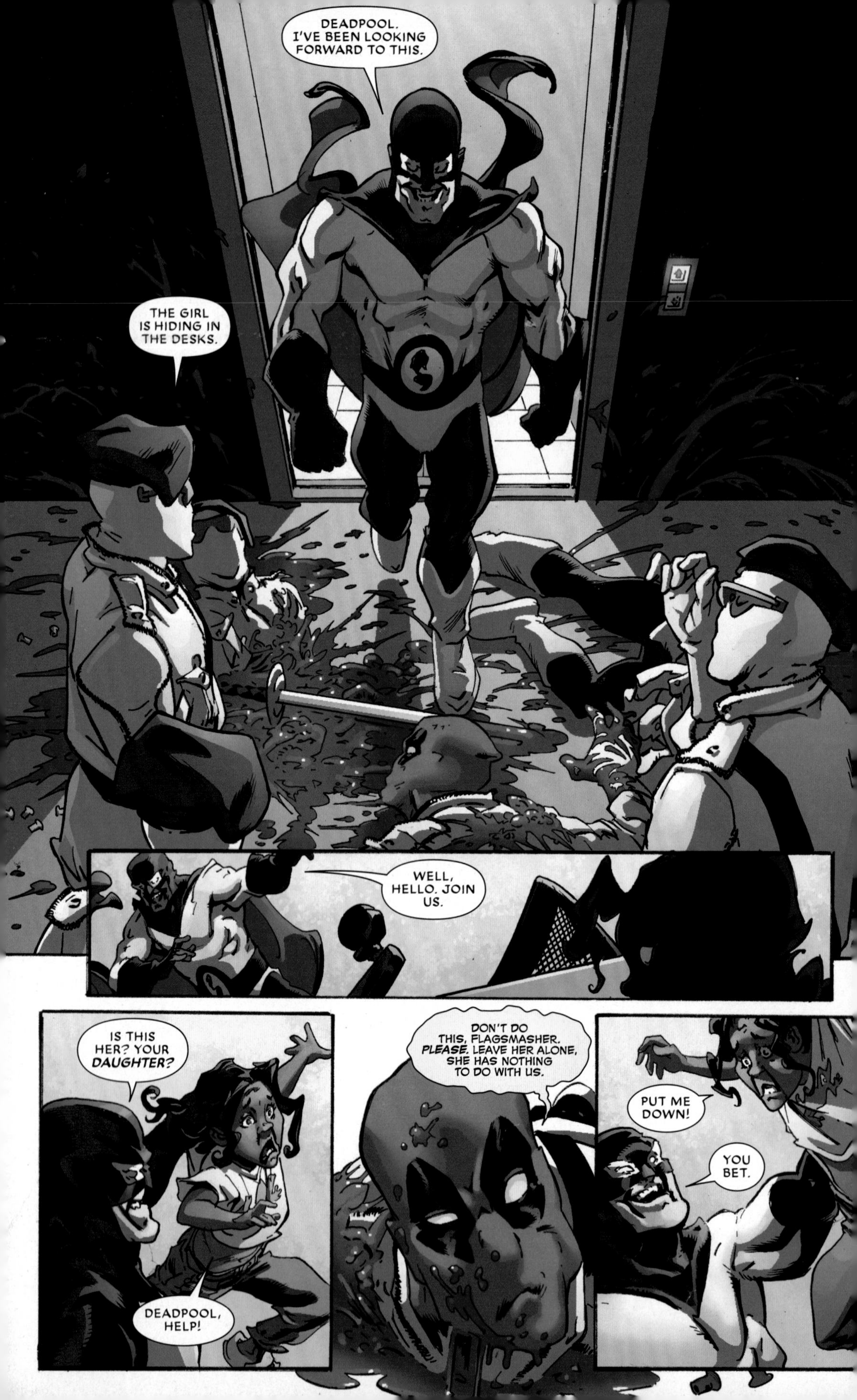
DEADPOOL. I'VE BEEN LOOKING FORWARD TO THIS.
THE GIRL IS HIDING IN THE DESKS.
WELL, HELLO. JOIN US.
IS THIS HER? YOUR *DAUGHTER?*
DEADPOOL, HELP!
DON'T DO THIS, FLAGSMASHER. *PLEASE.* LEAVE HER ALONE, SHE HAS NOTHING TO DO WITH US.
PUT ME DOWN!
YOU BET.

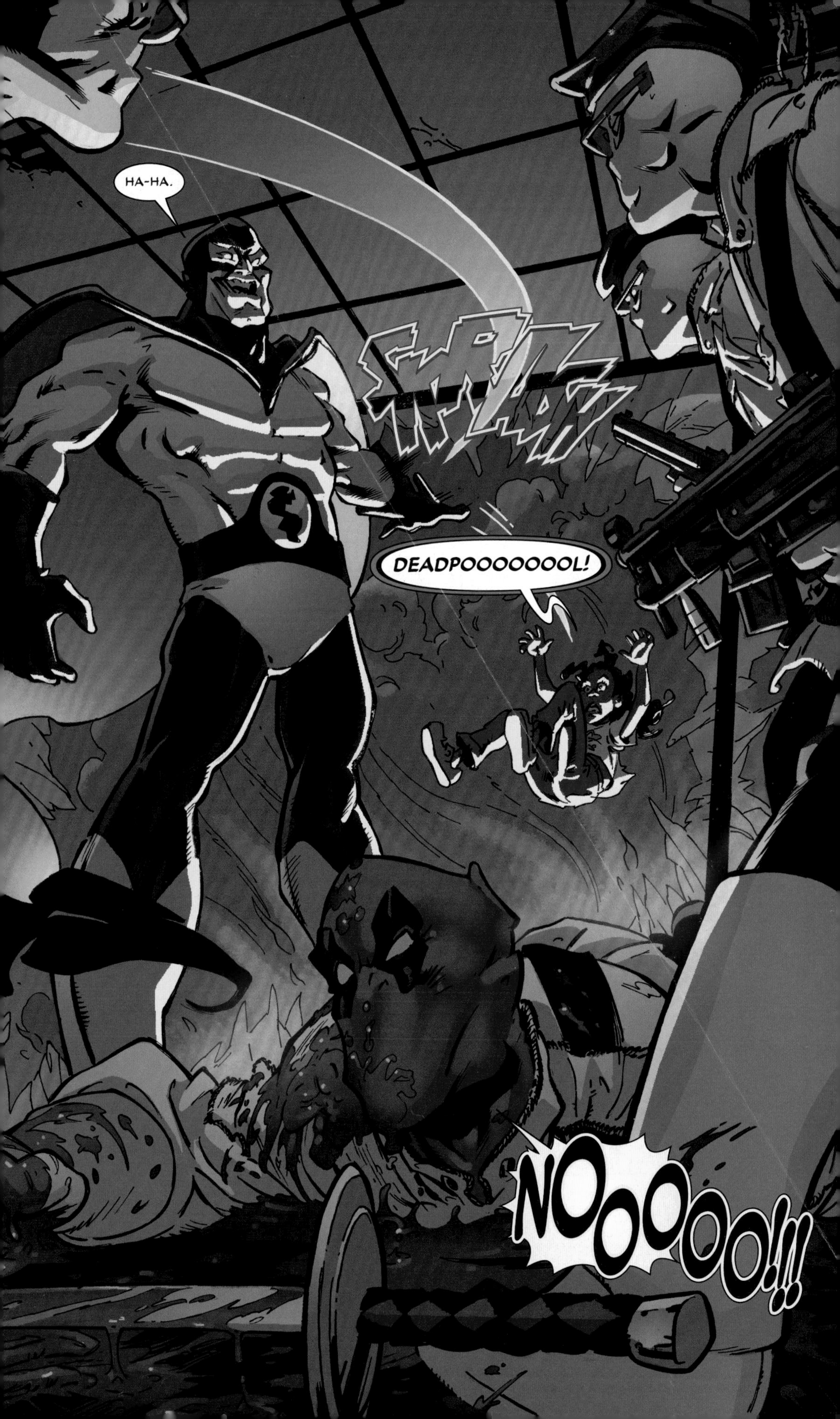
HA-HA.
DEADPOOOOOOOL!
NOOOOO!!!

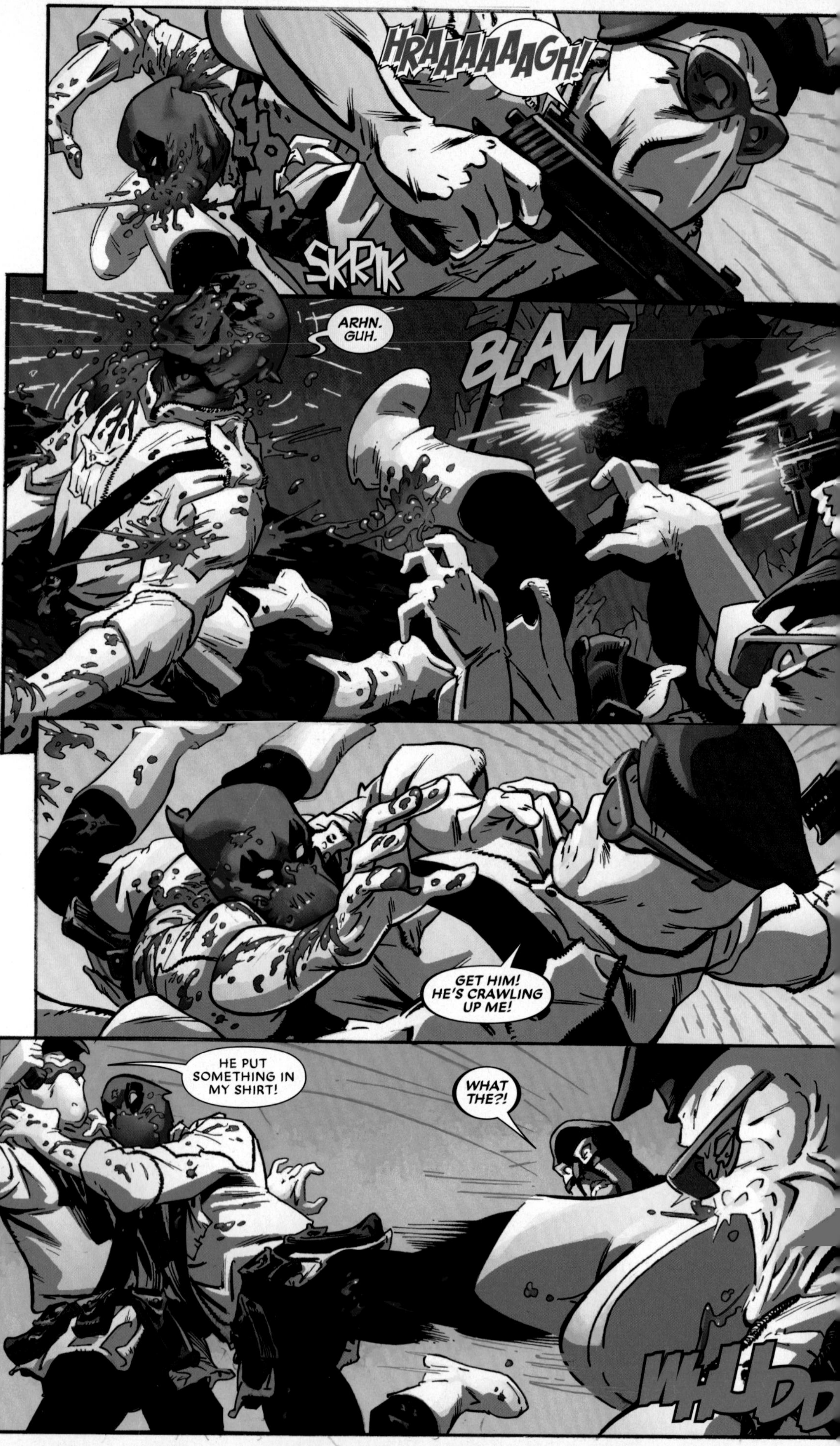
HRAAAAAAGH!
CHOMP
SKRIK
ARHN. GUH.
BLAM
GET HIM! HE'S CRAWLING UP ME!
HE PUT SOMETHING IN MY SHIRT!
WHAT THE?!
WHUDD

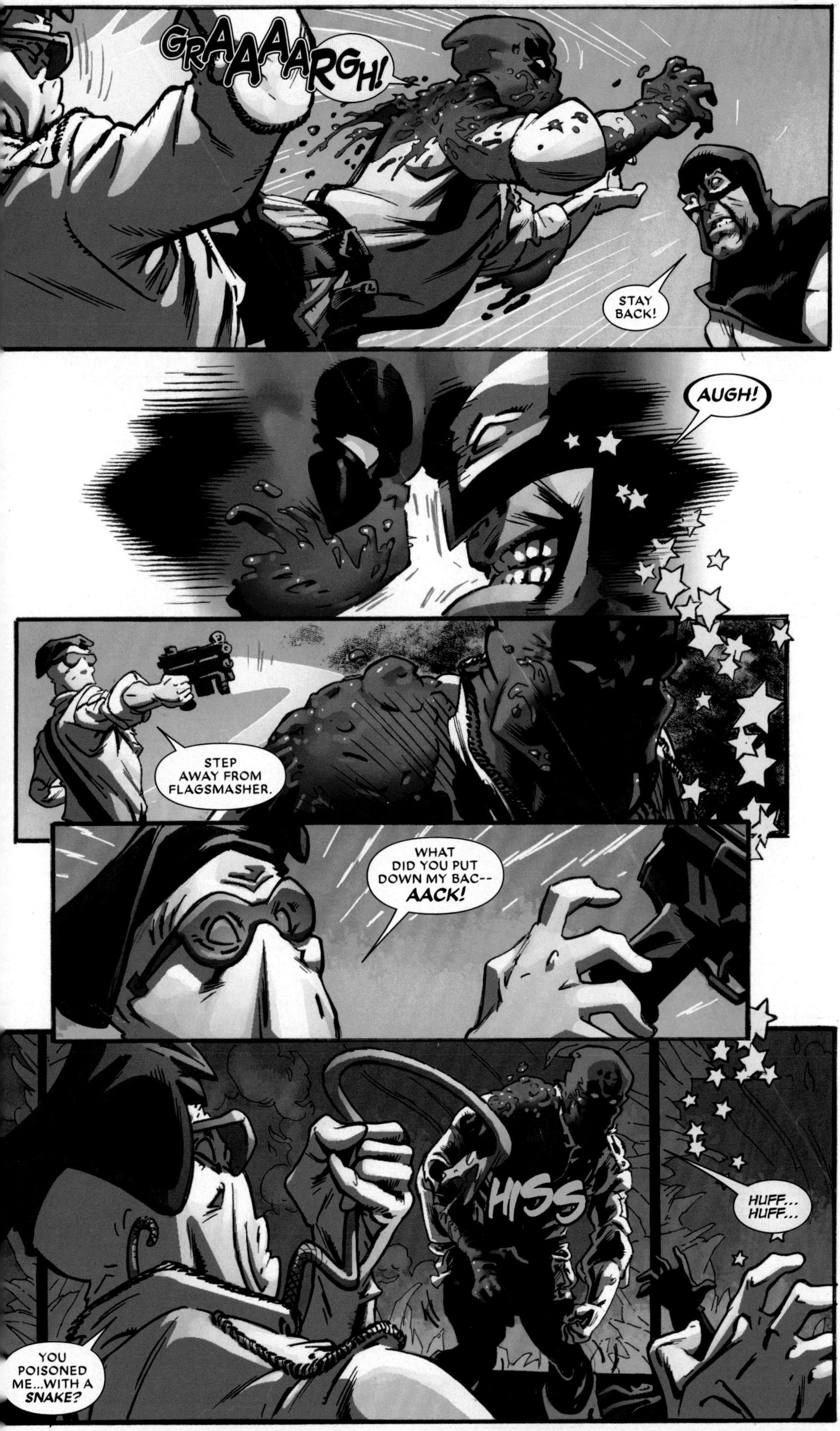
GRAAAARGH!
STAY BACK!
AUGH!
STEP AWAY FROM FLAGSMASHER.
WHAT DID YOU PUT DOWN MY BAC-- AACK!
YOU POISONED ME...WITH A SNAKE?
HISS
HUFF... HUFF...

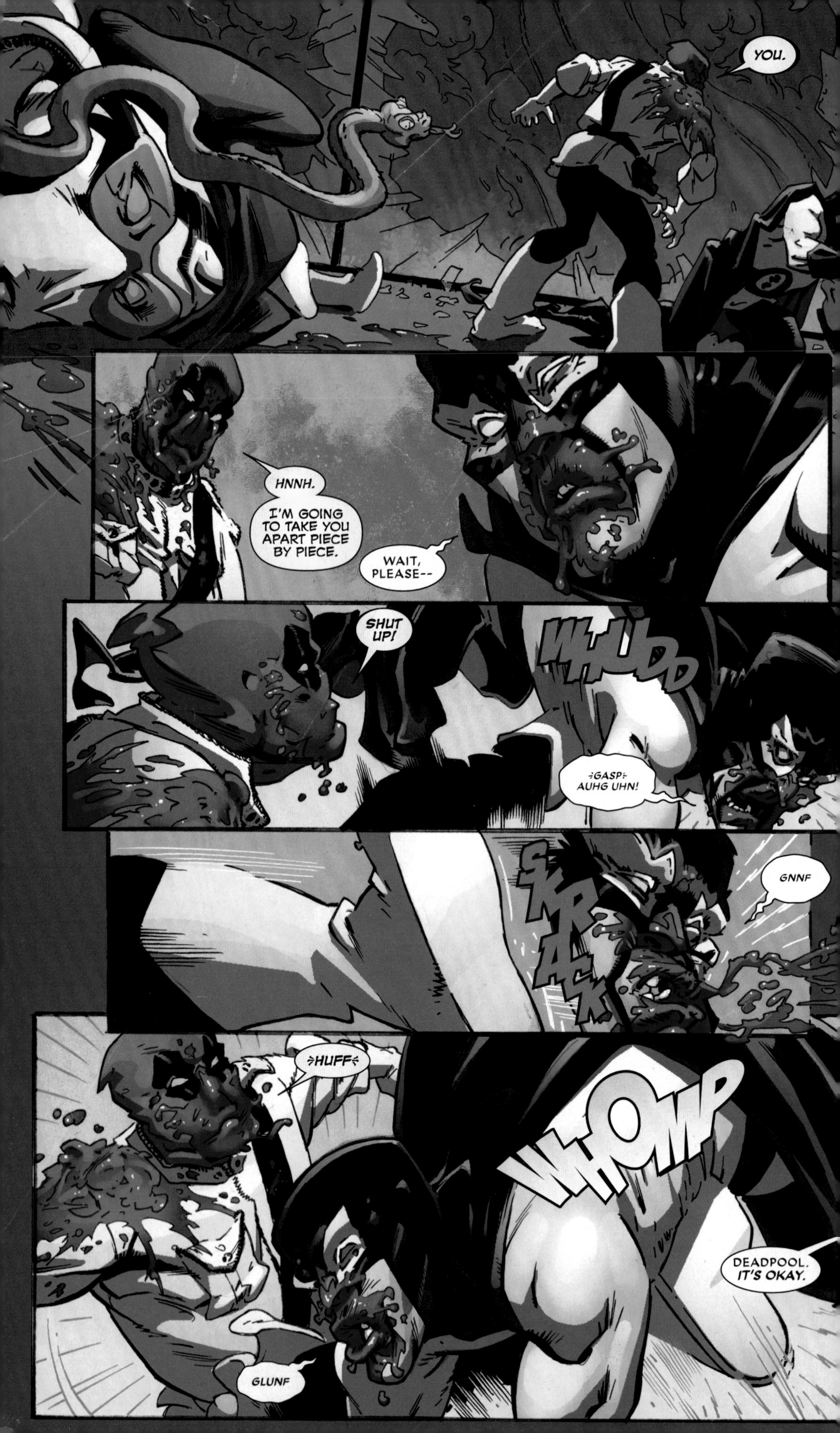
YOU.
HNNH.
I'M GOING TO TAKE YOU APART PIECE BY PIECE.
WAIT, PLEASE--
SHUT UP!
WHUDD
GASP AUHG UHN!
SKRACK
GNNF
HUFF
WHOMP
DEADPOOL. IT'S OKAY.
GLUNF

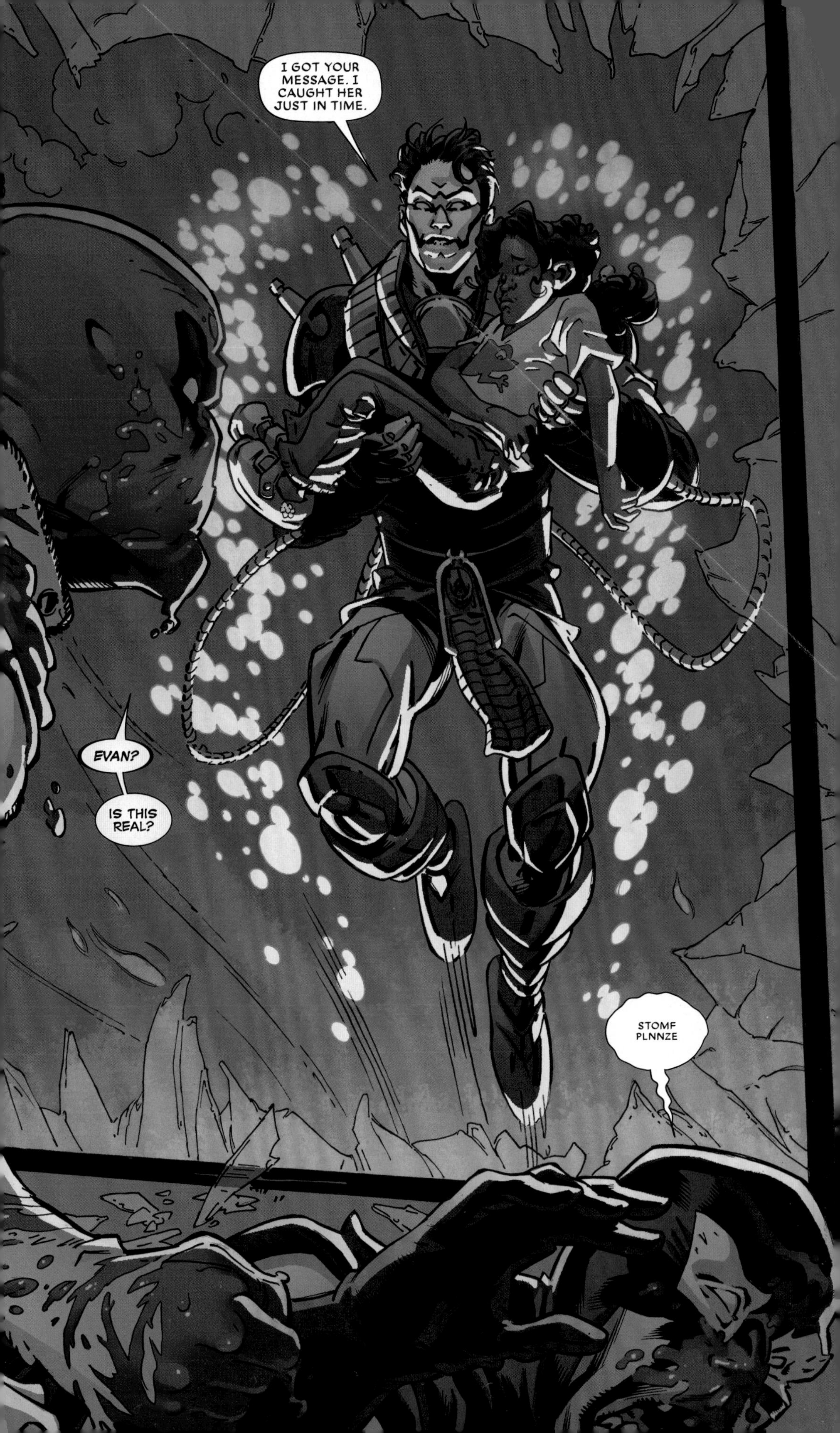
I GOT YOUR MESSAGE. I CAUGHT HER JUST IN TIME.
EVAN?
IS THIS REAL?
STOMF PLNNZE

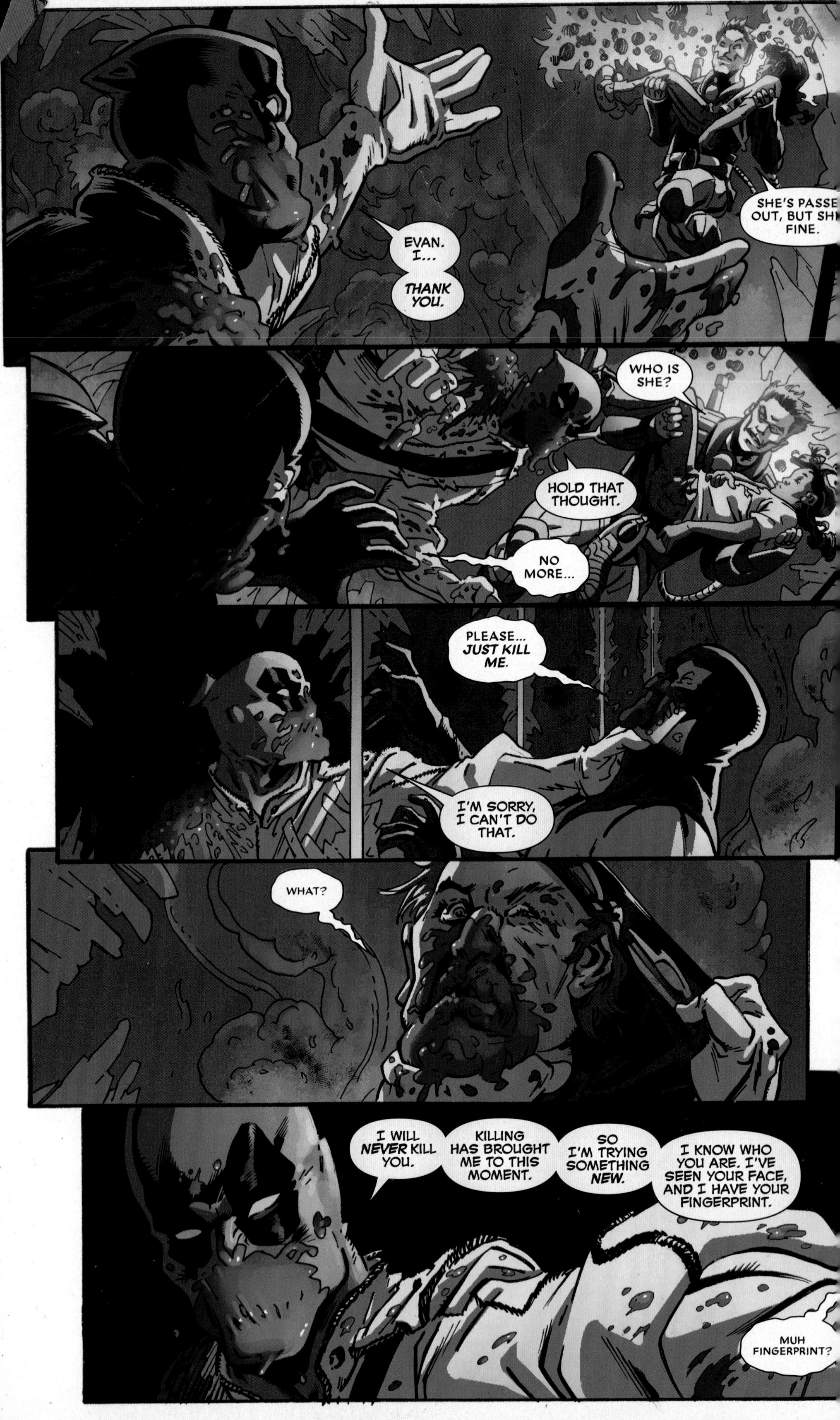

SHE'S PASSE OUT, BUT SH FINE.
EVAN. I...
THANK YOU.
WHO IS SHE?
HOLD THAT THOUGHT.
NO MORE...
PLEASE... JUST KILL ME.
I'M SORRY, I CAN'T DO THAT.
WHAT?
I WILL NEVER KILL YOU.
KILLING HAS BROUGHT ME TO THIS MOMENT.
SO I'M TRYING SOMETHING NEW.
I KNOW WHO YOU ARE. I'VE SEEN YOUR FACE, AND I HAVE YOUR FINGERPRINT.
MUH FINGERPRINT?

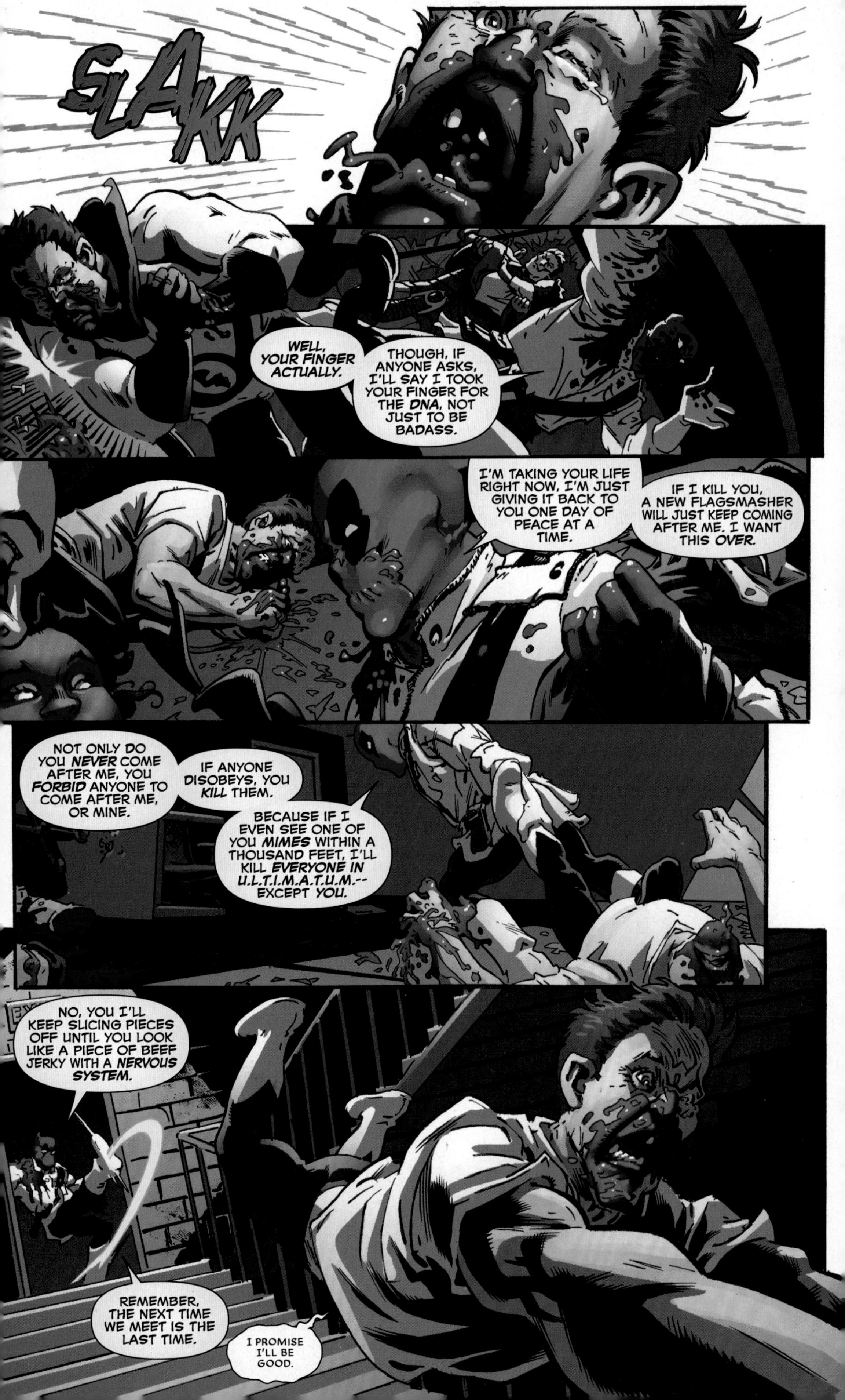
SLAKK
WELL, YOUR FINGER ACTUALLY.
THOUGH, IF ANYONE ASKS, I'LL SAY I TOOK YOUR FINGER FOR THE DNA, NOT JUST TO BE BADASS.
I'M TAKING YOUR LIFE RIGHT NOW, I'M JUST GIVING IT BACK TO YOU ONE DAY OF PEACE AT A TIME.
IF I KILL YOU, A NEW FLAGSMASHER WILL JUST KEEP COMING AFTER ME. I WANT THIS OVER.
NOT ONLY DO YOU NEVER COME AFTER ME, YOU FORBID ANYONE TO COME AFTER ME, OR MINE.
IF ANYONE DISOBEYS, YOU KILL THEM.
BECAUSE IF I EVEN SEE ONE OF YOU MIMES WITHIN A THOUSAND FEET, I'LL KILL EVERYONE IN U.L.T.I.M.A.T.U.M.--EXCEPT YOU.
NO, YOU I'LL KEEP SLICING PIECES OFF UNTIL YOU LOOK LIKE A PIECE OF BEEF JERKY WITH A NERVOUS SYSTEM.
REMEMBER, THE NEXT TIME WE MEET IS THE LAST TIME.
I PROMISE I'LL BE GOOD.

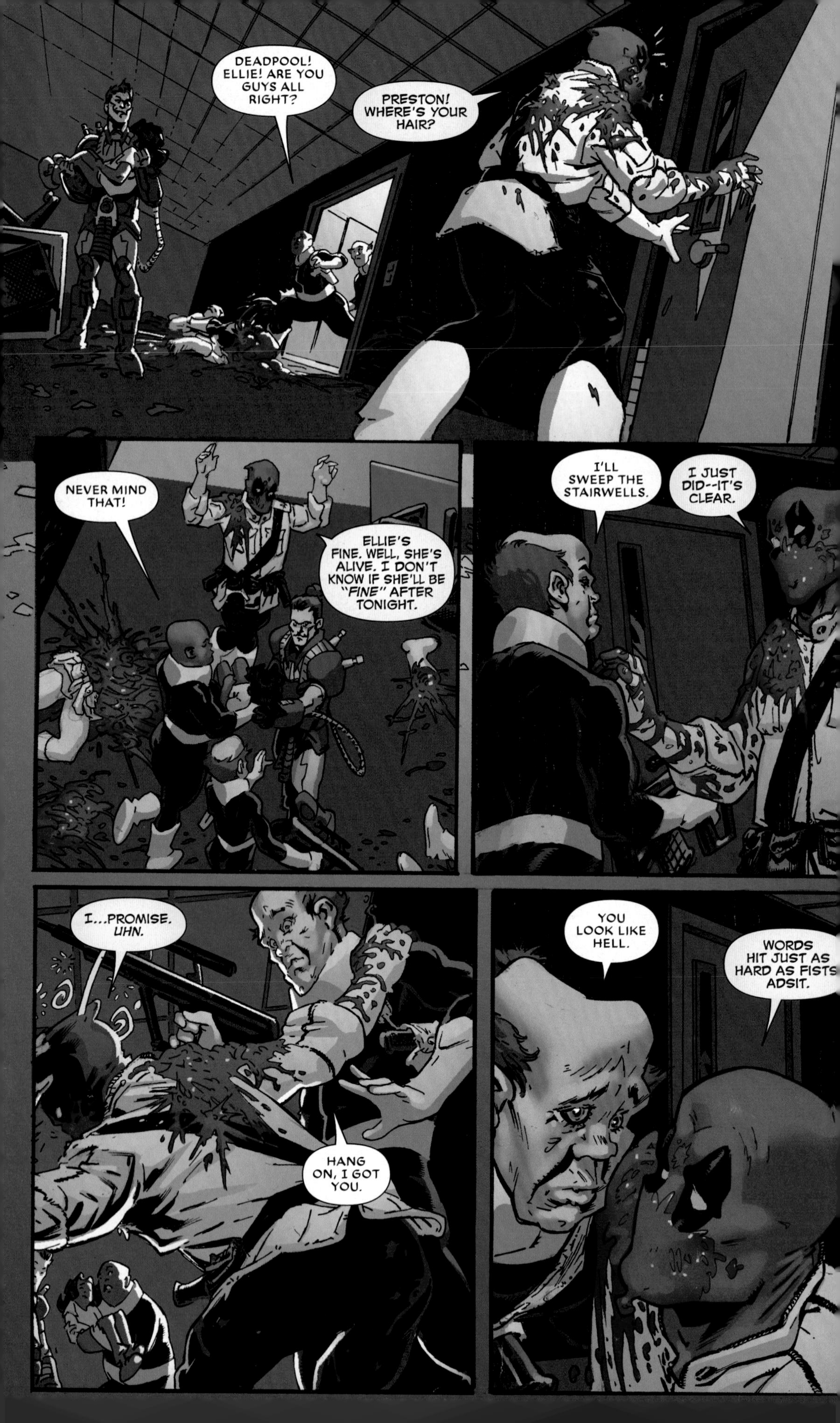
DEADPOOL! ELLIE! ARE YOU GUYS ALL RIGHT?
PRESTON! WHERE'S YOUR HAIR?
NEVER MIND THAT!
ELLIE'S FINE. WELL, SHE'S ALIVE. I DON'T KNOW IF SHE'LL BE "FINE" AFTER TONIGHT.
I'LL SWEEP THE STAIRWELLS.
I JUST DID--IT'S CLEAR.
I...PROMISE. UHN.
HANG ON, I GOT YOU.
YOU LOOK LIKE HELL.
WORDS HIT JUST AS HARD AS FISTS ADSIT.

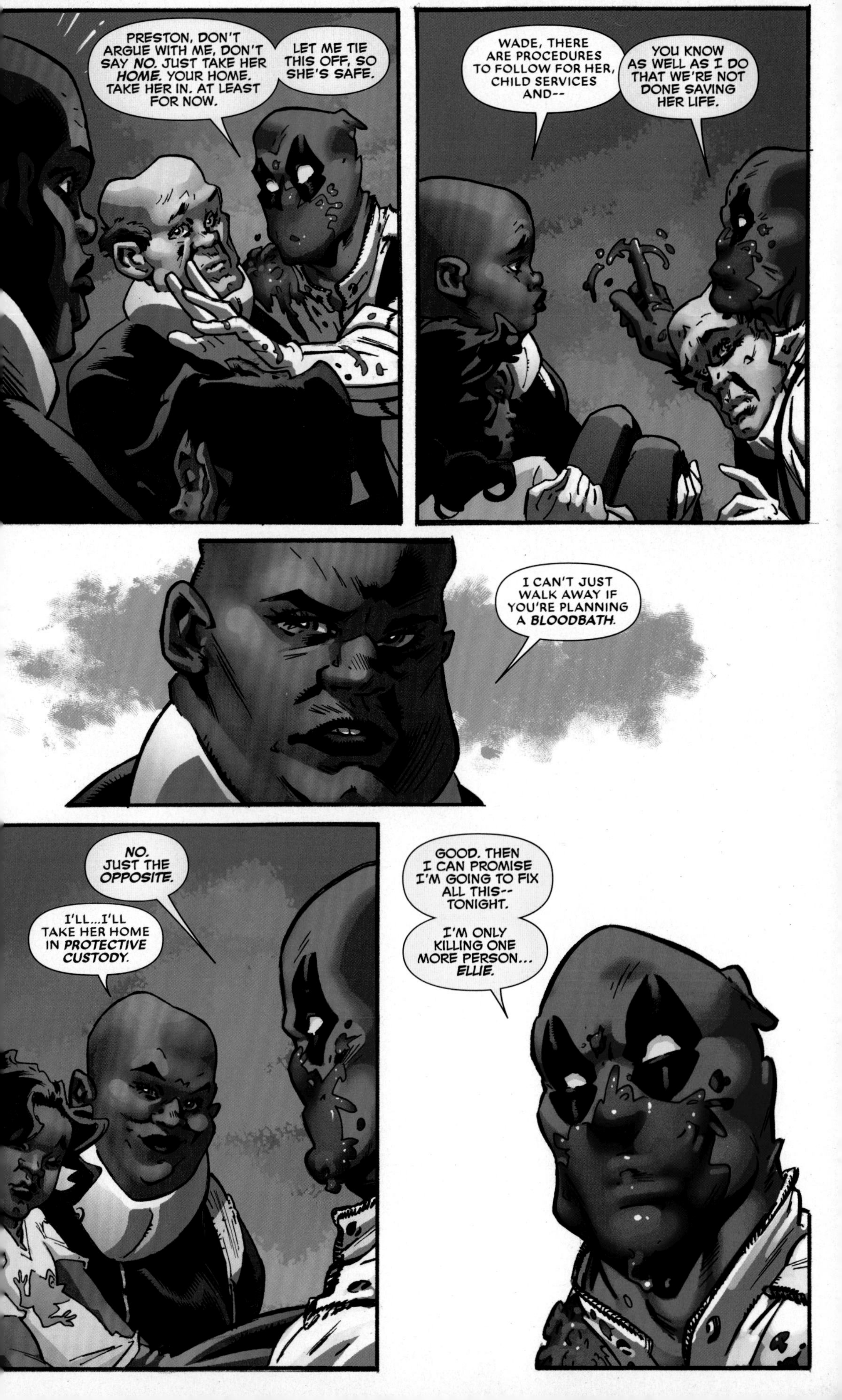
PRESTON, DON'T ARGUE WITH ME, DON'T SAY NO. JUST TAKE HER HOME. YOUR HOME. TAKE HER IN. AT LEAST FOR NOW.
LET ME TIE THIS OFF, SO SHE'S SAFE.
WADE, THERE ARE PROCEDURES TO FOLLOW FOR HER, CHILD SERVICES AND--
YOU KNOW AS WELL AS I DO THAT WE'RE NOT DONE SAVING HER LIFE.
I CAN'T JUST WALK AWAY IF YOU'RE PLANNING A BLOODBATH.
NO. JUST THE OPPOSITE.
I'LL...I'LL TAKE HER HOME IN PROTECTIVE CUSTODY.
GOOD. THEN I CAN PROMISE I'M GOING TO FIX ALL THIS-- TONIGHT.
I'M ONLY KILLING ONE MORE PERSON... ELLIE.

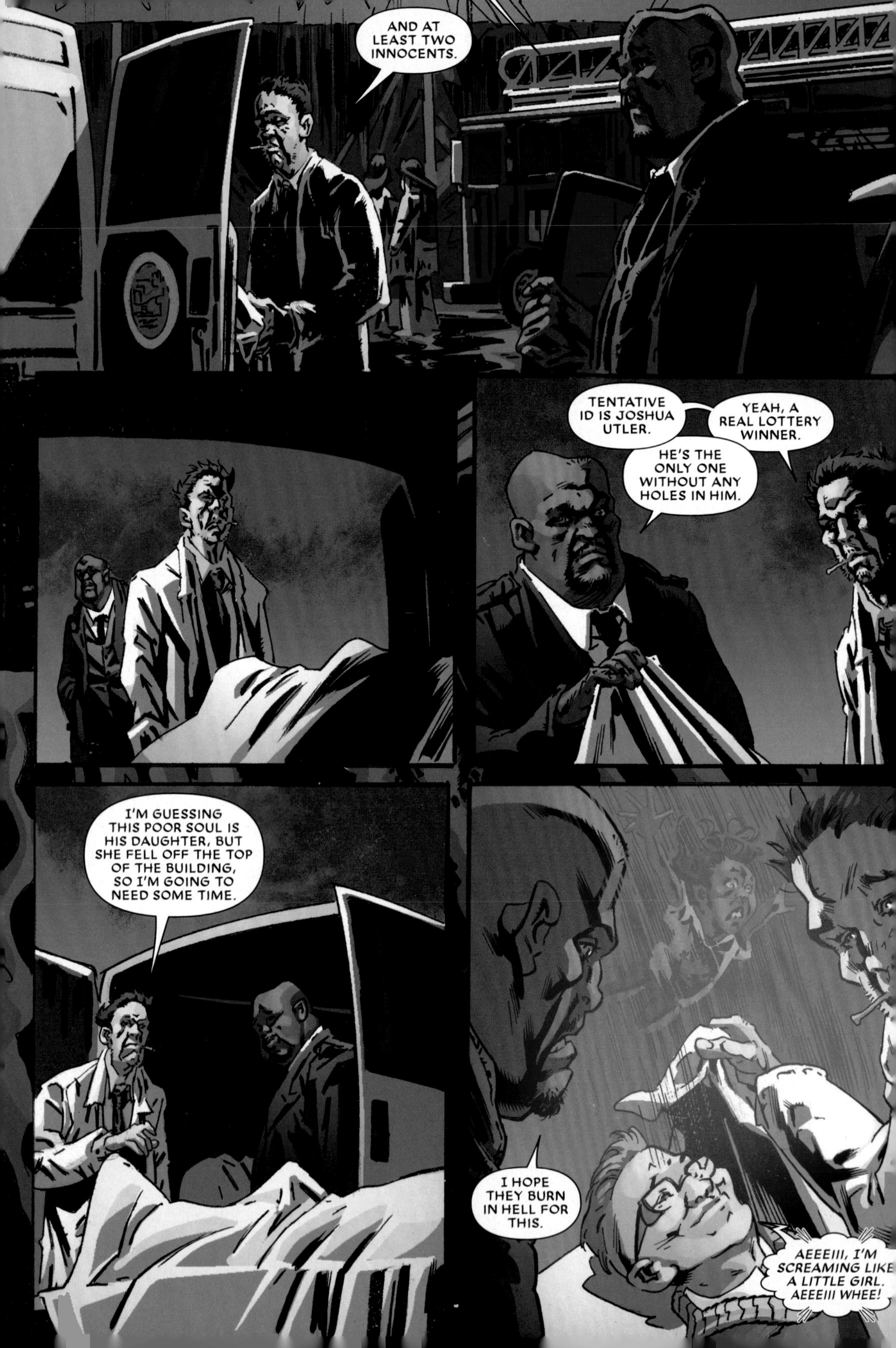
AND AT LEAST TWO INNOCENTS.
TENTATIVE ID IS JOSHUA UTLER.
YEAH, A REAL LOTTERY WINNER.
HE'S THE ONLY ONE WITHOUT ANY HOLES IN HIM.
I'M GUESSING THIS POOR SOUL IS HIS DAUGHTER, BUT SHE FELL OFF THE TOP OF THE BUILDING, SO I'M GOING TO NEED SOME TIME.
I HOPE THEY BURN IN HELL FOR THIS.
AEEEIII, I'M SCREAMING LIKE A LITTLE GIRL. AEEEIII WHEE!

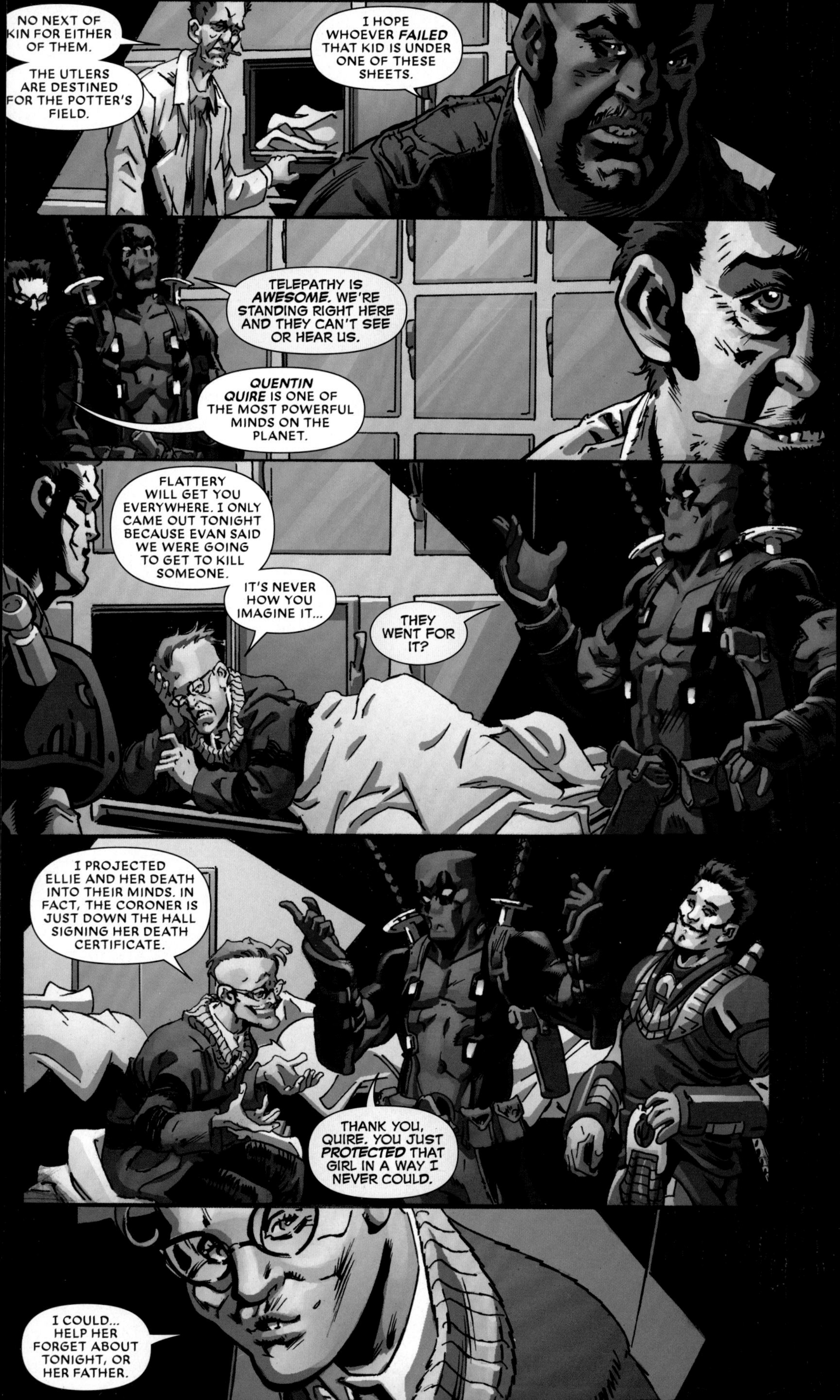

NO NEXT OF KIN FOR EITHER OF THEM.
THE UTLERS ARE DESTINED FOR THE POTTER'S FIELD.
I HOPE WHOEVER *FAILED* THAT KID IS UNDER ONE OF THESE SHEETS.
TELEPATHY IS *AWESOME.* WE'RE STANDING RIGHT HERE AND THEY CAN'T SEE OR HEAR US.
QUENTIN QUIRE IS ONE OF THE MOST POWERFUL MINDS ON THE PLANET.
FLATTERY WILL GET YOU EVERYWHERE. I ONLY CAME OUT TONIGHT BECAUSE EVAN SAID WE WERE GOING TO GET TO KILL SOMEONE.
IT'S NEVER HOW YOU IMAGINE IT...
THEY WENT FOR IT?
I PROJECTED ELLIE AND HER DEATH INTO THEIR MINDS. IN FACT, THE CORONER IS JUST DOWN THE HALL SIGNING HER DEATH CERTIFICATE.
THANK YOU, QUIRE. YOU JUST *PROTECTED* THAT GIRL IN A WAY I NEVER COULD.
I COULD... HELP HER FORGET ABOUT TONIGHT, OR HER FATHER.

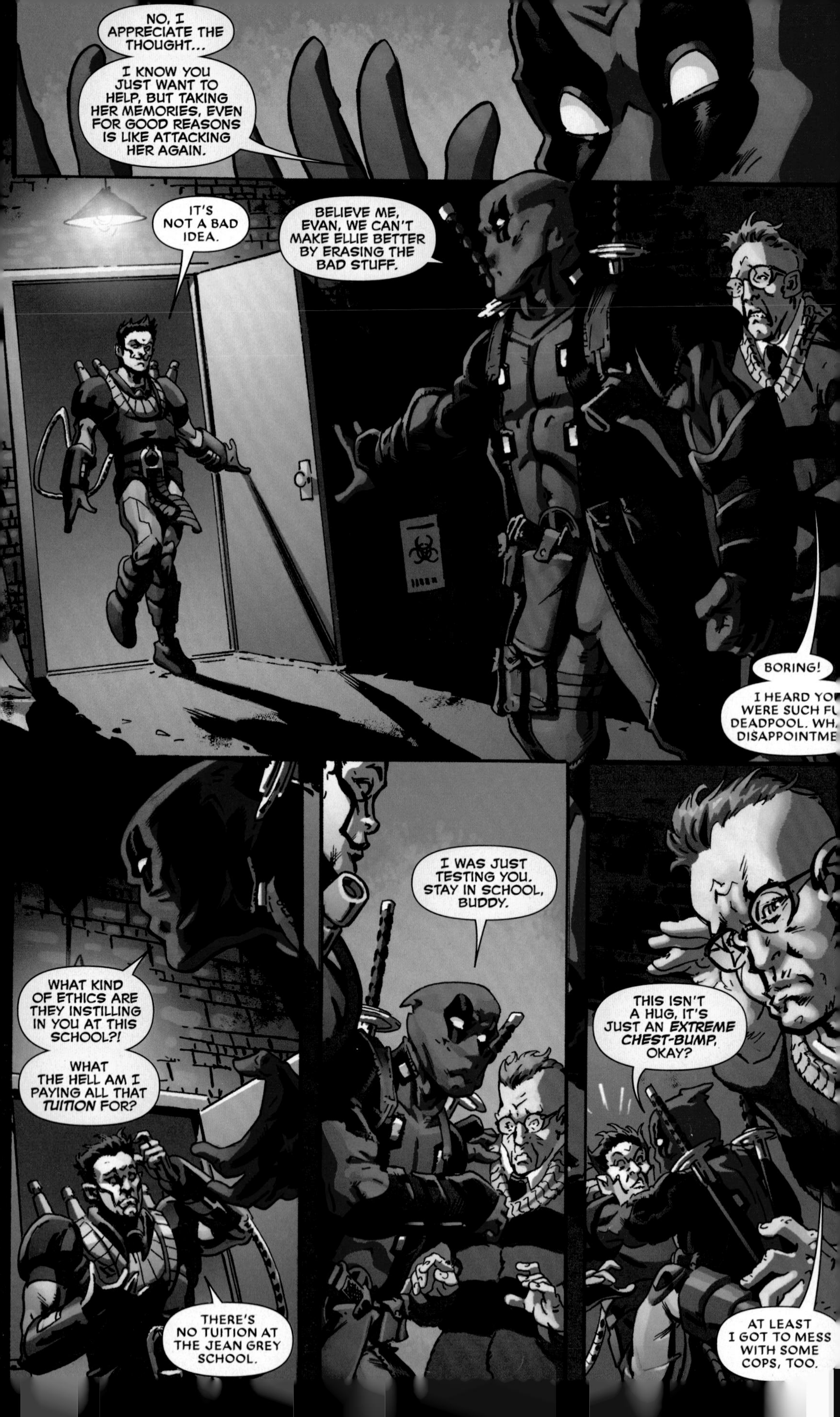
NO, I APPRECIATE THE THOUGHT...
I KNOW YOU JUST WANT TO HELP, BUT TAKING HER MEMORIES, EVEN FOR GOOD REASONS IS LIKE ATTACKING HER AGAIN.
IT'S NOT A BAD IDEA.
BELIEVE ME, EVAN, WE CAN'T MAKE ELLIE BETTER BY ERASING THE BAD STUFF.
BORING!
I HEARD YO WERE SUCH FU DEADPOOL. WHA DISAPPOINTME
WHAT KIND OF ETHICS ARE THEY INSTILLING IN YOU AT THIS SCHOOL?!
WHAT THE HELL AM I PAYING ALL THAT *TUITION* FOR?
THERE'S NO TUITION AT THE JEAN GREY SCHOOL.
I WAS JUST TESTING YOU. STAY IN SCHOOL, BUDDY.
THIS ISN'T A HUG, IT'S JUST AN *EXTREME CHEST-BUMP*, OKAY?
AT LEAST I GOT TO MESS WITH SOME COPS, TOO.

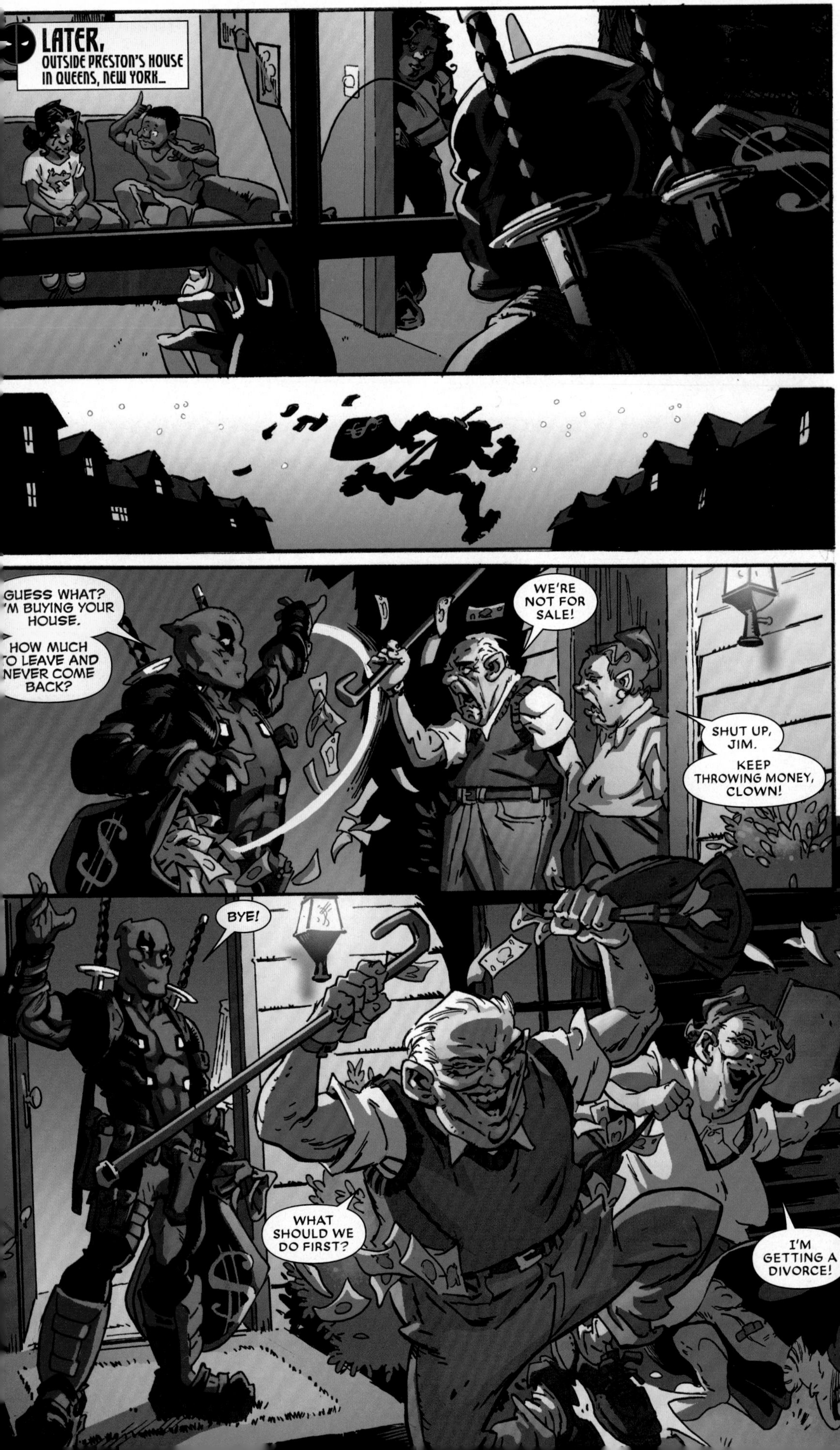
LATER, OUTSIDE PRESTON'S HOUSE IN QUEENS, NEW YORK...
GUESS WHAT? I'M BUYING YOUR HOUSE.
HOW MUCH TO LEAVE AND NEVER COME BACK?
WE'RE NOT FOR SALE!
SHUT UP, JIM.
KEEP THROWING MONEY, CLOWN!
BYE!
WHAT SHOULD WE DO FIRST?
I'M GETTING A DIVORCE!

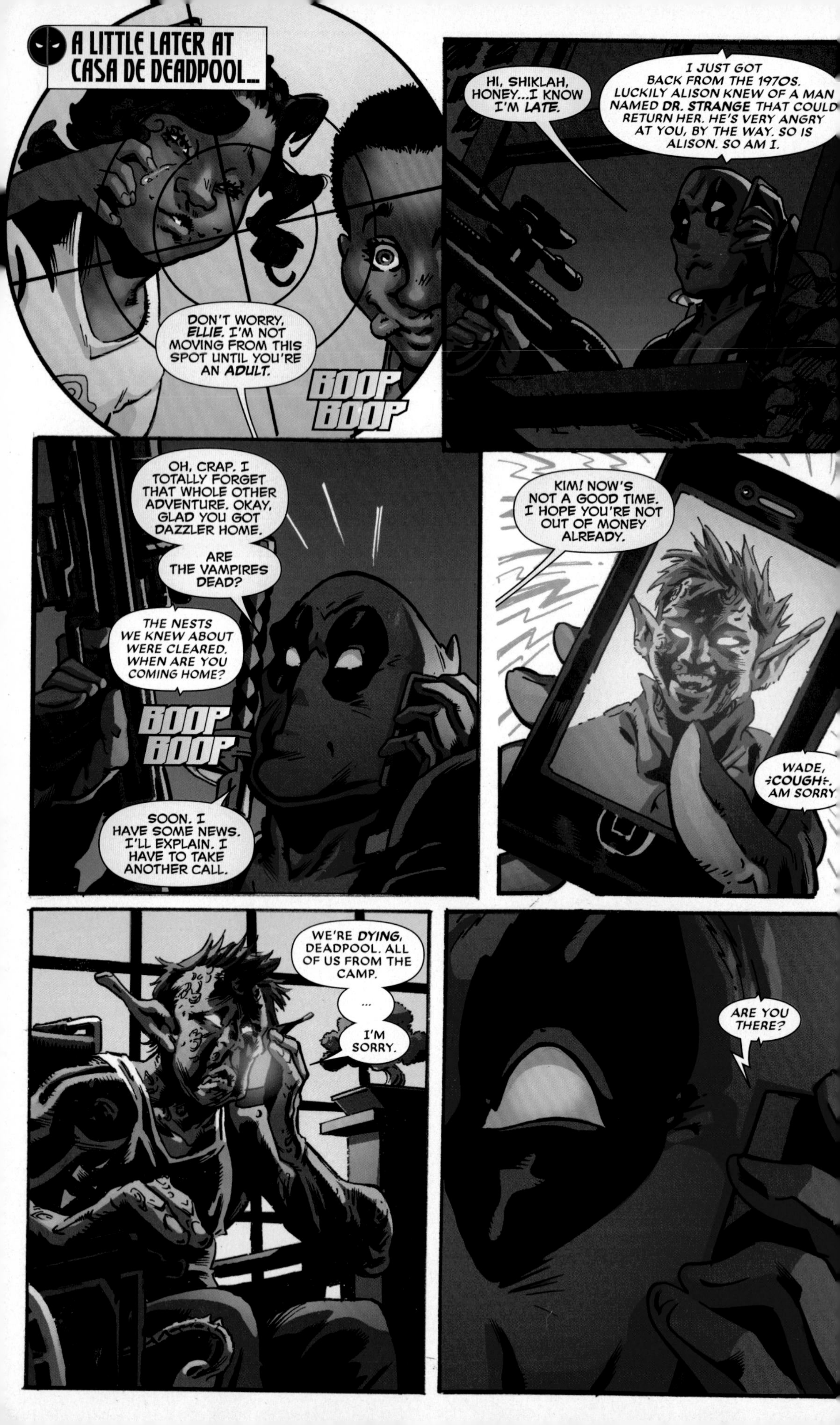

A LITTLE LATER AT CASA DE DEADPOOL...
DON'T WORRY, ELLIE. I'M NOT MOVING FROM THIS SPOT UNTIL YOU'RE AN ADULT.
BOOP BOOP
HI, SHIKLAH, HONEY...I KNOW I'M LATE.
I JUST GOT BACK FROM THE 1970S. LUCKILY ALISON KNEW OF A MAN NAMED DR. STRANGE THAT COULD RETURN HER. HE'S VERY ANGRY AT YOU, BY THE WAY. SO IS ALISON. SO AM I.
OH, CRAP. I TOTALLY FORGET THAT WHOLE OTHER ADVENTURE. OKAY, GLAD YOU GOT DAZZLER HOME.
ARE THE VAMPIRES DEAD?
THE NESTS WE KNEW ABOUT WERE CLEARED. WHEN ARE YOU COMING HOME?
BOOP BOOP
SOON. I HAVE SOME NEWS. I'LL EXPLAIN. I HAVE TO TAKE ANOTHER CALL.
KIM! NOW'S NOT A GOOD TIME. I HOPE YOU'RE NOT OUT OF MONEY ALREADY.
WADE, -COUGH-. AM SORRY
WE'RE DYING, DEADPOOL. ALL OF US FROM THE CAMP.
...
I'M SORRY.
ARE YOU THERE?

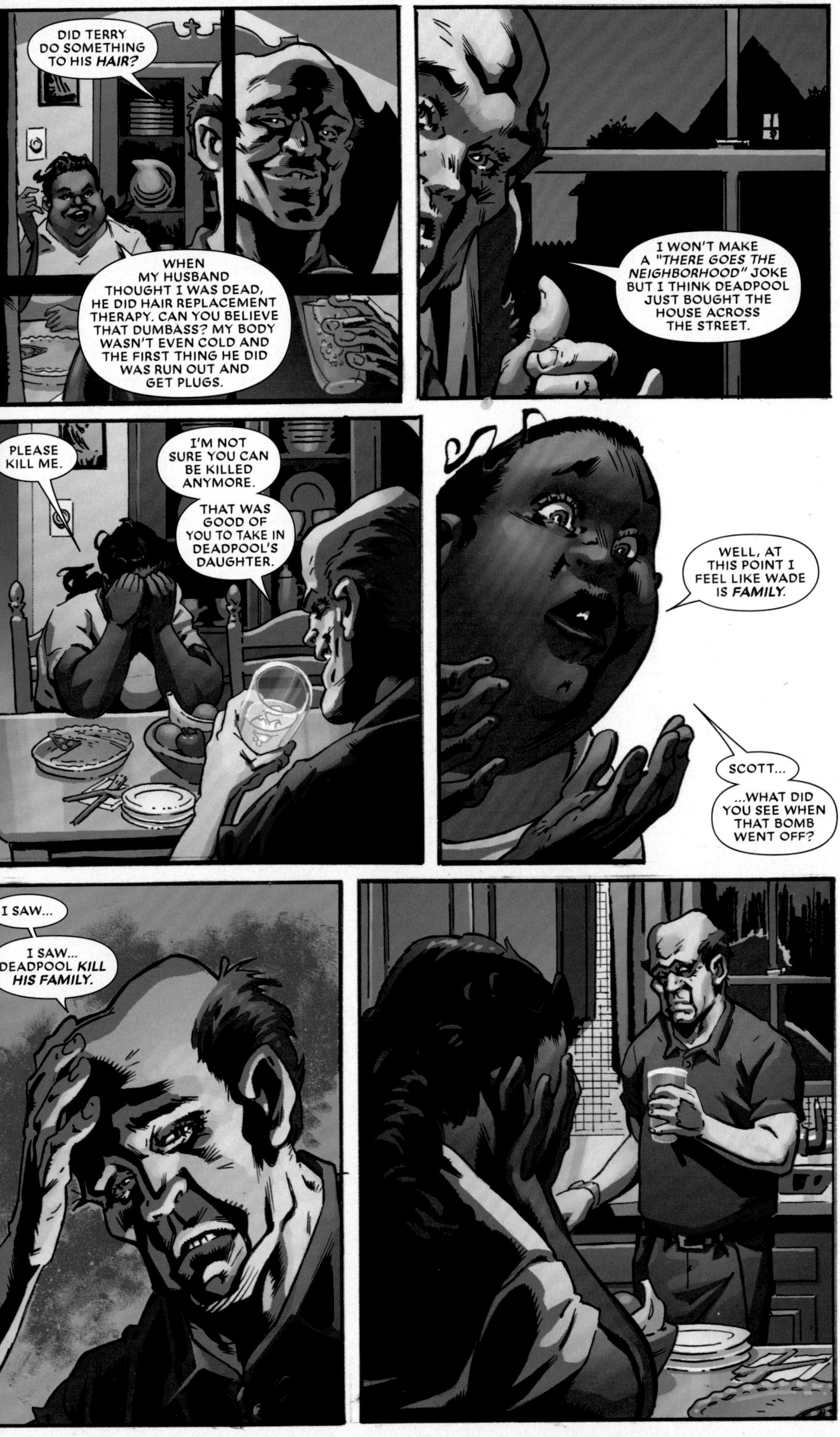
DID TERRY DO SOMETHING TO HIS *HAIR?*
WHEN MY HUSBAND THOUGHT I WAS DEAD, HE DID HAIR REPLACEMENT THERAPY. CAN YOU BELIEVE THAT DUMBASS? MY BODY WASN'T EVEN COLD AND THE FIRST THING HE DID WAS RUN OUT AND GET PLUGS.
I WON'T MAKE A *"THERE GOES THE NEIGHBORHOOD"* JOKE BUT I THINK DEADPOOL JUST BOUGHT THE HOUSE ACROSS THE STREET.
PLEASE KILL ME.
I'M NOT SURE YOU CAN BE KILLED ANYMORE.
THAT WAS GOOD OF YOU TO TAKE IN DEADPOOL'S DAUGHTER.
WELL, AT THIS POINT I FEEL LIKE WADE IS *FAMILY.*
SCOTT...
...WHAT DID YOU SEE WHEN THAT BOMB WENT OFF?
I SAW...
I SAW... DEADPOOL *KILL HIS FAMILY.*

LENTICULAR COVER FRAMES

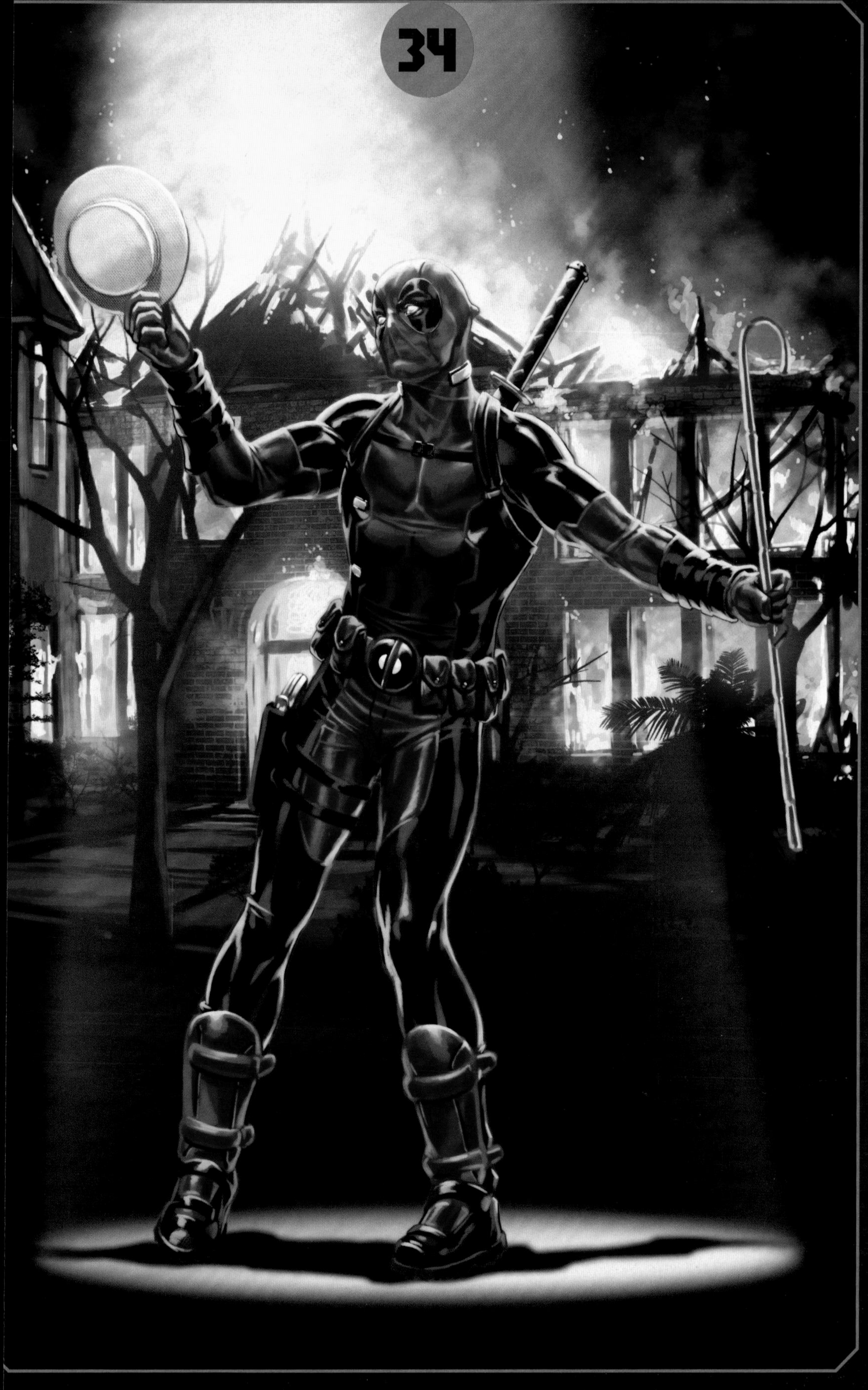
34

THE ONE WITH THE SUPER-RARE 3-D COVER!

Possibly the world's most skilled mercenary, definitely the world' most annoying, Wade Wilson was chosen for a top-secret governmen program that gave him a healing factor allowing him to heal fro any wound. Now, Wade makes his way as a gun for hire, shootin his prey's faces off while talking his friends' ears off. Call hi the Merc with the Mouth...call him the Regeneratin' Degenerate.. call him...**DEADPOOL**.

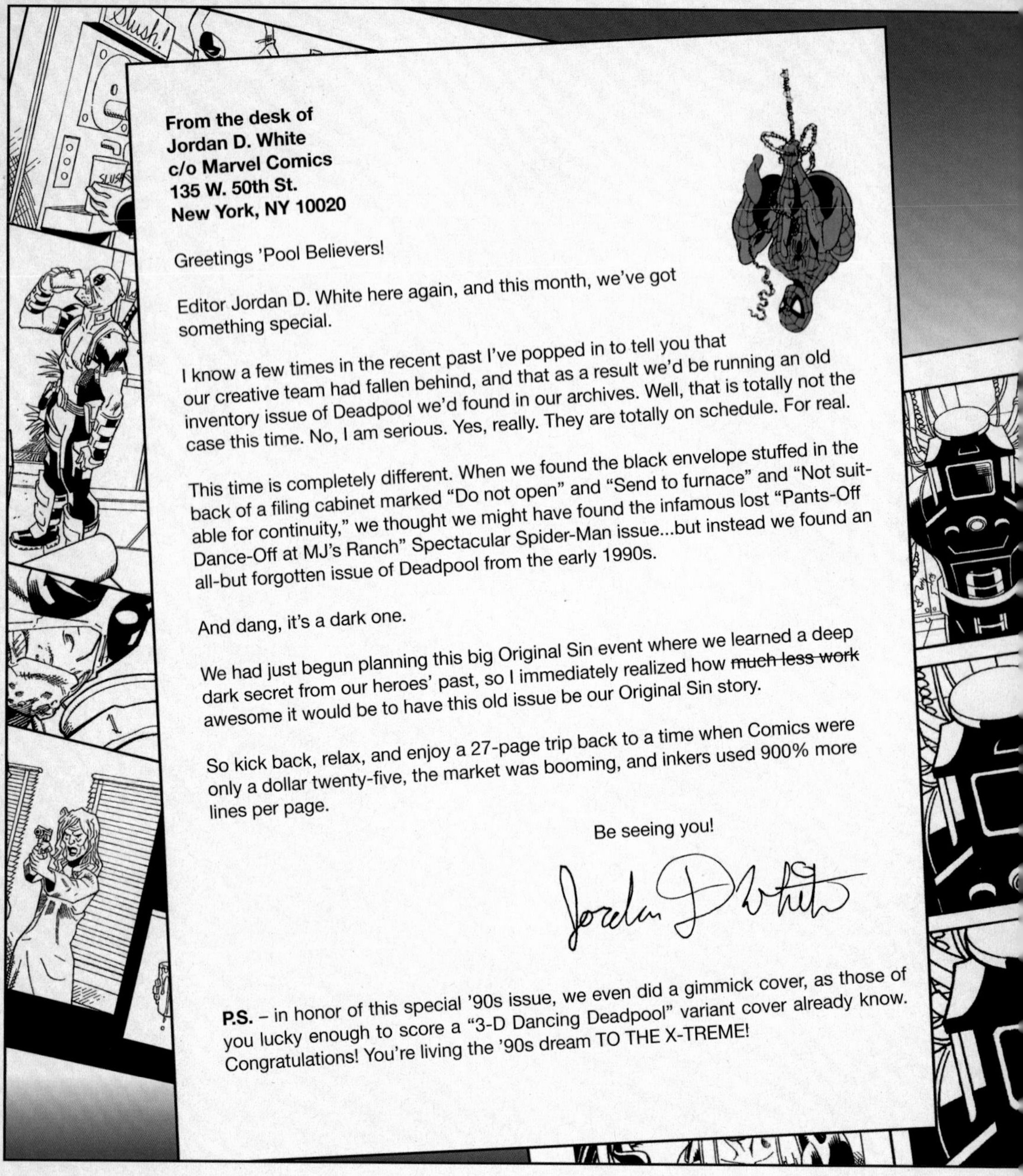

From the desk of
Jordan D. White
c/o Marvel Comics
135 W. 50th St.
New York, NY 10020

Greetings 'Pool Believers!

Editor Jordan D. White here again, and this month, we've got something special.

I know a few times in the recent past I've popped in to tell you that our creative team had fallen behind, and that as a result we'd be running an old inventory issue of Deadpool we'd found in our archives. Well, that is totally not the case this time. No, I am serious. Yes, really. They are totally on schedule. For real.

This time is completely different. When we found the black envelope stuffed in the back of a filing cabinet marked "Do not open" and "Send to furnace" and "Not suitable for continuity," we thought we might have found the infamous lost "Pants-Off Dance-Off at MJ's Ranch" Spectacular Spider-Man issue...but instead we found an all-but forgotten issue of Deadpool from the early 1990s.

And dang, it's a dark one.

We had just begun planning this big Original Sin event where we learned a deep dark secret from our heroes' past, so I immediately realized how ~~much less work~~ awesome it would be to have this old issue be our Original Sin story.

So kick back, relax, and enjoy a 27-page trip back to a time when Comics were only a dollar twenty-five, the market was booming, and inkers used 900% more lines per page.

Be seeing you!

Jordan D. White

P.S. – in honor of this special '90s issue, we even did a gimmick cover, as those of you lucky enough to score a "3-D Dancing Deadpool" variant cover already know. Congratulations! You're living the '90s dream TO THE X-TREME!

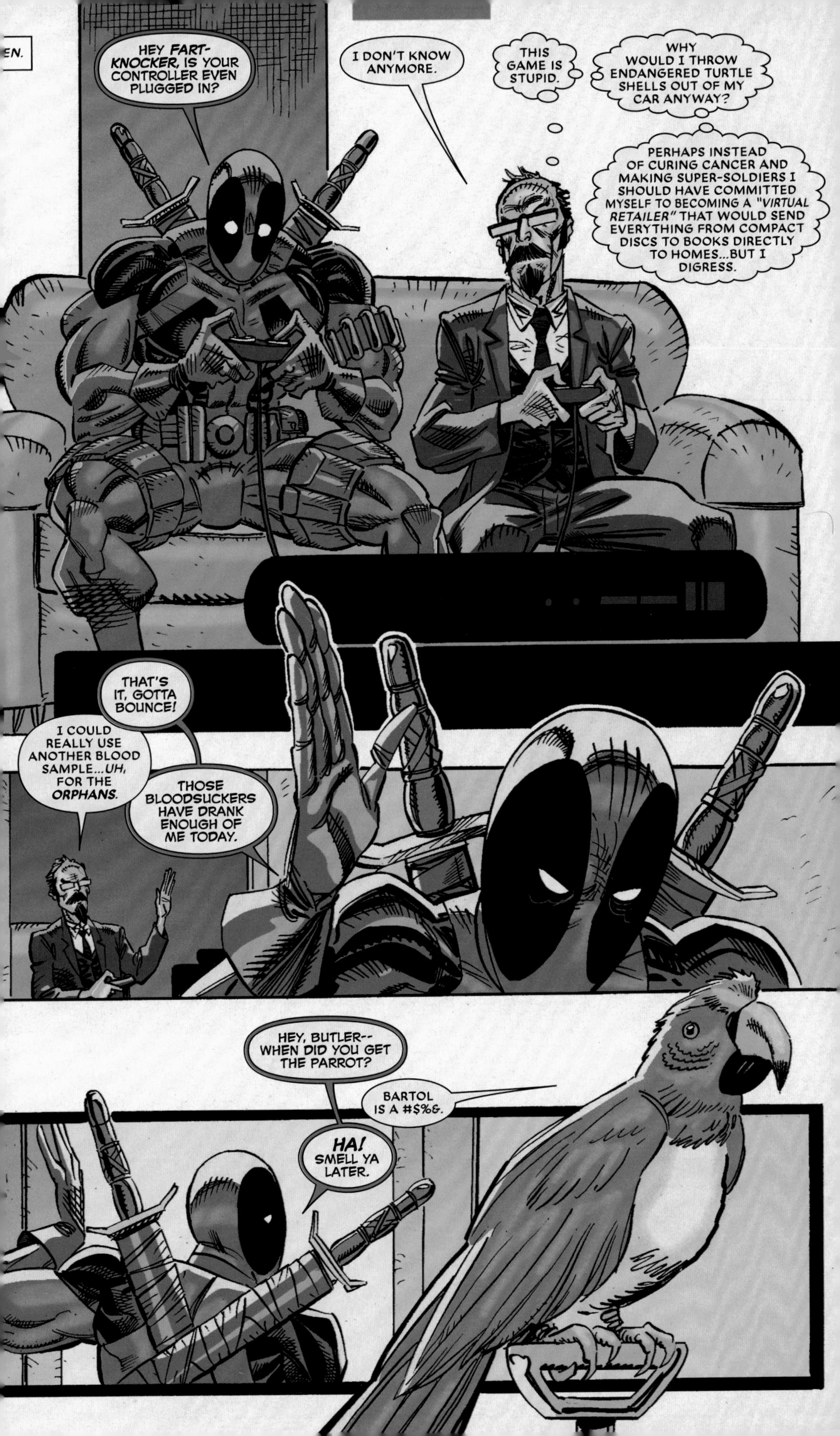

EN.
HEY FART-KNOCKER, IS YOUR CONTROLLER EVEN PLUGGED IN?
I DON'T KNOW ANYMORE.
THIS GAME IS STUPID.
WHY WOULD I THROW ENDANGERED TURTLE SHELLS OUT OF MY CAR ANYWAY?
PERHAPS INSTEAD OF CURING CANCER AND MAKING SUPER-SOLDIERS I SHOULD HAVE COMMITTED MYSELF TO BECOMING A "VIRTUAL RETAILER" THAT WOULD SEND EVERYTHING FROM COMPACT DISCS TO BOOKS DIRECTLY TO HOMES...BUT I DIGRESS.
THAT'S IT, GOTTA BOUNCE!
I COULD REALLY USE ANOTHER BLOOD SAMPLE...UH, FOR THE ORPHANS.
THOSE BLOODSUCKERS HAVE DRANK ENOUGH OF ME TODAY.
HEY, BUTLER--WHEN DID YOU GET THE PARROT?
BARTOL IS A #$%&.
HA! SMELL YA LATER.

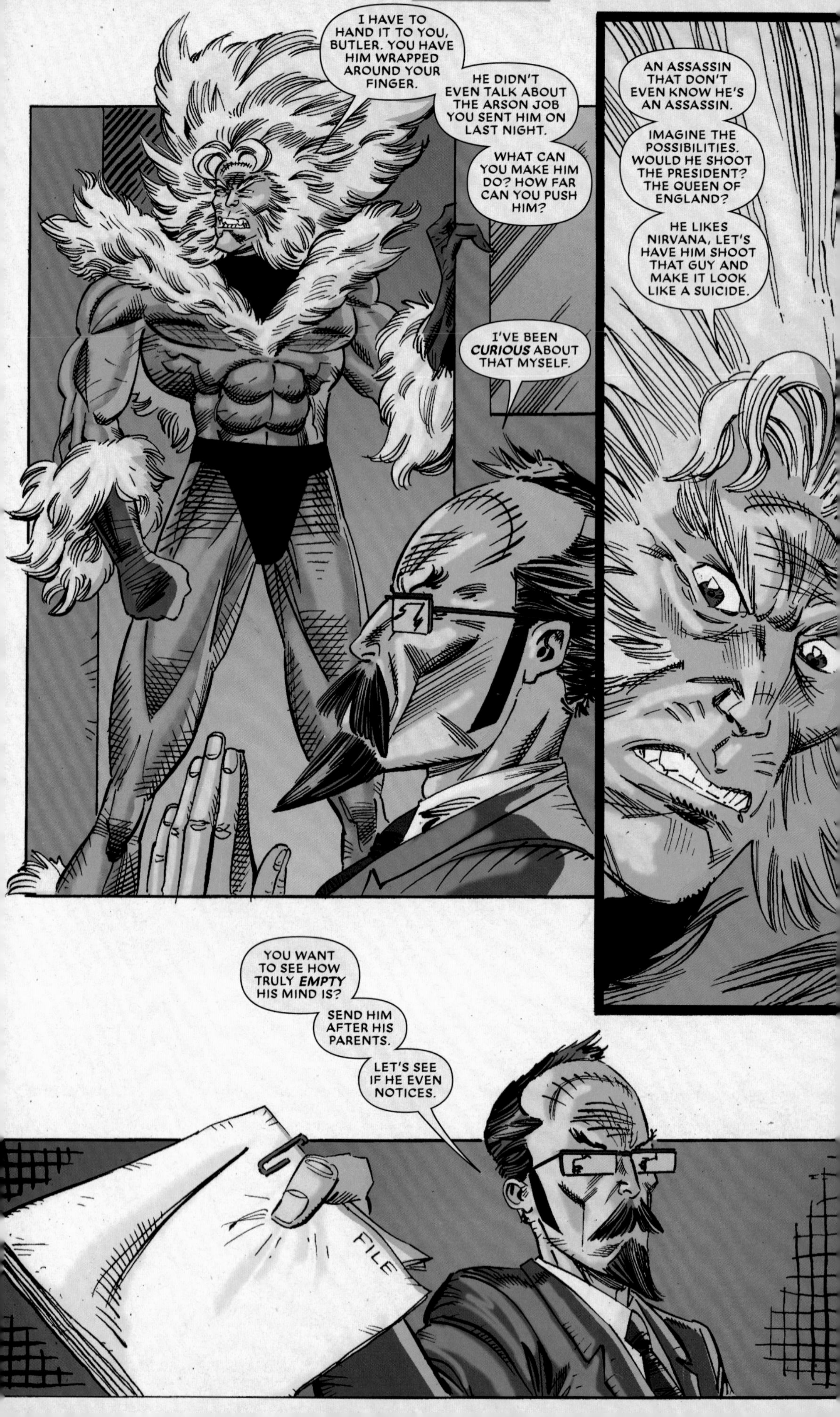

I HAVE TO HAND IT TO YOU, BUTLER. YOU HAVE HIM WRAPPED AROUND YOUR FINGER.
HE DIDN'T EVEN TALK ABOUT THE ARSON JOB YOU SENT HIM ON LAST NIGHT.
WHAT CAN YOU MAKE HIM DO? HOW FAR CAN YOU PUSH HIM?
I'VE BEEN *CURIOUS* ABOUT THAT MYSELF.
AN ASSASSIN THAT DON'T EVEN KNOW HE'S AN ASSASSIN.
IMAGINE THE POSSIBILITIES. WOULD HE SHOOT THE PRESIDENT? THE QUEEN OF ENGLAND?
HE LIKES NIRVANA, LET'S HAVE HIM SHOOT THAT GUY AND MAKE IT LOOK LIKE A SUICIDE.
YOU WANT TO SEE HOW TRULY *EMPTY* HIS MIND IS?
SEND HIM AFTER HIS PARENTS.
LET'S SEE IF HE EVEN NOTICES.
FILE

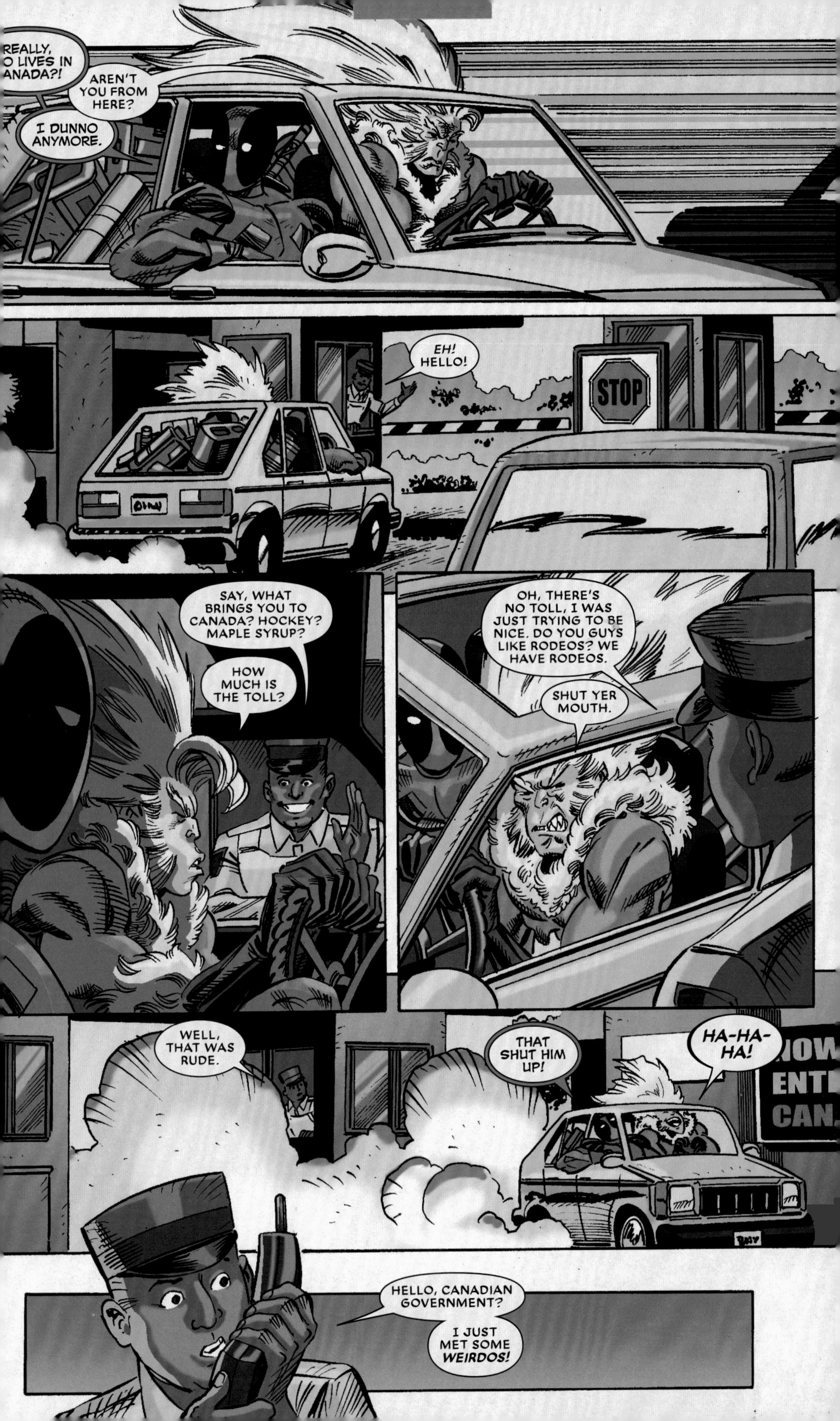
REALLY, O LIVES IN ANADA?!
AREN'T YOU FROM HERE?
I DUNNO ANYMORE.
EH! HELLO!
STOP
SAY, WHAT BRINGS YOU TO CANADA? HOCKEY? MAPLE SYRUP?
HOW MUCH IS THE TOLL?
OH, THERE'S NO TOLL, I WAS JUST TRYING TO BE NICE. DO YOU GUYS LIKE RODEOS? WE HAVE RODEOS.
SHUT YER MOUTH.
WELL, THAT WAS RUDE.
THAT SHUT HIM UP!
HA-HA-HA!
HELLO, CANADIAN GOVERNMENT?
I JUST MET SOME WEIRDOS!

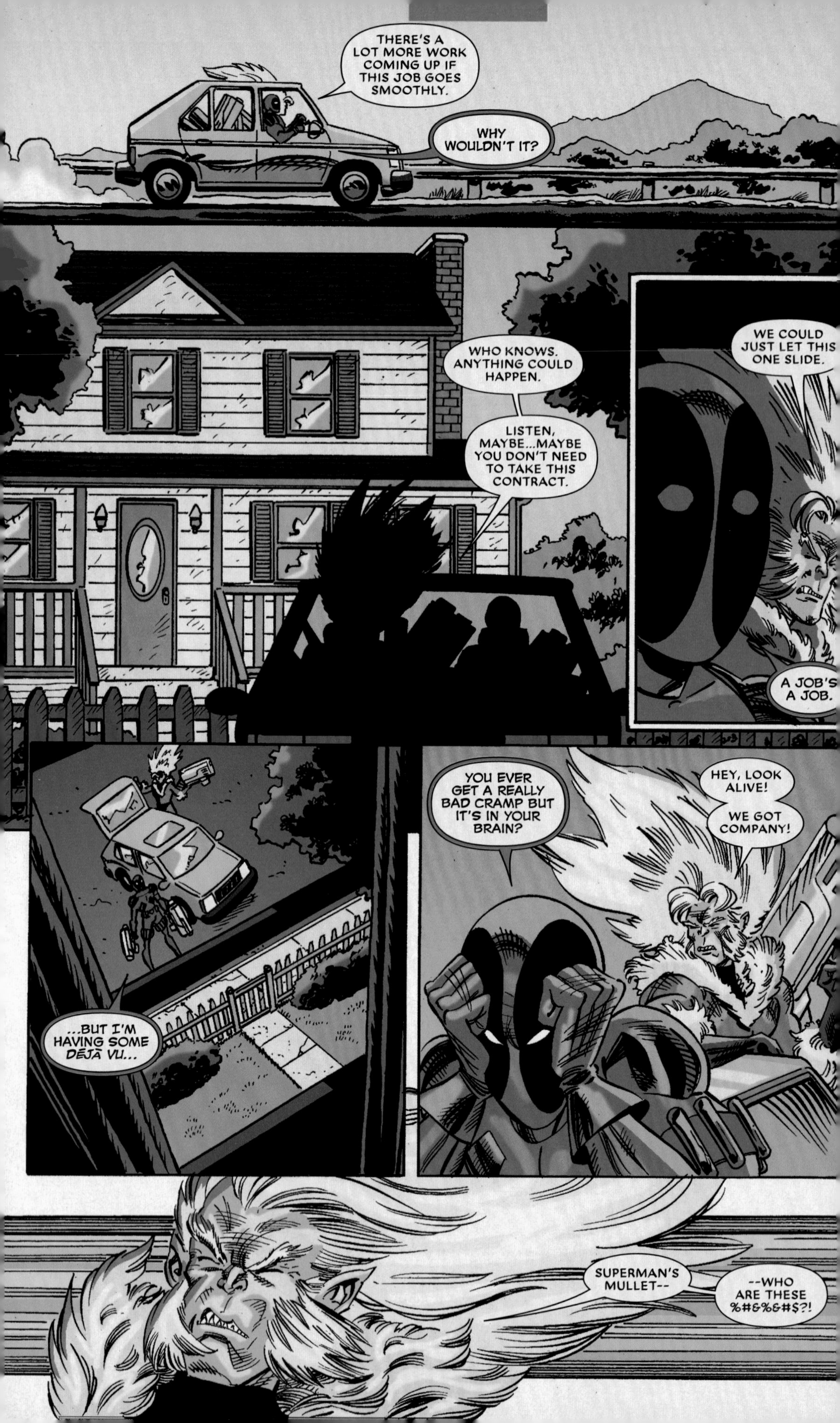

THERE'S A LOT MORE WORK COMING UP IF THIS JOB GOES SMOOTHLY.
WHY WOULDN'T IT?
WHO KNOWS. ANYTHING COULD HAPPEN.
LISTEN, MAYBE...MAYBE YOU DON'T NEED TO TAKE THIS CONTRACT.
WE COULD JUST LET THIS ONE SLIDE.
A JOB'S A JOB.
...BUT I'M HAVING SOME DÉJÀ VU...
YOU EVER GET A REALLY BAD CRAMP BUT IT'S IN YOUR BRAIN?
HEY, LOOK ALIVE!
WE GOT COMPANY!
SUPERMAN'S MULLET--
--WHO ARE THESE %#&%&#$?!

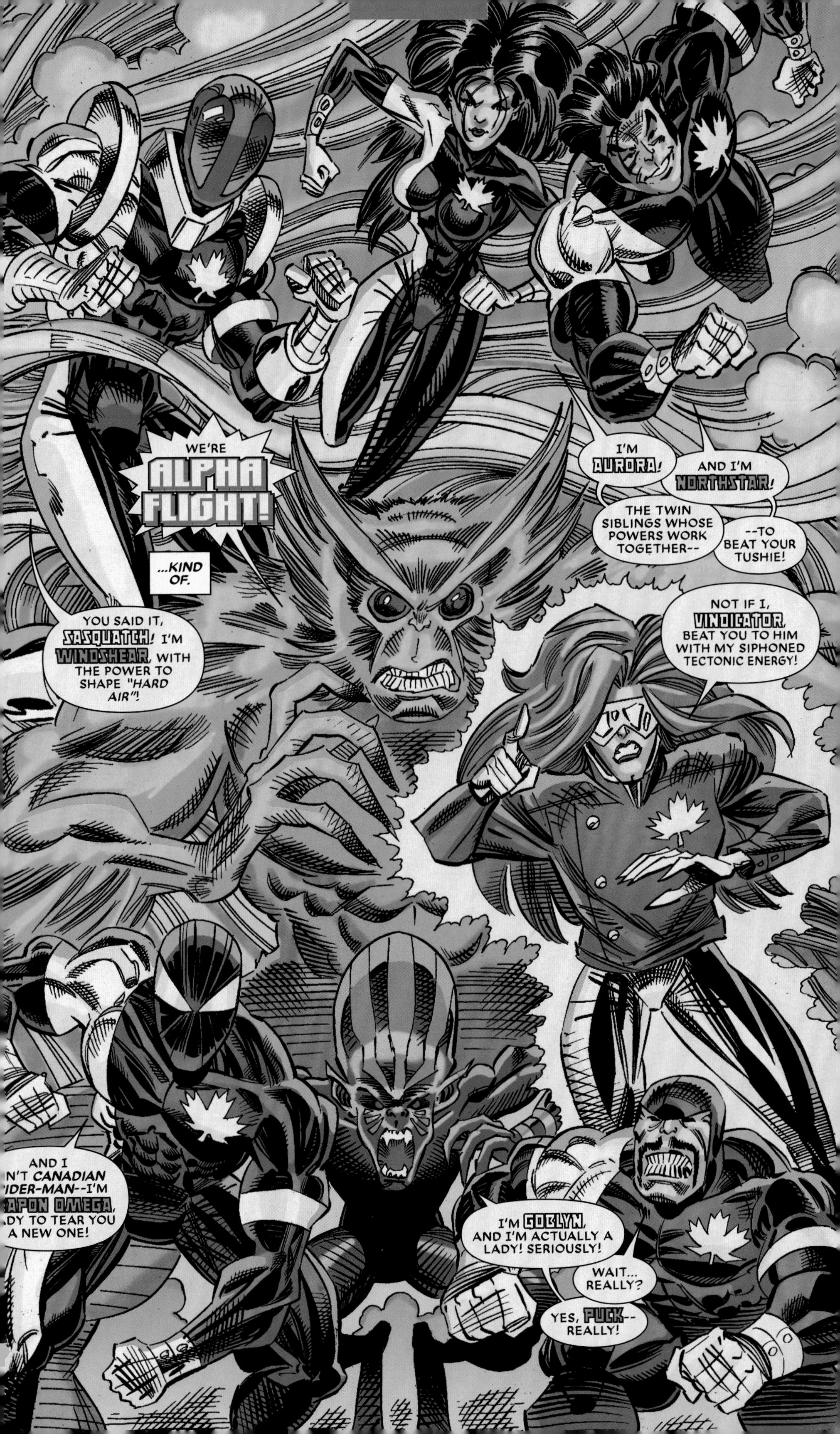

WE'RE ALPHA FLIGHT!
...KIND OF.
YOU SAID IT, SASQUATCH! I'M WINDSHEAR, WITH THE POWER TO SHAPE "HARD AIR"!
I'M AURORA!
AND I'M NORTHSTAR!
THE TWIN SIBLINGS WHOSE POWERS WORK TOGETHER--
--TO BEAT YOUR TUSHIE!
NOT IF I, VINDICATOR, BEAT YOU TO HIM WITH MY SIPHONED TECTONIC ENERGY!
AND I N'T CANADIAN IDER-MAN--I'M APON OMEGA, DY TO TEAR YOU A NEW ONE!
I'M GOBLYN, AND I'M ACTUALLY A LADY! SERIOUSLY!
WAIT... REALLY?
YES, PUCK--REALLY!

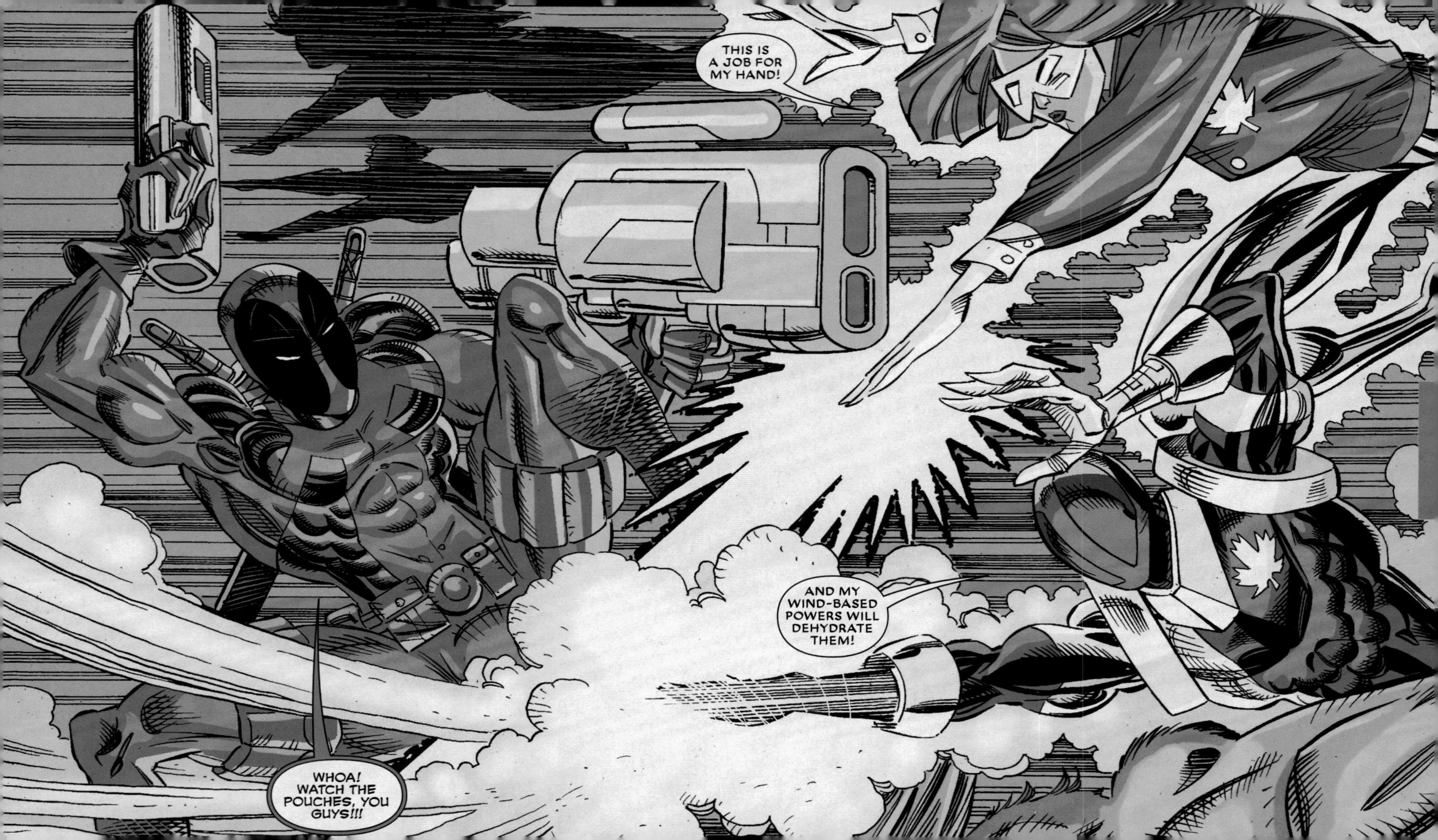
THIS IS A JOB FOR MY HAND!
AND MY WIND-BASED POWERS WILL DEHYDRATE THEM!
WHOA! WATCH THE POUCHES, YOU GUYS!!!

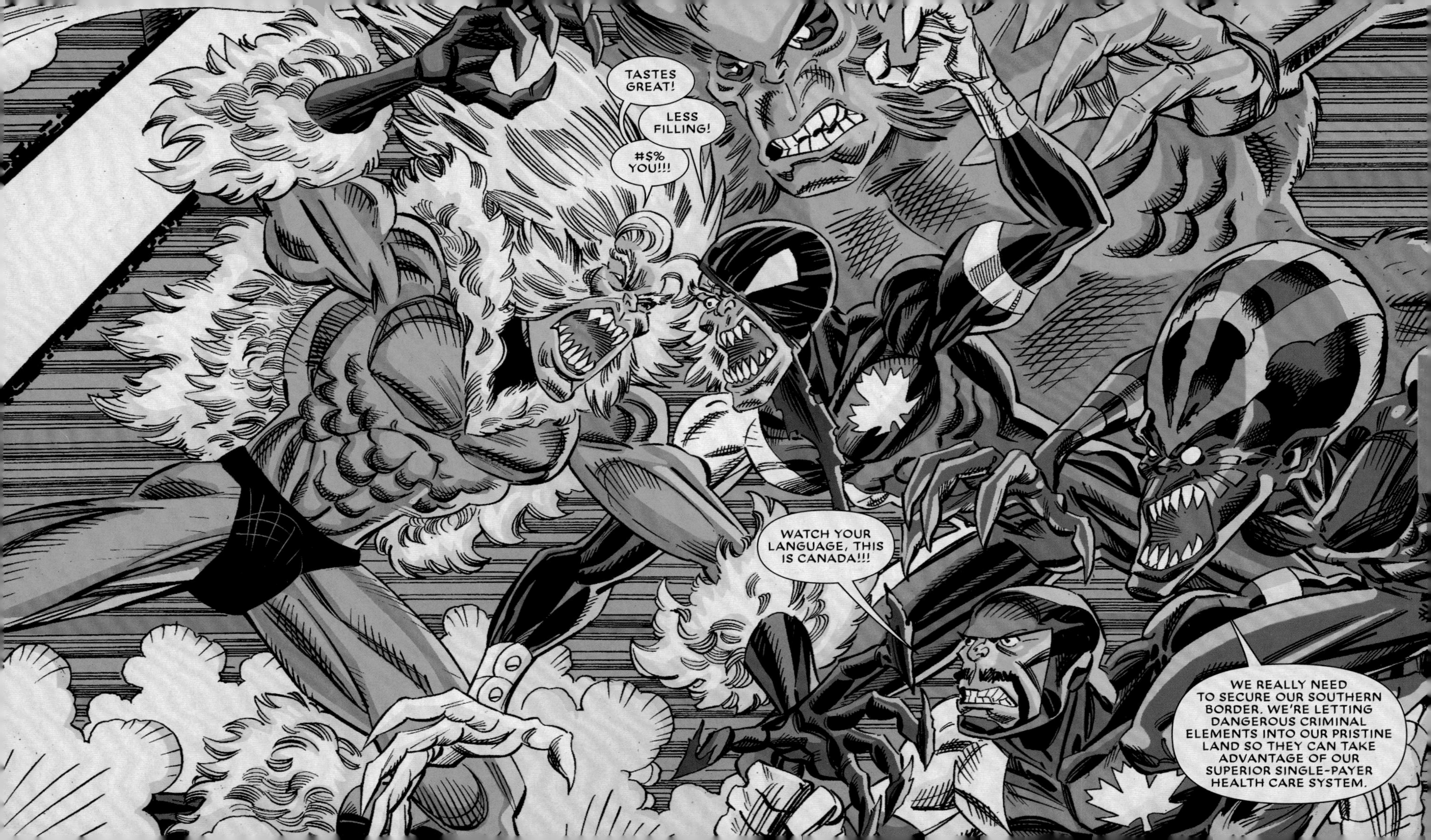
TASTES GREAT!
LESS FILLING!
#$% YOU!!!
WATCH YOUR LANGUAGE, THIS IS CANADA!!!
WE REALLY NEED TO SECURE OUR SOUTHERN BORDER. WE'RE LETTING DANGEROUS CRIMINAL ELEMENTS INTO OUR PRISTINE LAND SO THEY CAN TAKE ADVANTAGE OF OUR SUPERIOR SINGLE-PAYER HEALTH CARE SYSTEM.

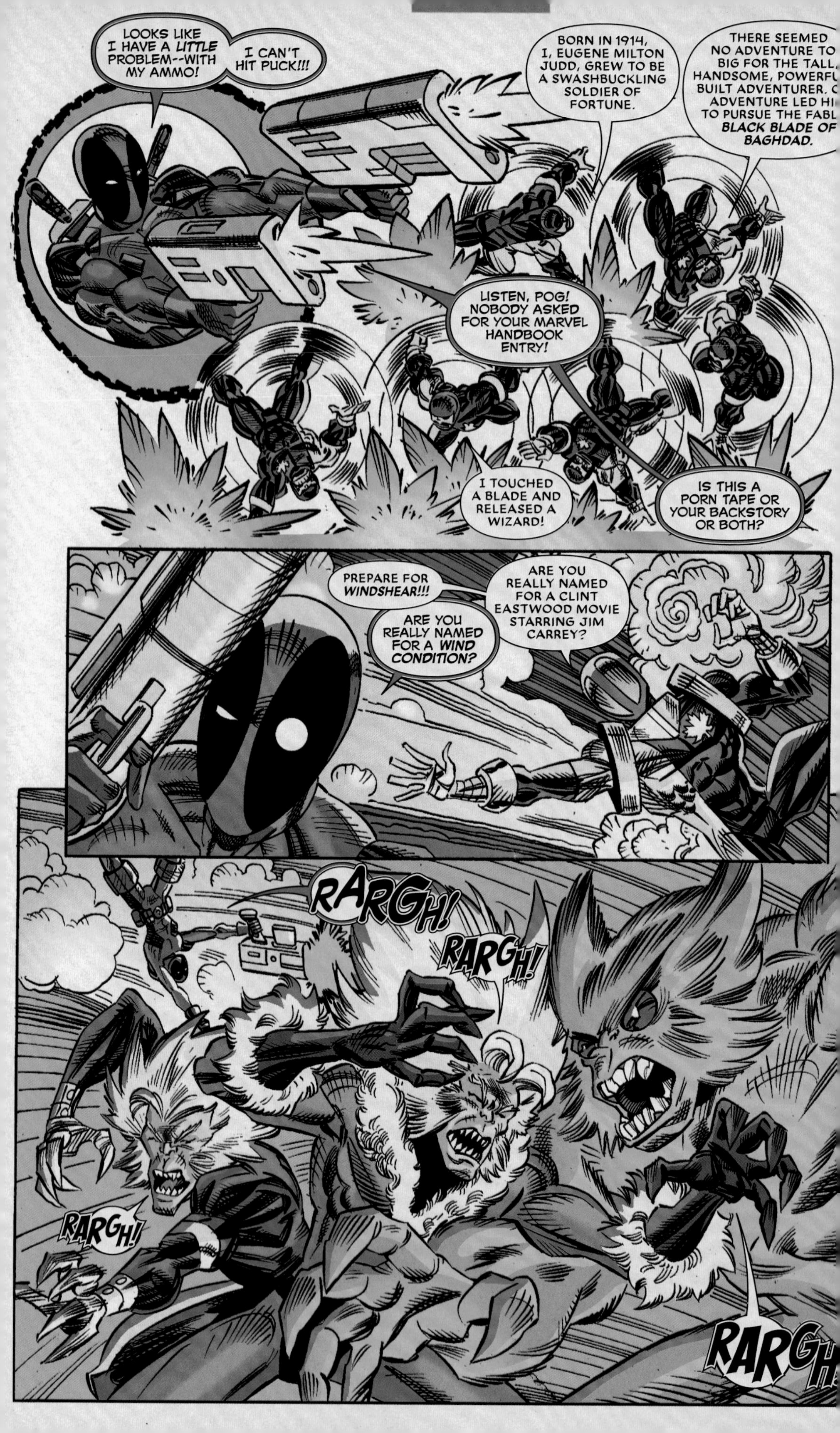
LOOKS LIKE I HAVE A LITTLE PROBLEM--WITH MY AMMO!
I CAN'T HIT PUCK!!!
BORN IN 1914, I, EUGENE MILTON JUDD, GREW TO BE A SWASHBUCKLING SOLDIER OF FORTUNE.
LISTEN, POG! NOBODY ASKED FOR YOUR MARVEL HANDBOOK ENTRY!
I TOUCHED A BLADE AND RELEASED A WIZARD!
IS THIS A PORN TAPE OR YOUR BACKSTORY OR BOTH?
PREPARE FOR WINDSHEAR!!!
ARE YOU REALLY NAMED FOR A WIND CONDITION?
ARE YOU REALLY NAMED FOR A CLINT EASTWOOD MOVIE STARRING JIM CARREY?
RARGH!
RARGH!
RARGH!

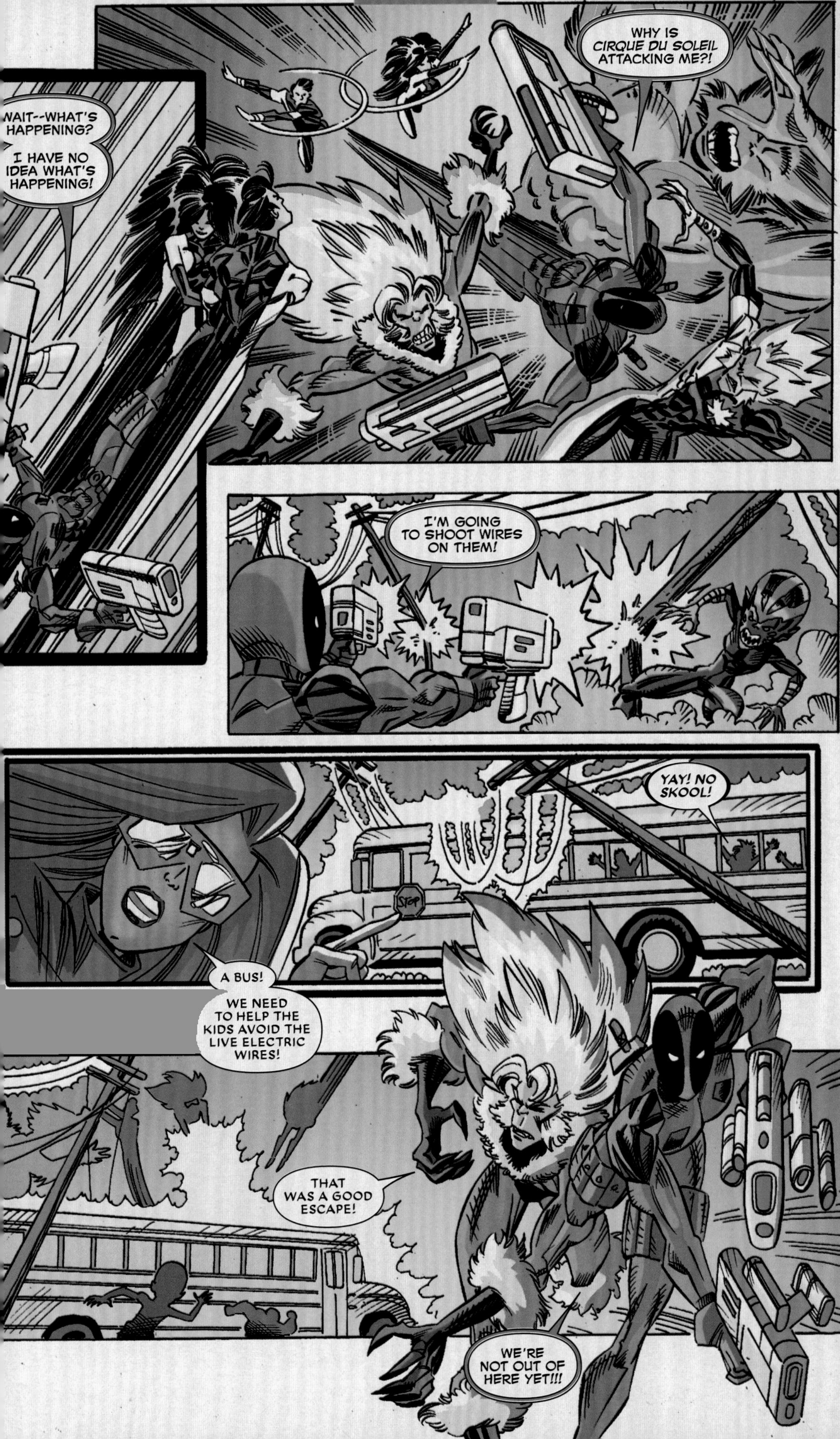
WAIT--WHAT'S HAPPENING?
I HAVE NO IDEA WHAT'S HAPPENING!
WHY IS CIRQUE DU SOLEIL ATTACKING ME?!
I'M GOING TO SHOOT WIRES ON THEM!
YAY! NO SKOOL!
A BUS!
WE NEED TO HELP THE KIDS AVOID THE LIVE ELECTRIC WIRES!
THAT WAS A GOOD ESCAPE!
WE'RE NOT OUT OF HERE YET!!!

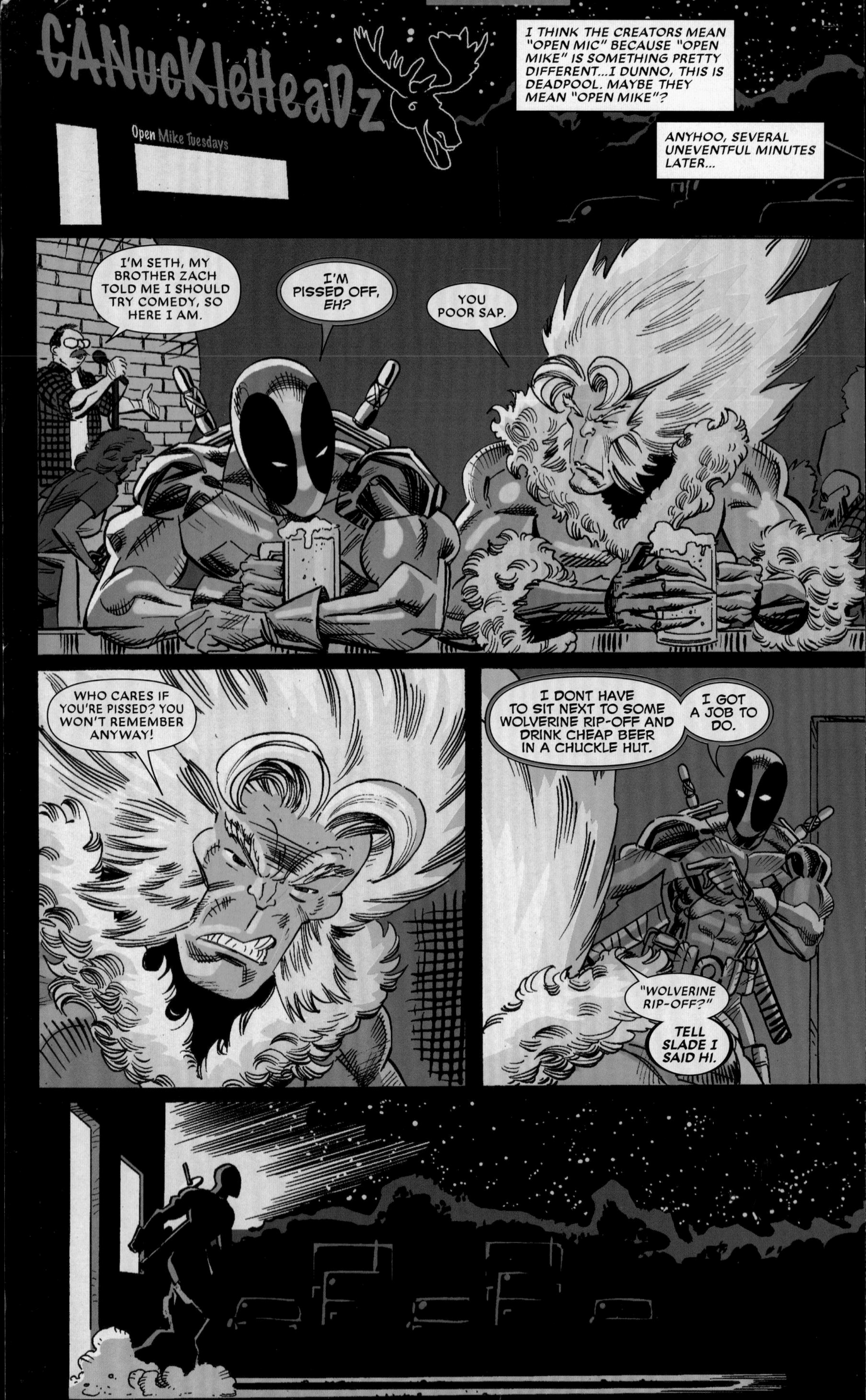
CANucKleHeaDz
Open Mike Tuesdays
I THINK THE CREATORS MEAN "OPEN MIC" BECAUSE "OPEN MIKE" IS SOMETHING PRETTY DIFFERENT...I DUNNO, THIS IS DEADPOOL. MAYBE THEY MEAN "OPEN MIKE"?
ANYHOO, SEVERAL UNEVENTFUL MINUTES LATER...
I'M SETH, MY BROTHER ZACH TOLD ME I SHOULD TRY COMEDY, SO HERE I AM.
I'M PISSED OFF, EH?
YOU POOR SAP.
WHO CARES IF YOU'RE PISSED? YOU WON'T REMEMBER ANYWAY!
I DONT HAVE TO SIT NEXT TO SOME WOLVERINE RIP-OFF AND DRINK CHEAP BEER IN A CHUCKLE HUT.
I GOT A JOB TO DO.
"WOLVERINE RIP-OFF?"
TELL SLADE I SAID HI.

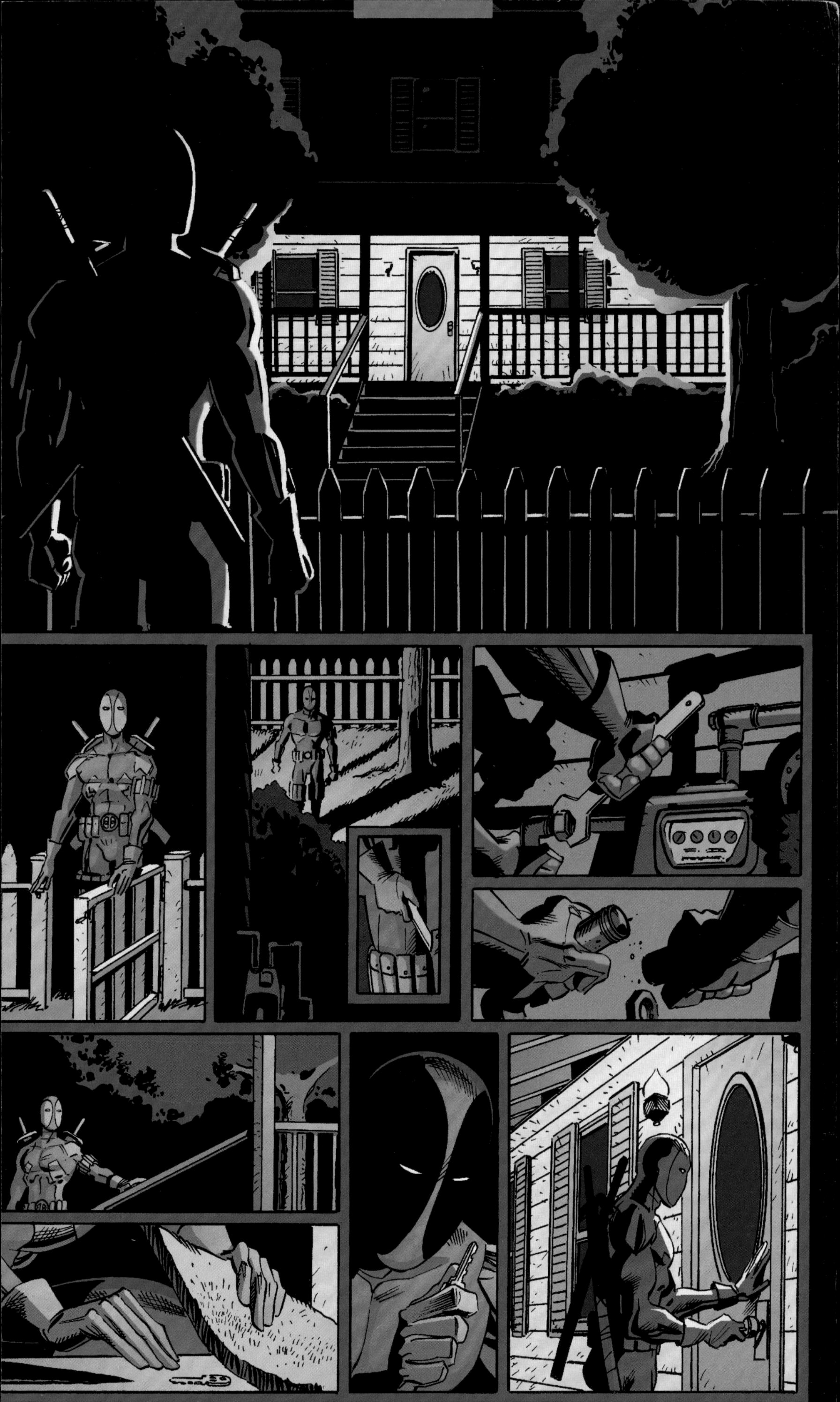

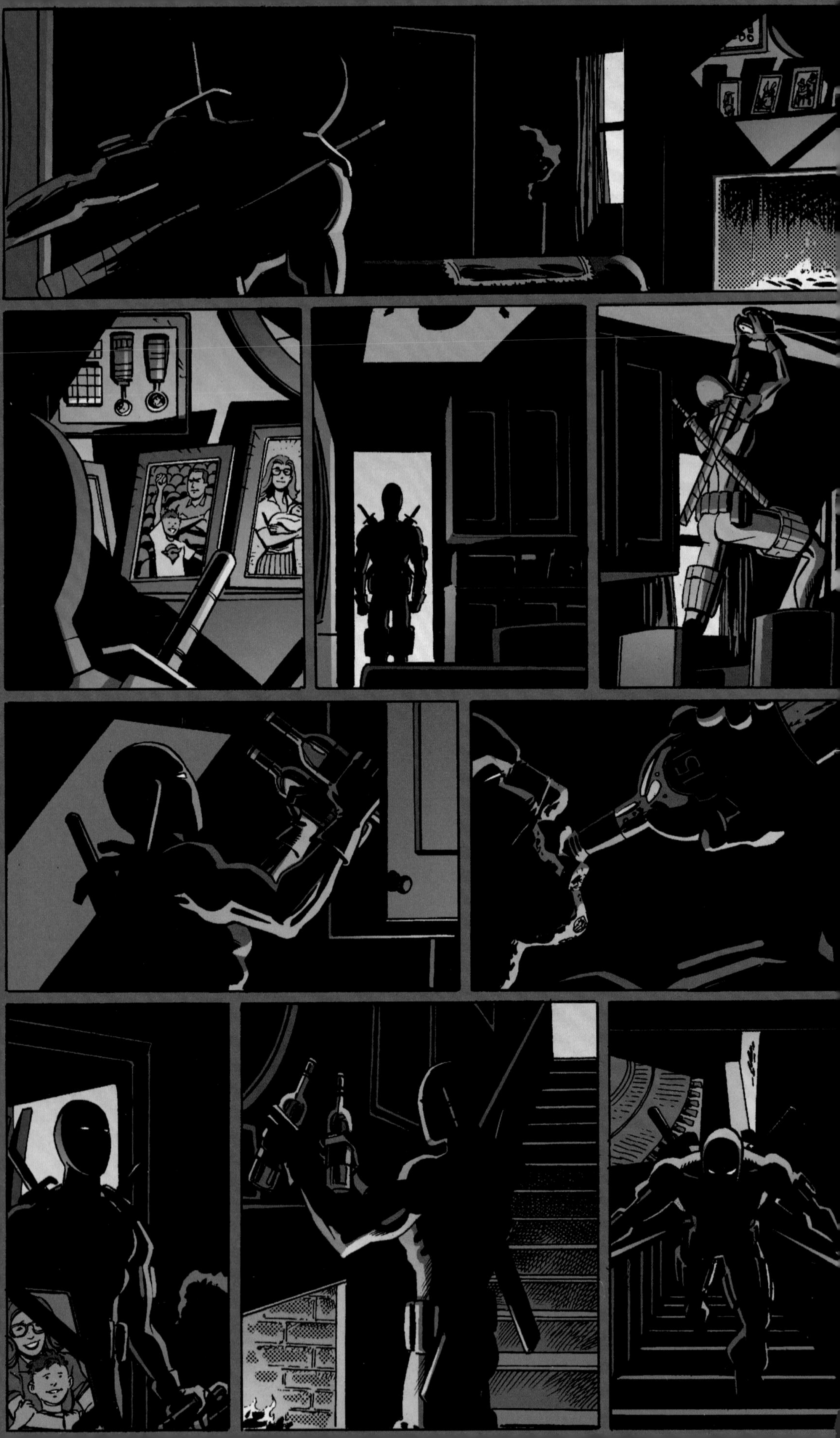

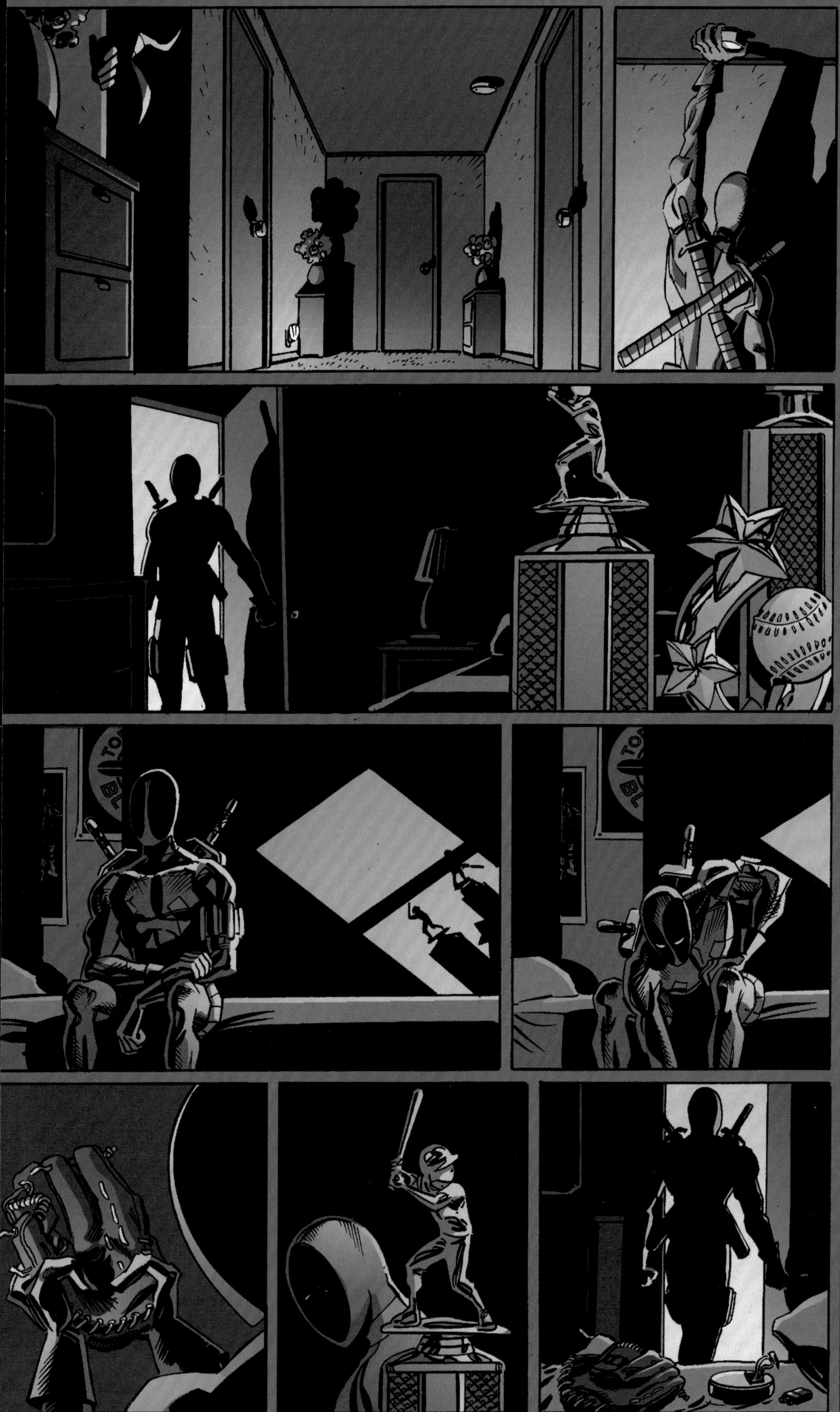

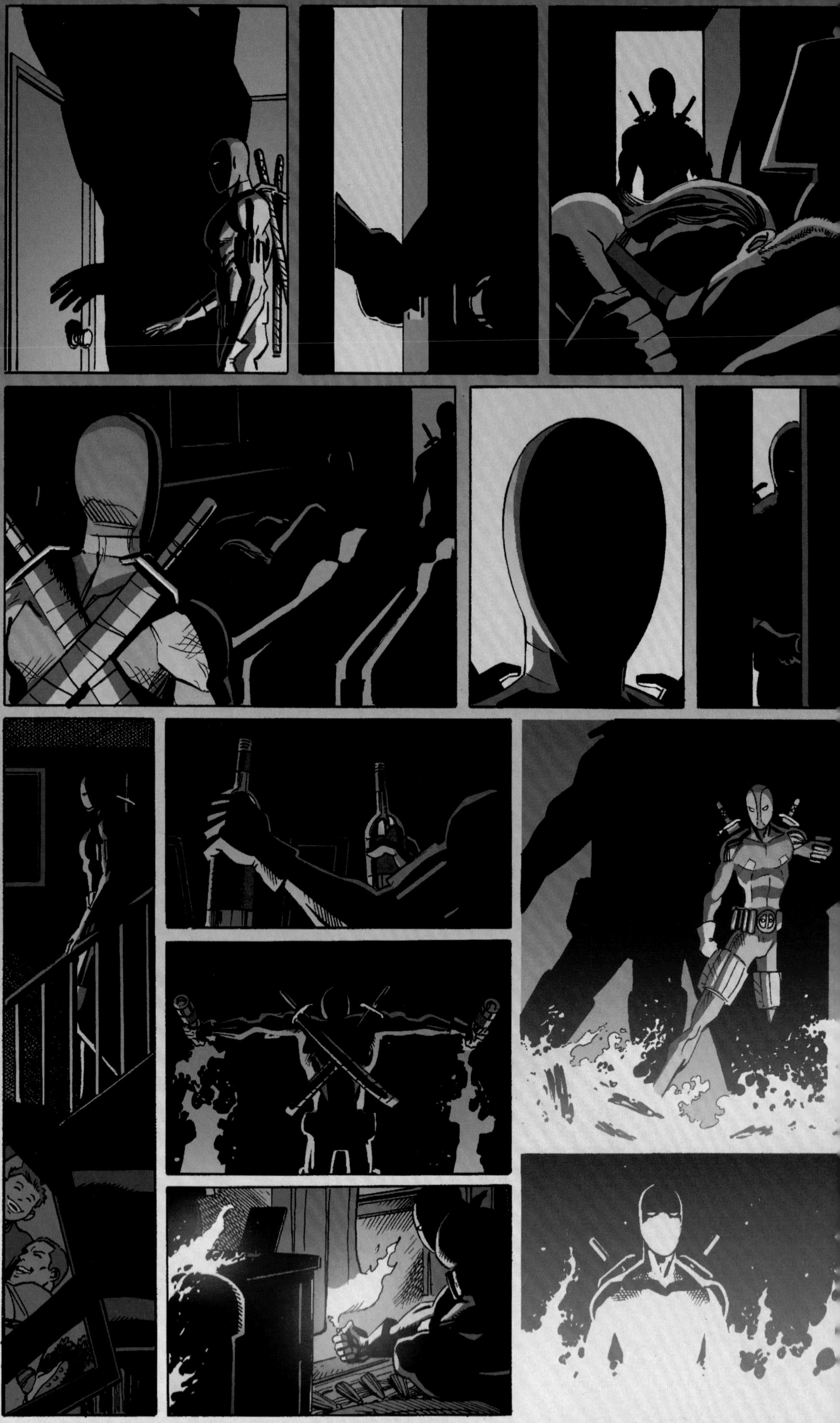

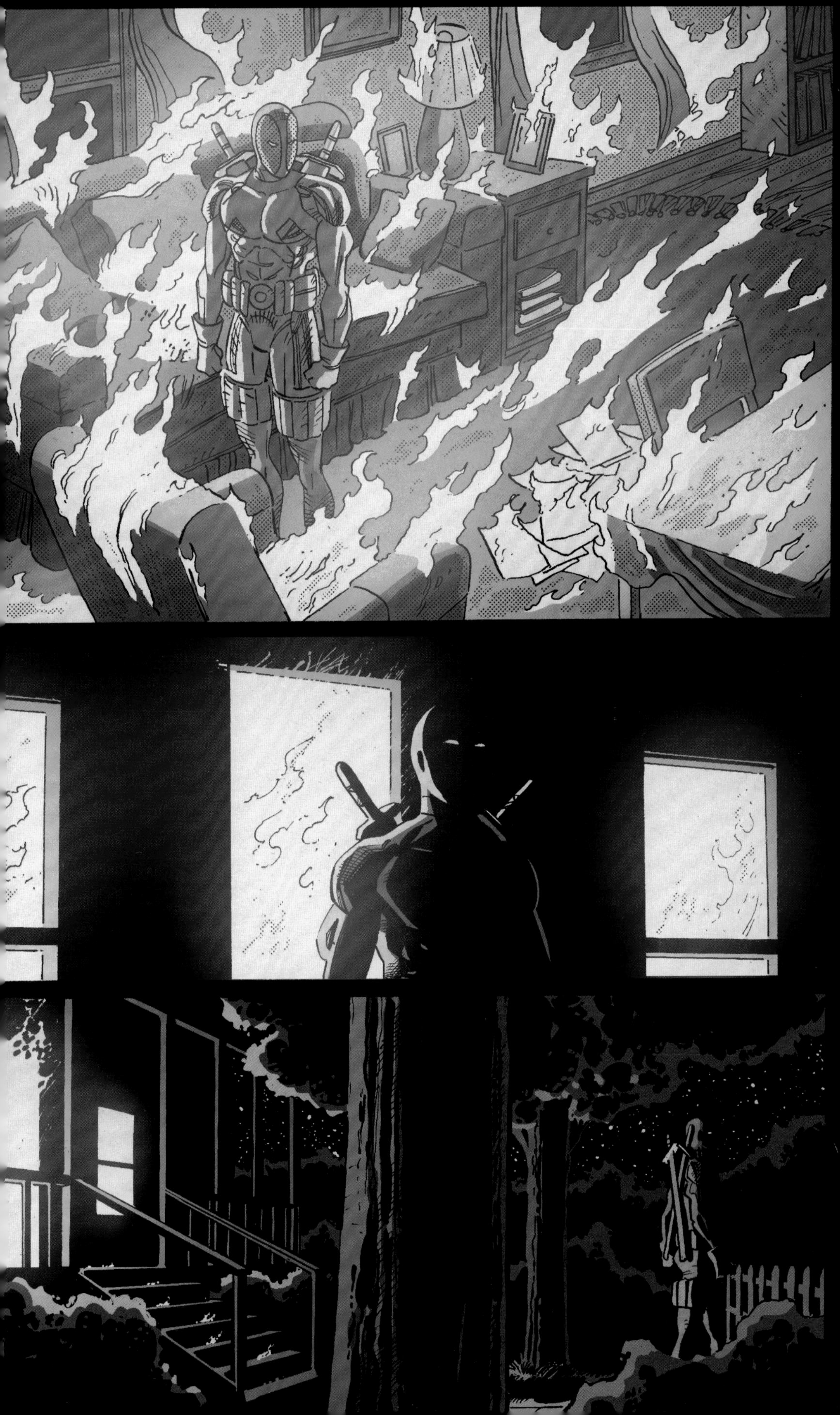

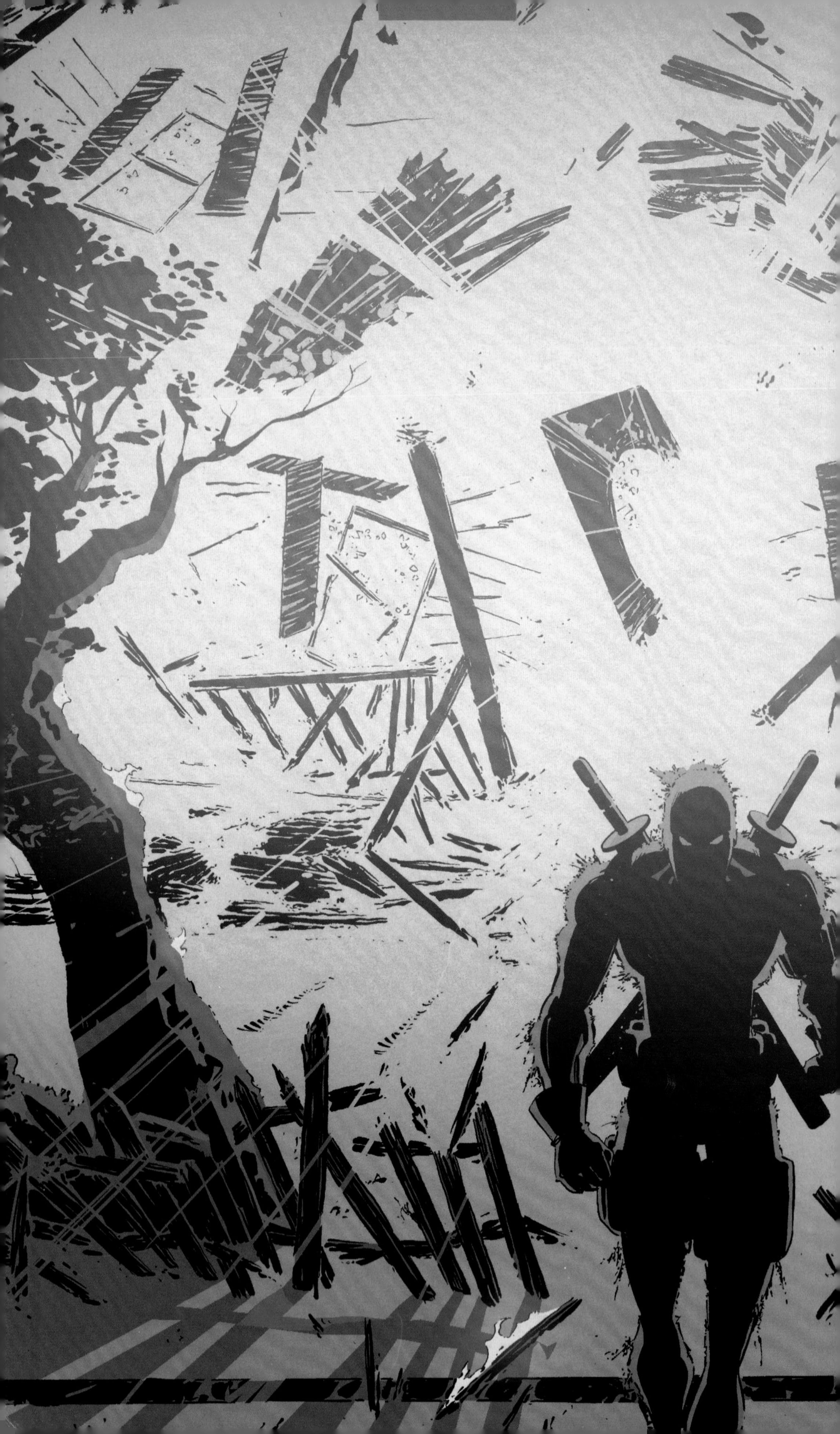

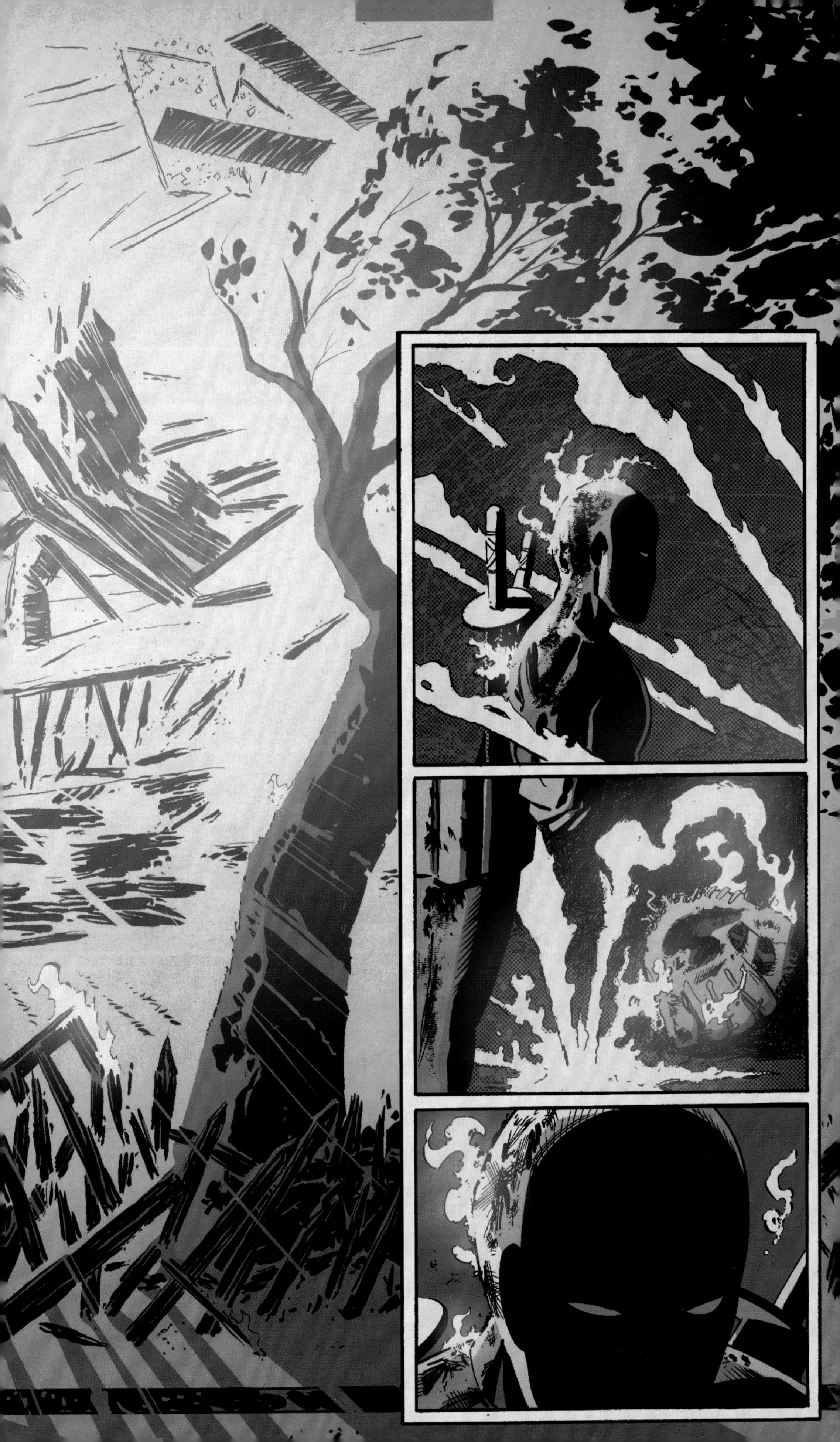

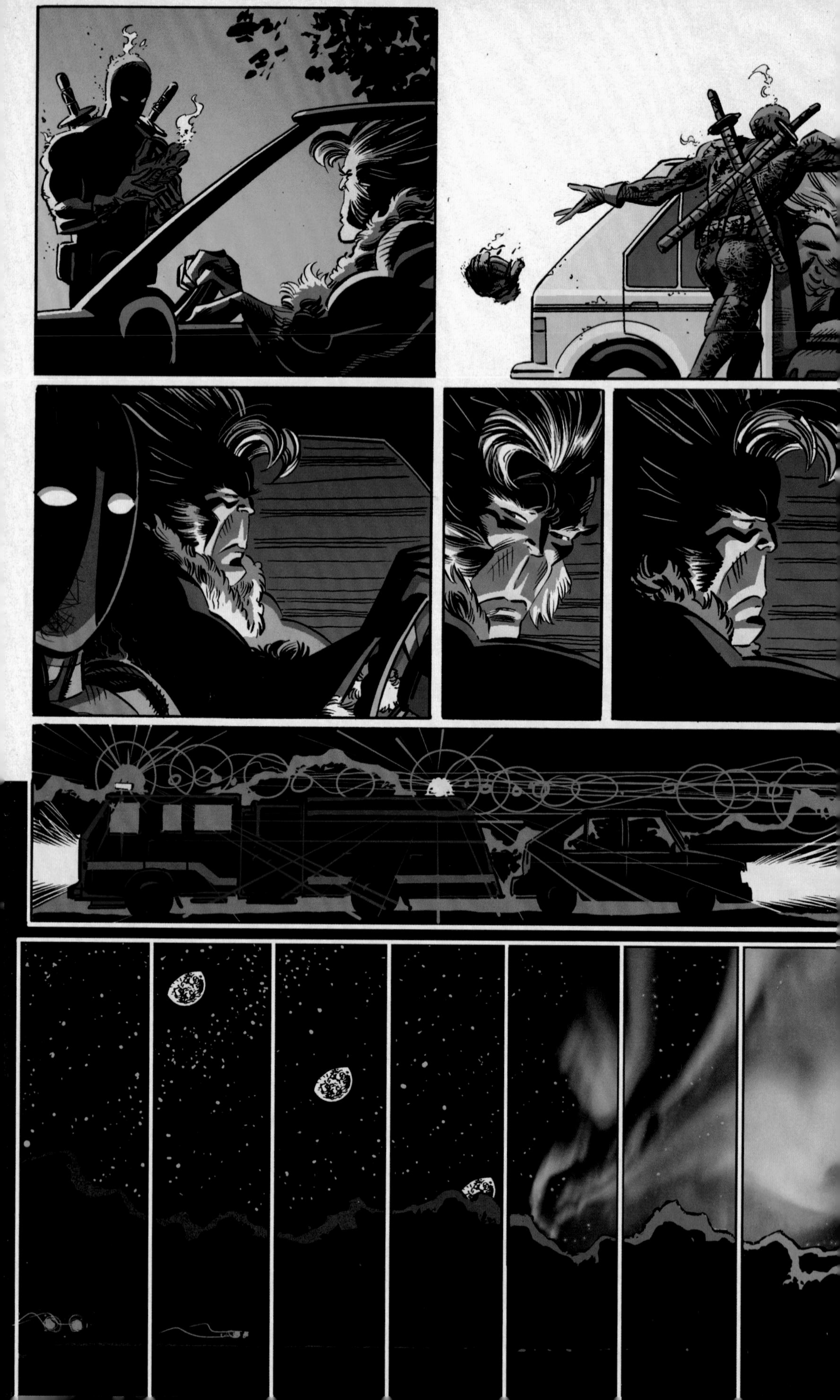

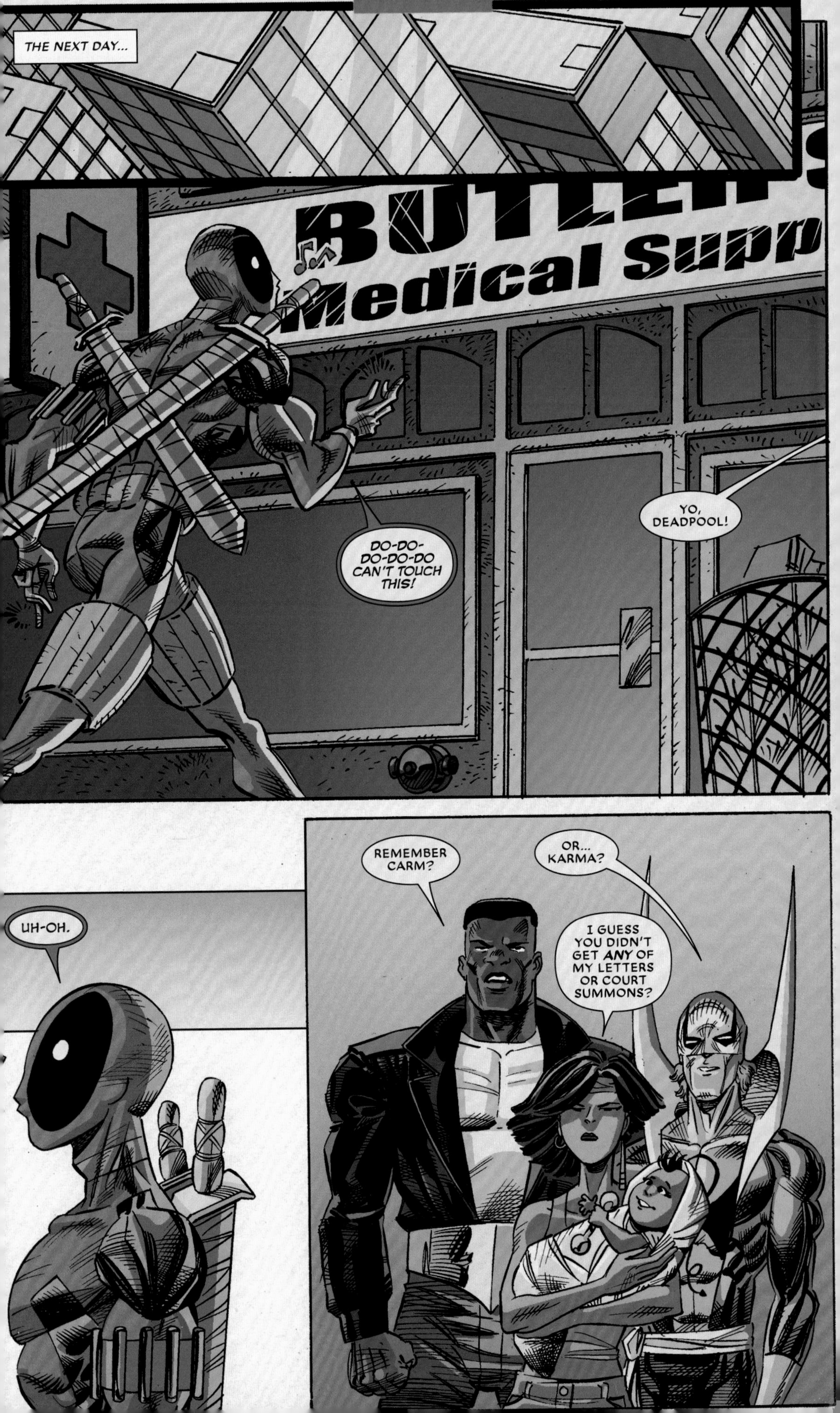
THE NEXT DAY...
BUTLER'S
Medical Supp
DO-DO-DO-DO-DO CAN'T TOUCH THIS!
YO, DEADPOOL!
UH-OH.
REMEMBER CARM?
OR... KARMA?
I GUESS YOU DIDN'T GET ANY OF MY LETTERS OR COURT SUMMONS?

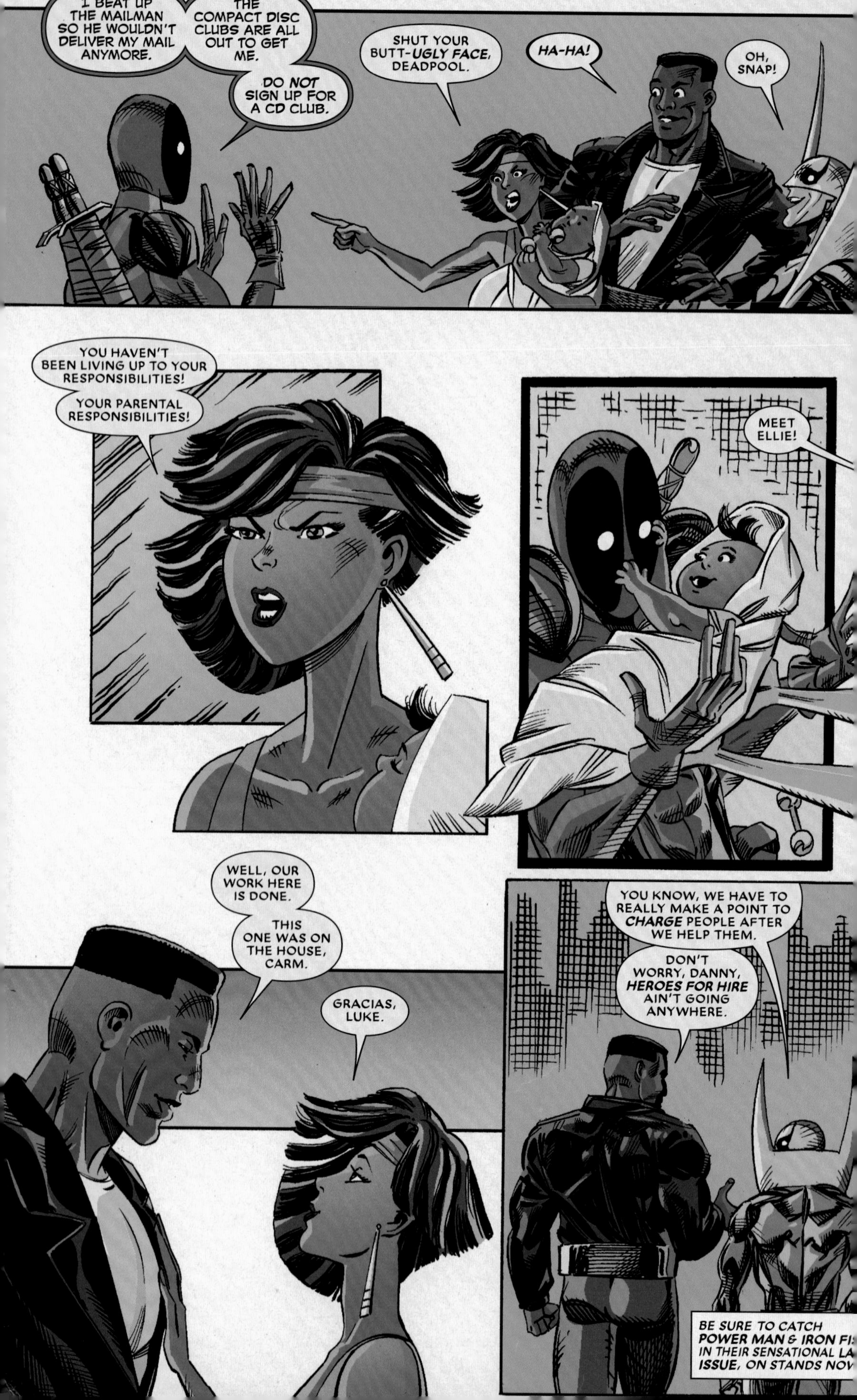
I BEAT UP THE MAILMAN SO HE WOULDN'T DELIVER MY MAIL ANYMORE.
THE COMPACT DISC CLUBS ARE ALL OUT TO GET ME.
DO NOT SIGN UP FOR A CD CLUB.
SHUT YOUR BUTT-UGLY FACE, DEADPOOL.
HA-HA!
OH, SNAP!
YOU HAVEN'T BEEN LIVING UP TO YOUR RESPONSIBILITIES!
YOUR PARENTAL RESPONSIBILITIES!
MEET ELLIE!
WELL, OUR WORK HERE IS DONE.
THIS ONE WAS ON THE HOUSE, CARM.
GRACIAS, LUKE.
YOU KNOW, WE HAVE TO REALLY MAKE A POINT TO CHARGE PEOPLE AFTER WE HELP THEM.
DON'T WORRY, DANNY, HEROES FOR HIRE AIN'T GOING ANYWHERE.
BE SURE TO CATCH POWER MAN & IRON FI IN THEIR SENSATIONAL LA ISSUE, ON STANDS NOV

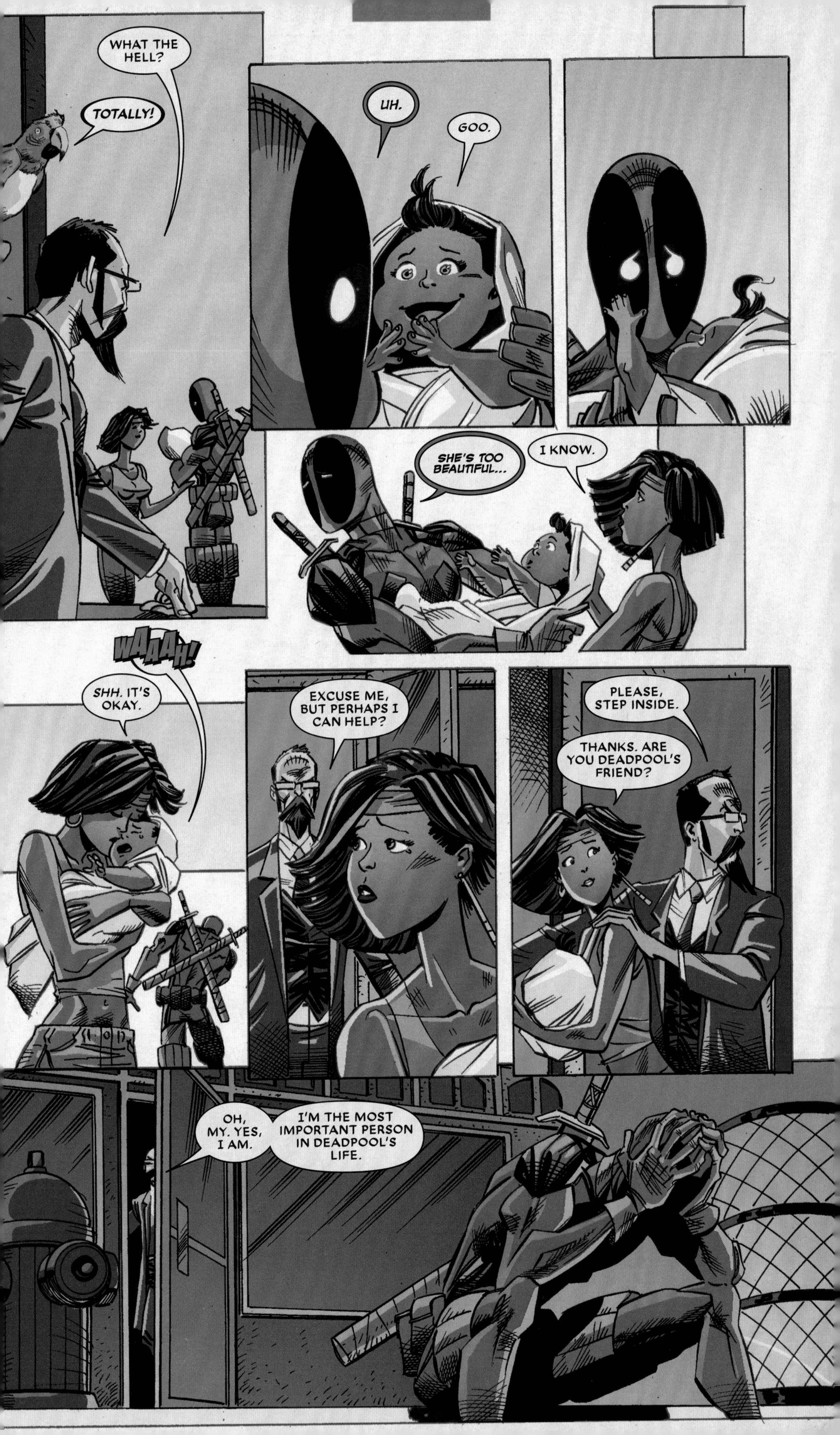
WHAT THE HELL?
TOTALLY!
UH.
GOO.
SHE'S TOO BEAUTIFUL...
I KNOW.
WAAAH!
SHH. IT'S OKAY.
EXCUSE ME, BUT PERHAPS I CAN HELP?
PLEASE, STEP INSIDE.
THANKS. ARE YOU DEADPOOL'S FRIEND?
OH, MY. YES, I AM.
I'M THE MOST IMPORTANT PERSON IN DEADPOOL'S LIFE.

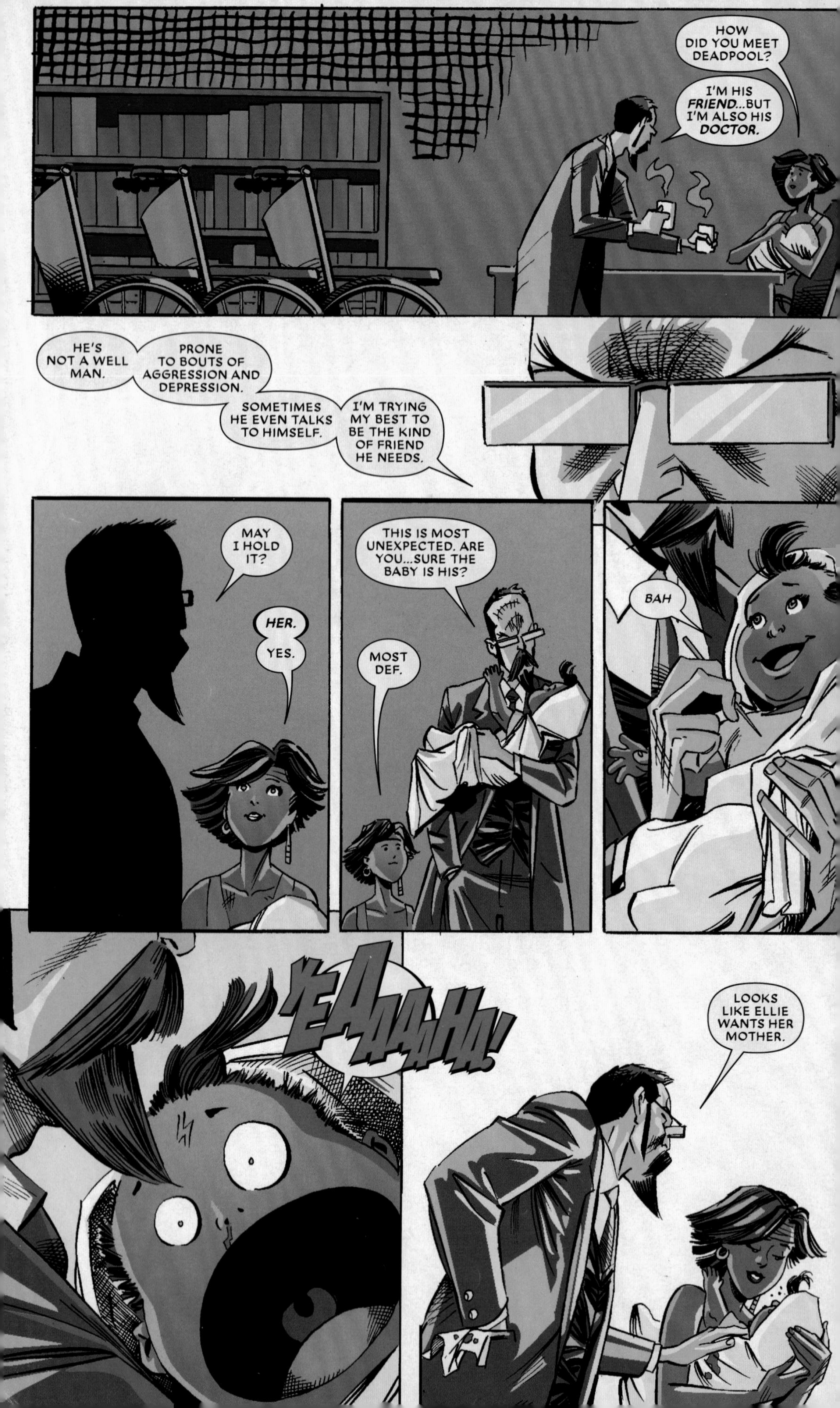
HOW DID YOU MEET DEADPOOL?
I'M HIS *FRIEND*...BUT I'M ALSO HIS *DOCTOR.*
HE'S NOT A WELL MAN.
PRONE TO BOUTS OF AGGRESSION AND DEPRESSION.
SOMETIMES HE EVEN TALKS TO HIMSELF.
I'M TRYING MY BEST TO BE THE KIND OF FRIEND HE NEEDS.
MAY I HOLD IT?
HER.
YES.
THIS IS MOST UNEXPECTED. ARE YOU...SURE THE BABY IS HIS?
MOST DEF.
BAH
YEAAAAHA!
LOOKS LIKE ELLIE WANTS HER MOTHER.

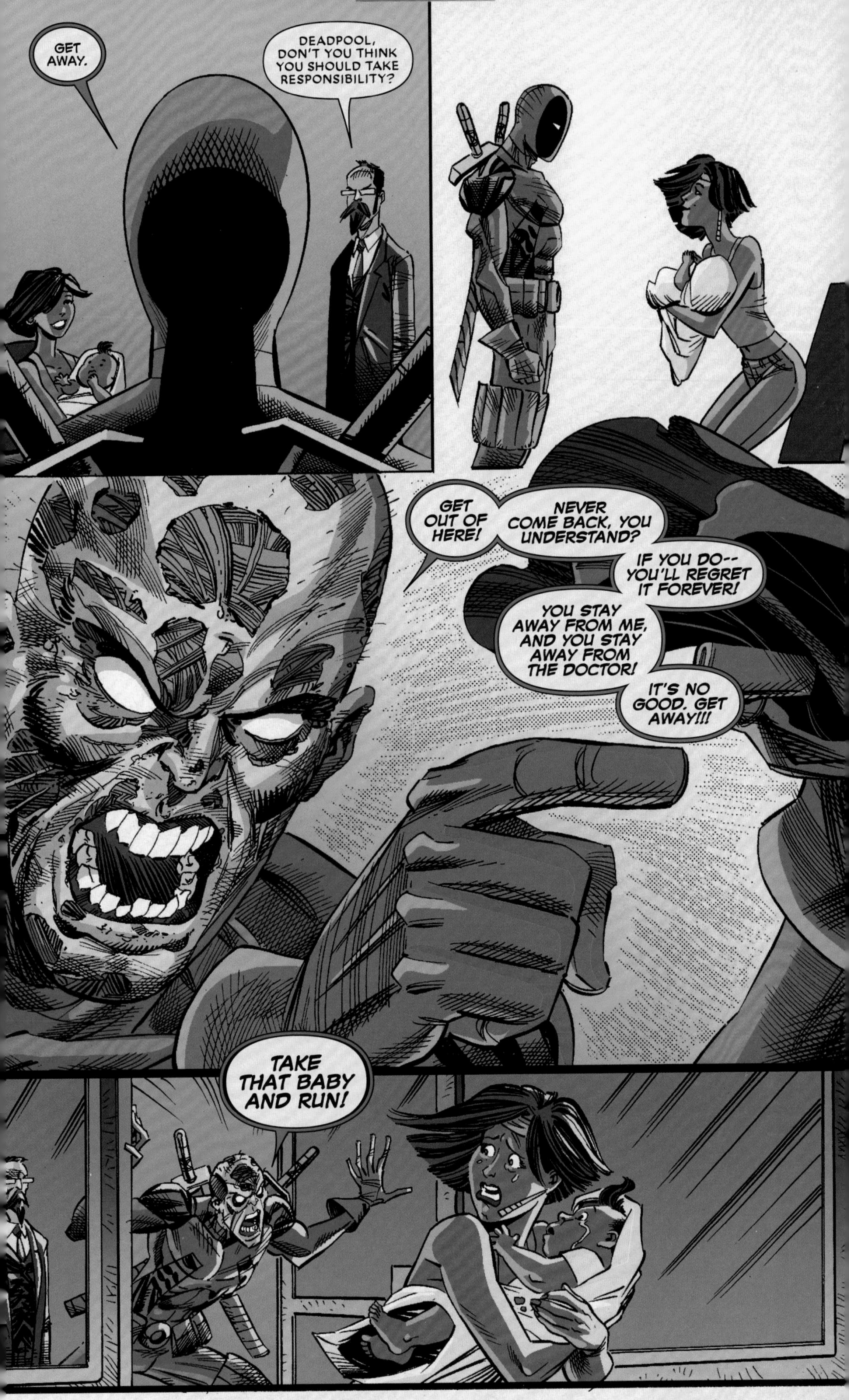
GET AWAY.
DEADPOOL, DON'T YOU THINK YOU SHOULD TAKE RESPONSIBILITY?
GET OUT OF HERE!
NEVER COME BACK, YOU UNDERSTAND?
IF YOU DO-- YOU'LL REGRET IT FOREVER!
YOU STAY AWAY FROM ME, AND YOU STAY AWAY FROM THE DOCTOR!
IT'S NO GOOD. GET AWAY!!!
TAKE THAT BABY AND RUN!

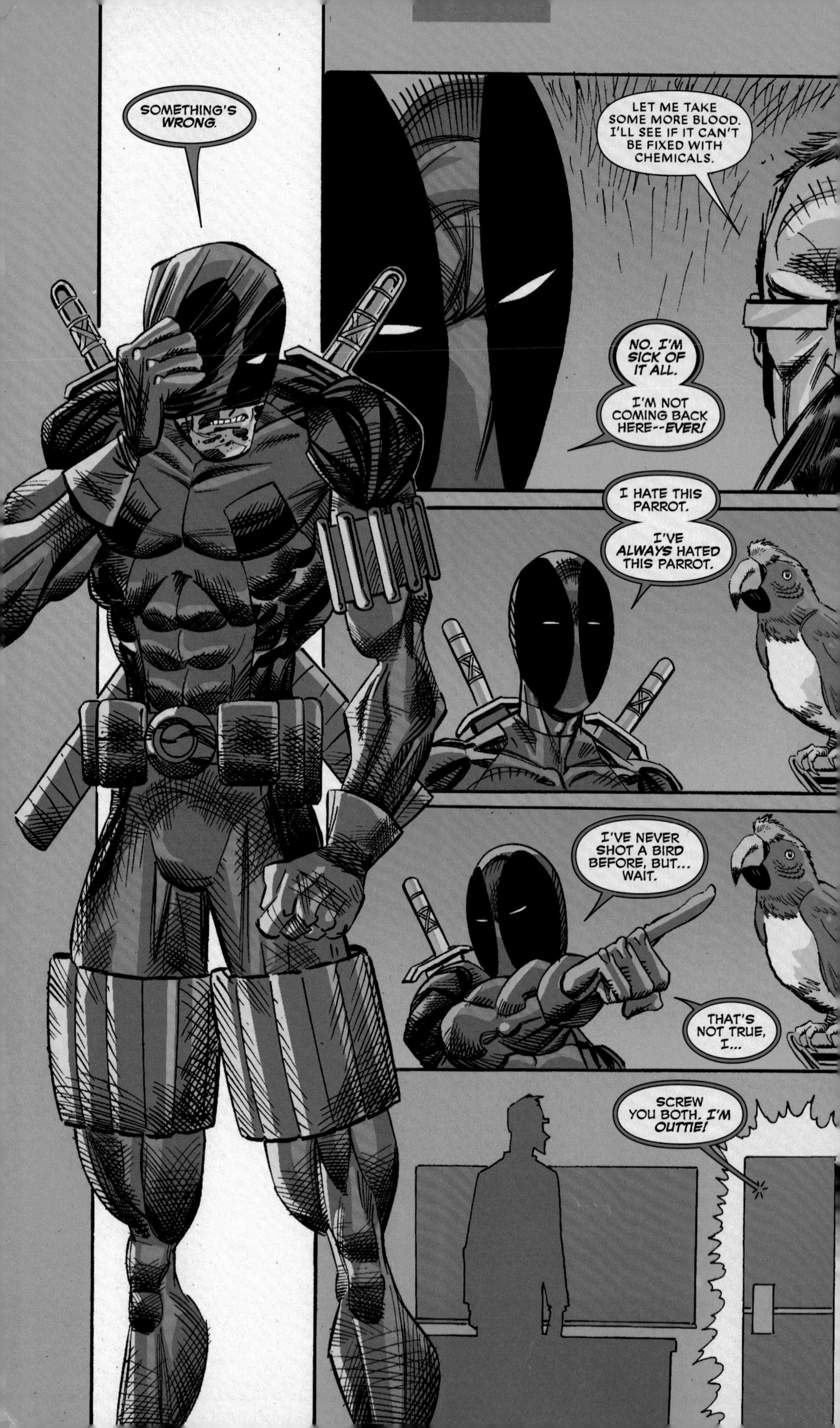
SOMETHING'S WRONG.
LET ME TAKE SOME MORE BLOOD. I'LL SEE IF IT CAN'T BE FIXED WITH CHEMICALS.
NO. I'M SICK OF IT ALL.
I'M NOT COMING BACK HERE--EVER!
I HATE THIS PARROT.
I'VE ALWAYS HATED THIS PARROT.
I'VE NEVER SHOT A BIRD BEFORE, BUT... WAIT.
THAT'S NOT TRUE, I...
SCREW YOU BOTH. I'M OUTTIE!

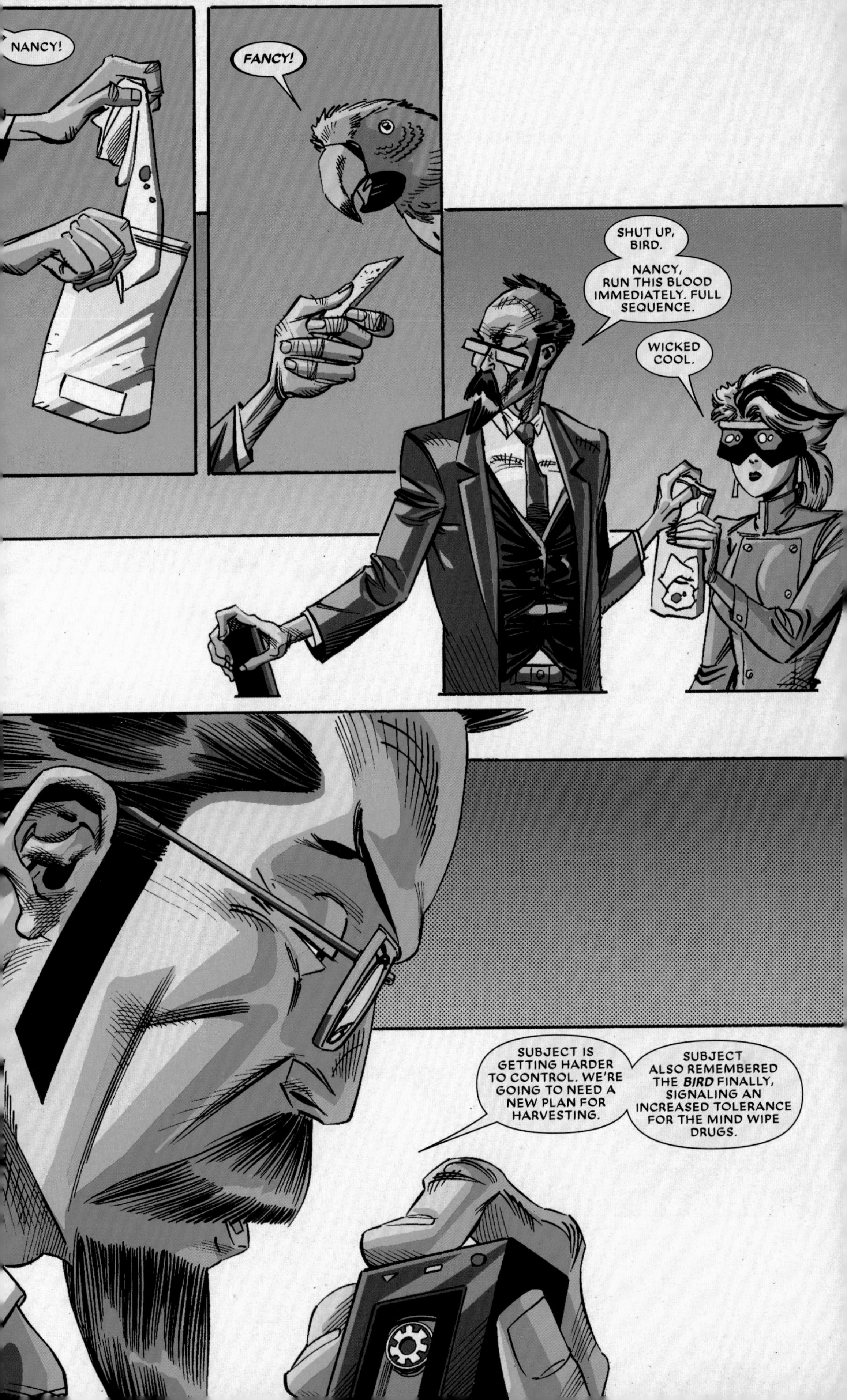
NANCY!
FANCY!
SHUT UP, BIRD.
NANCY, RUN THIS BLOOD IMMEDIATELY. FULL SEQUENCE.
WICKED COOL.
SUBJECT IS GETTING HARDER TO CONTROL. WE'RE GOING TO NEED A NEW PLAN FOR HARVESTING.
SUBJECT ALSO REMEMBERED THE *BIRD* FINALLY, SIGNALING AN INCREASED TOLERANCE FOR THE MIND WIPE DRUGS.

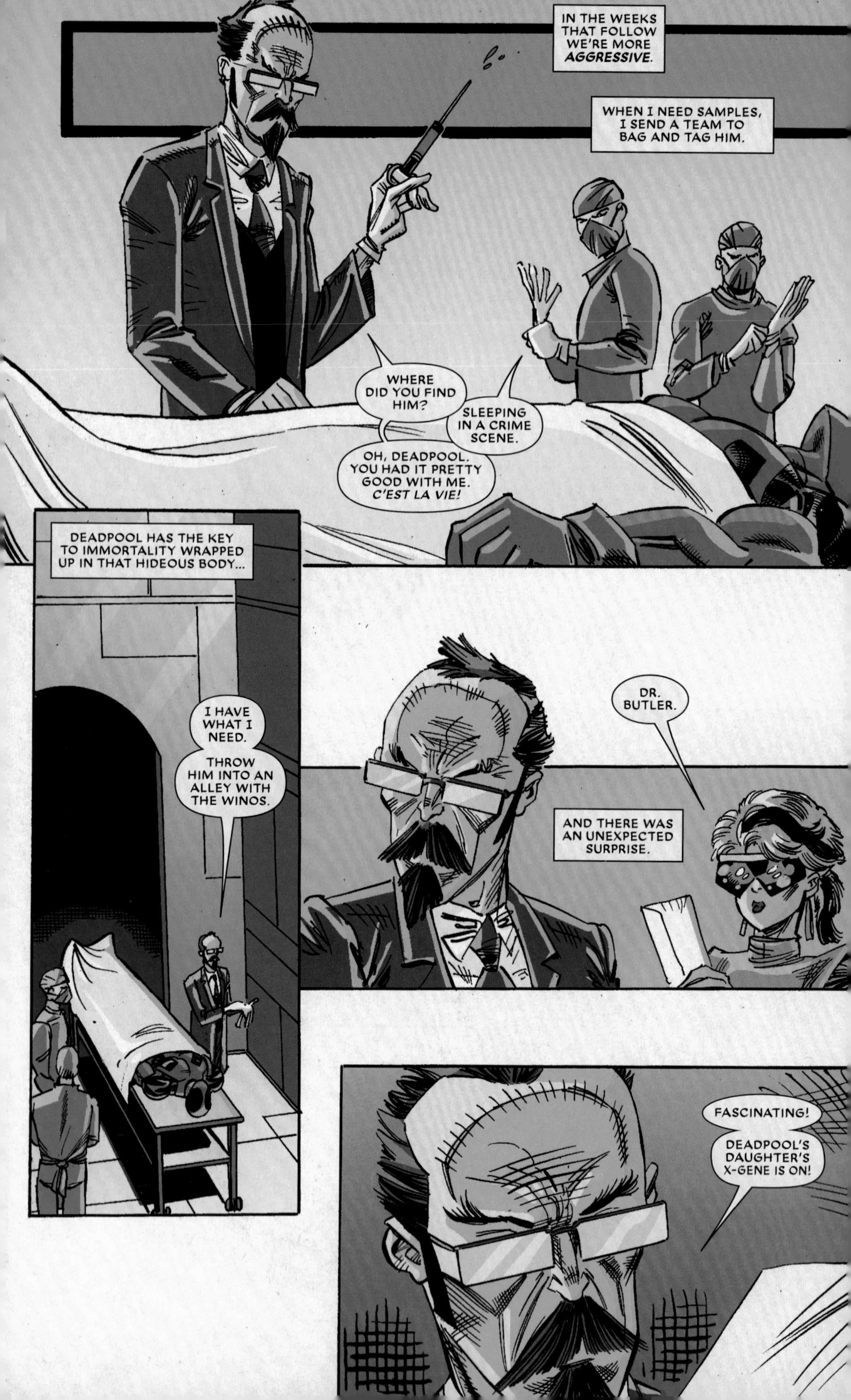
IN THE WEEKS THAT FOLLOW WE'RE MORE AGGRESSIVE.
WHEN I NEED SAMPLES, I SEND A TEAM TO BAG AND TAG HIM.
WHERE DID YOU FIND HIM?
SLEEPING IN A CRIME SCENE.
OH, DEADPOOL. YOU HAD IT PRETTY GOOD WITH ME. C'EST LA VIE!
DEADPOOL HAS THE KEY TO IMMORTALITY WRAPPED UP IN THAT HIDEOUS BODY...
I HAVE WHAT I NEED.
THROW HIM INTO AN ALLEY WITH THE WINOS.
DR. BUTLER.
AND THERE WAS AN UNEXPECTED SURPRISE.
FASCINATING!
DEADPOOL'S DAUGHTER'S X-GENE IS ON!

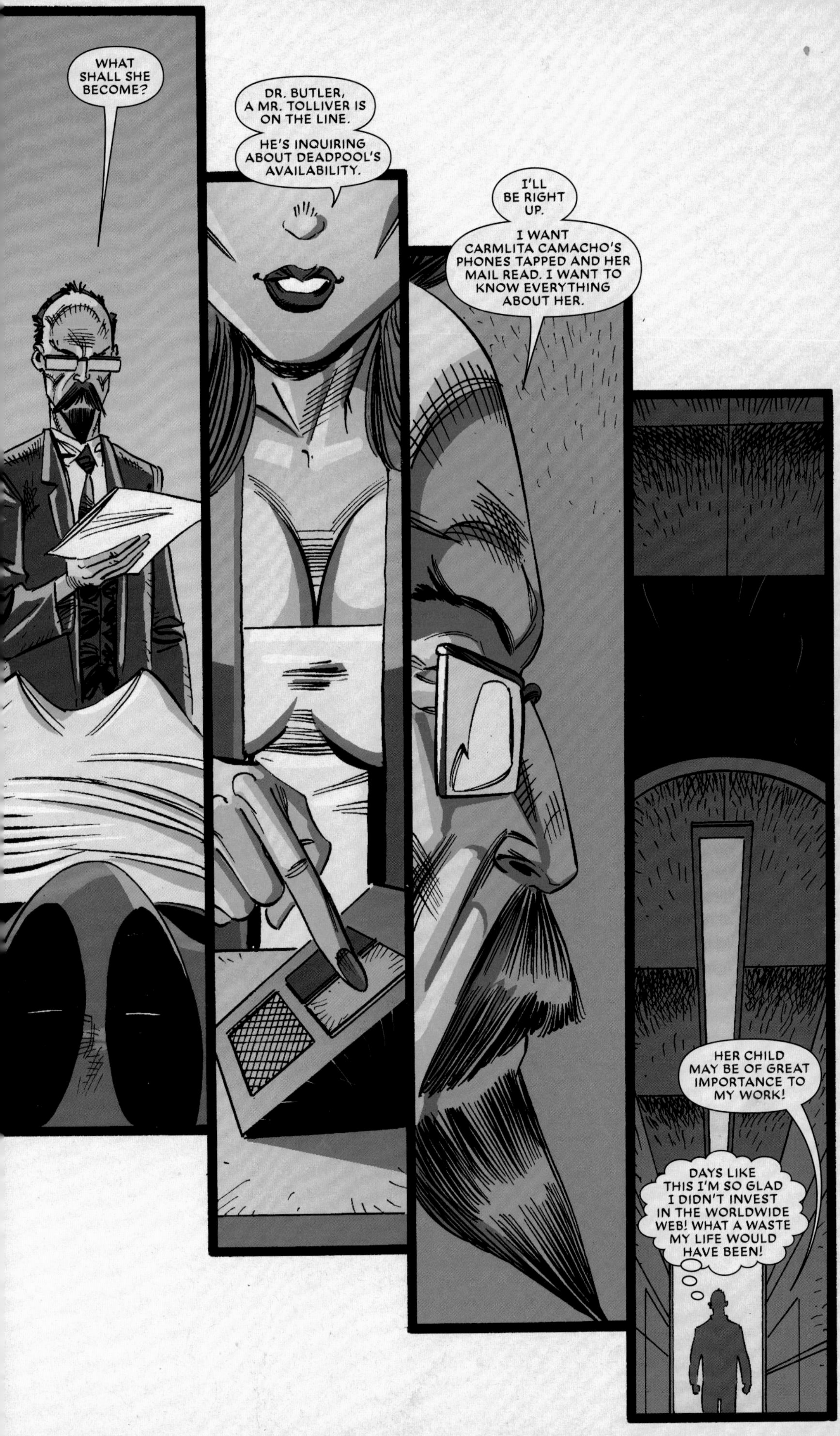
WHAT SHALL SHE BECOME?
DR. BUTLER, A MR. TOLLIVER IS ON THE LINE.
HE'S INQUIRING ABOUT DEADPOOL'S AVAILABILITY.
I'LL BE RIGHT UP.
I WANT CARMLITA CAMACHO'S PHONES TAPPED AND HER MAIL READ. I WANT TO KNOW EVERYTHING ABOUT HER.
HER CHILD MAY BE OF GREAT IMPORTANCE TO MY WORK!
DAYS LIKE THIS I'M SO GLAD I DIDN'T INVEST IN THE WORLDWIDE WEB! WHAT A WASTE MY LIFE WOULD HAVE BEEN!

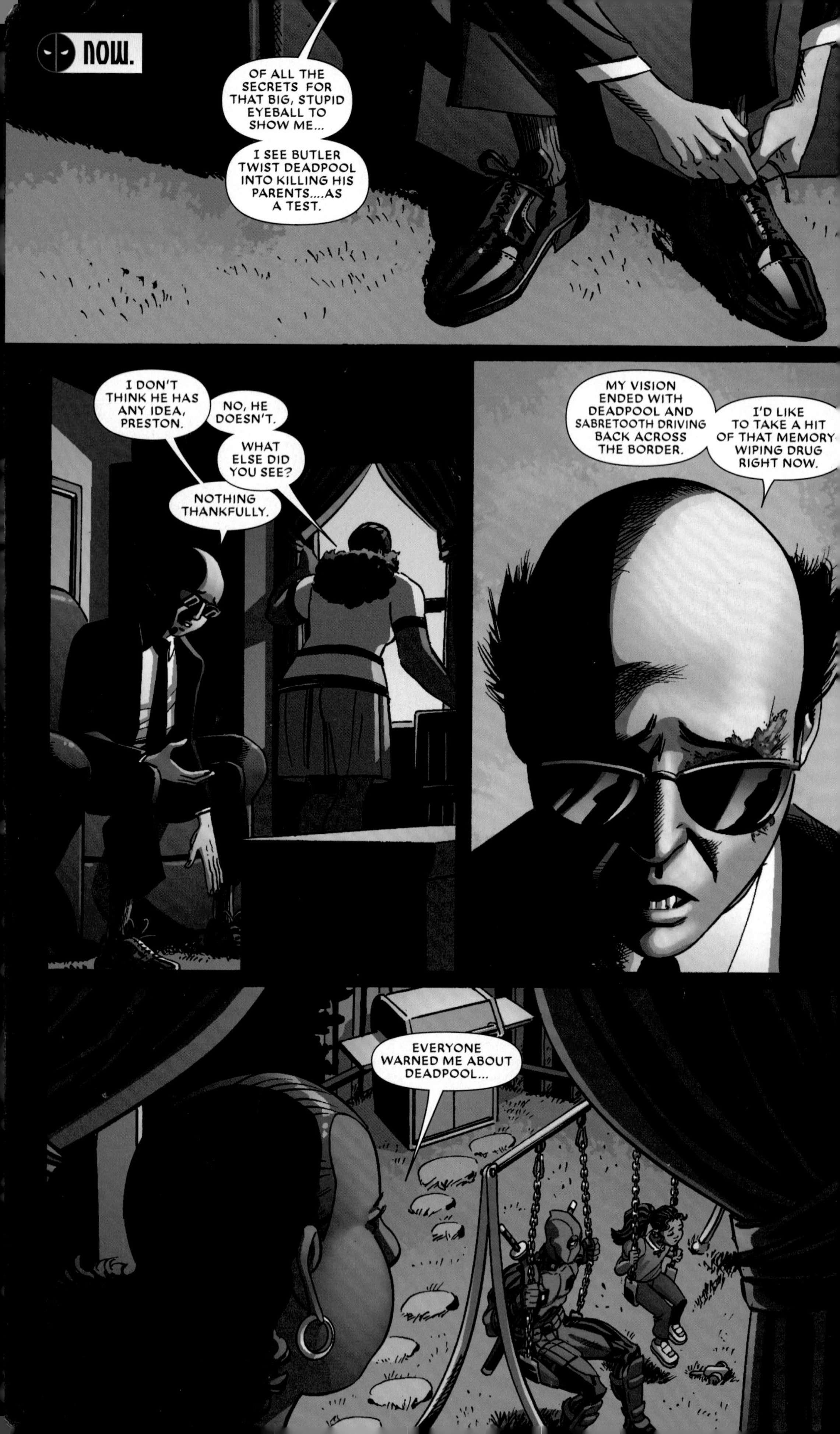
NOW.
OF ALL THE SECRETS FOR THAT BIG, STUPID EYEBALL TO SHOW ME...
I SEE BUTLER TWIST DEADPOOL INTO KILLING HIS PARENTS....AS A TEST.
I DON'T THINK HE HAS ANY IDEA, PRESTON.
NO, HE DOESN'T.
WHAT ELSE DID YOU SEE?
NOTHING THANKFULLY.
MY VISION ENDED WITH DEADPOOL AND SABRETOOTH DRIVING BACK ACROSS THE BORDER.
I'D LIKE TO TAKE A HIT OF THAT MEMORY WIPING DRUG RIGHT NOW.
EVERYONE WARNED ME ABOUT DEADPOOL...

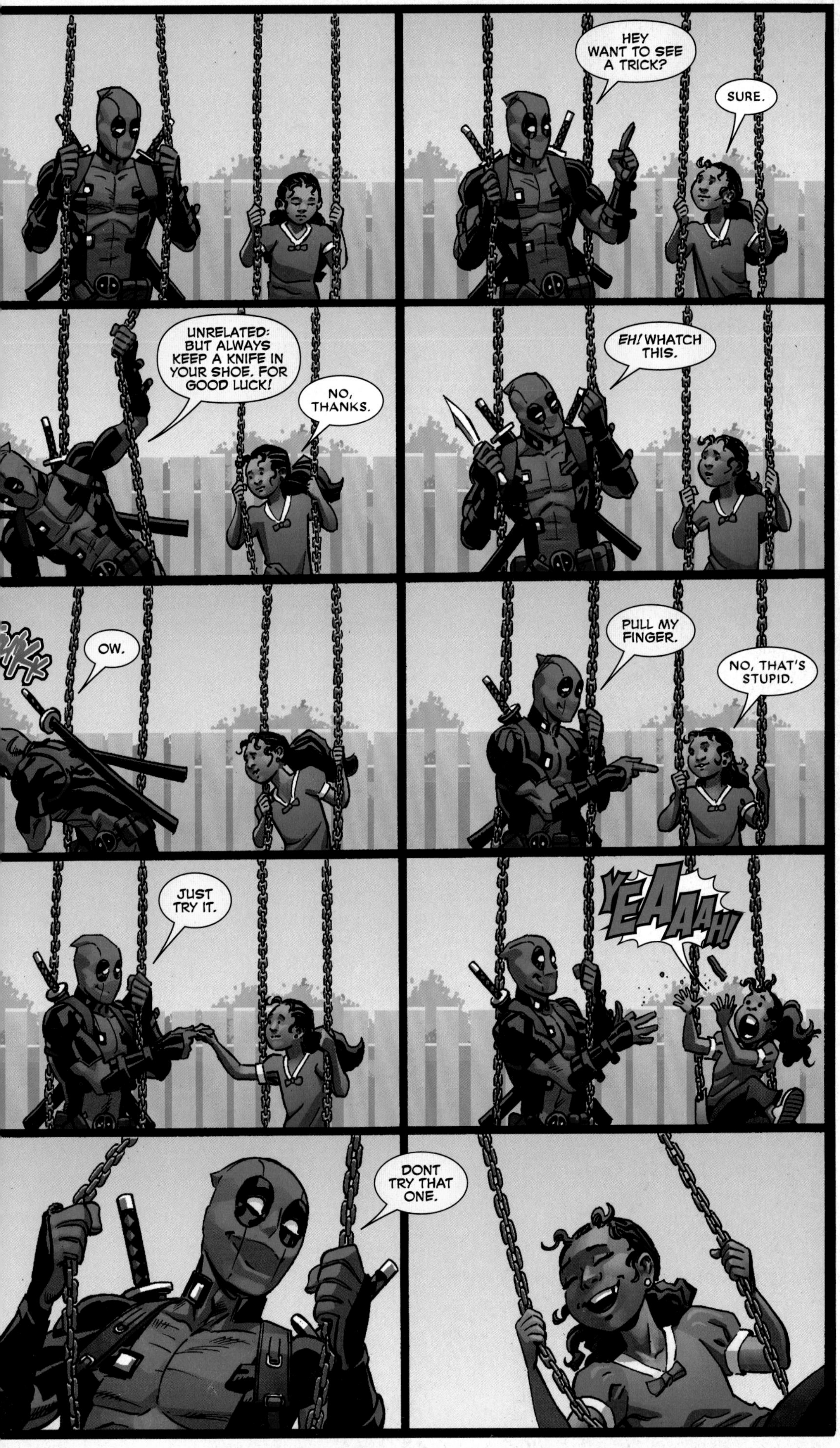
HEY WANT TO SEE A TRICK?
SURE.
UNRELATED: BUT ALWAYS KEEP A KNIFE IN YOUR SHOE. FOR GOOD LUCK!
NO, THANKS.
EH! WHATCH THIS.
OW.
PULL MY FINGER.
NO, THAT'S STUPID.
JUST TRY IT.
YEAAAH!
DONT TRY THAT ONE.

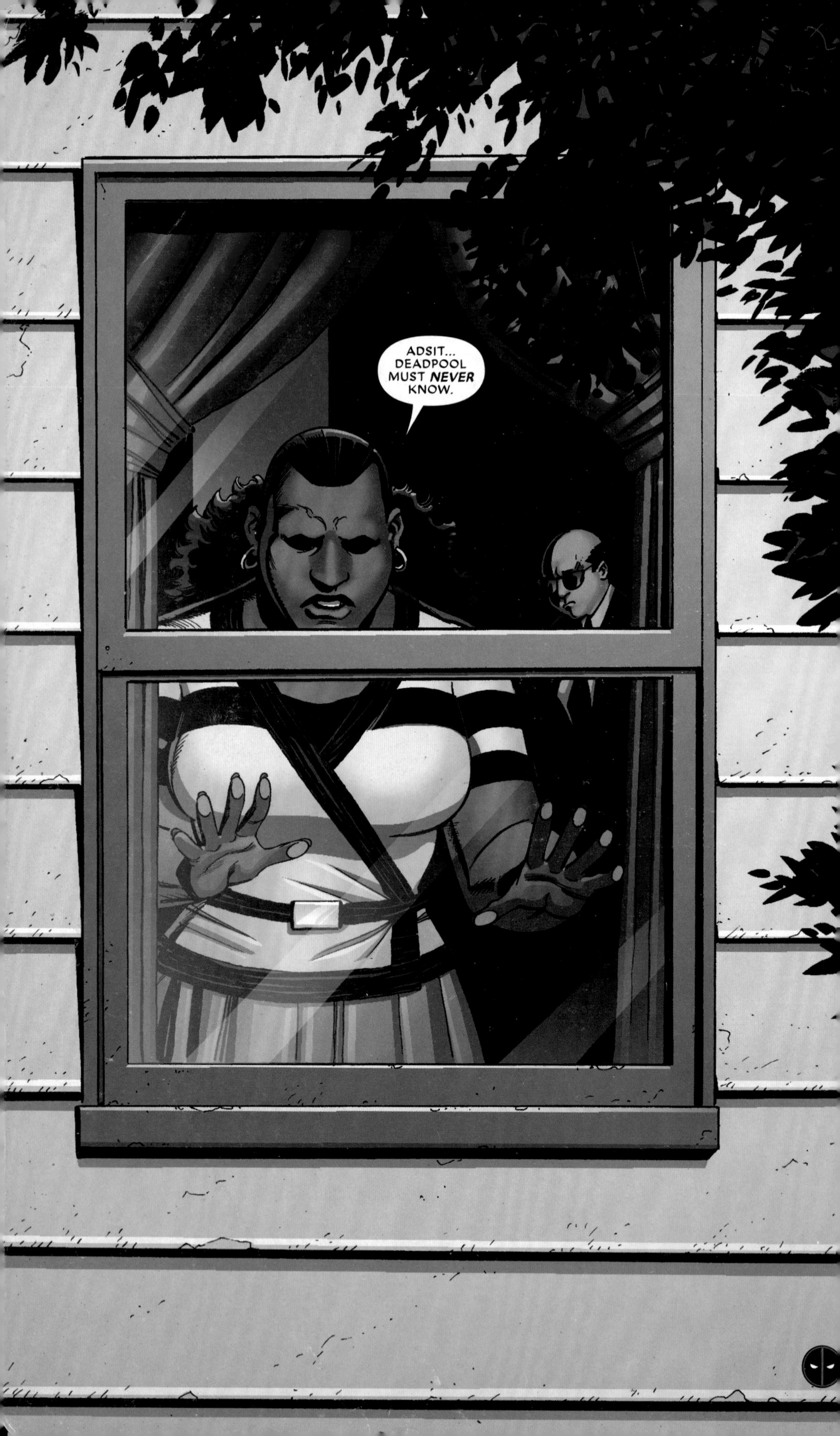
ADSIT... DEADPOOL MUST NEVER KNOW.